Historic Britain

WESTMINSTER HALL

Historic Britain

BRITAIN'S HERITAGE

OF FAMOUS PLACES AND PEOPLE

THROUGH THE AGES

Advisory Editor

Graham Fisher

ODHAMS BOOKS

Published for Odhams Books
by The Hamlyn Publishing Group Limited
Hamlyn House, 42 The Centre, Feltham, Middlesex.

*Made and Printed in Great Britain
by Odhams (Watford) Limited,
Watford, Herts.*
6007   0419   X/R6

CONTENTS

THE CATHEDRAL OF WINCHESTER

Winchester was the capital of all England in Saxon days. Even in Norman times there are indications that it continued to be joint capital city with London for a time. The cathedral was begun about 1080, and the greater part of the Norman church was finished before the end of the century. The only parts of the building which retain their Norman workmanship unchanged are the transepts. The beautiful Gothic additions to the cathedral date chiefly from the fourteenth century.

6

INTRODUCTION

THIS book shows how the wayfarer in Britain's varied countryside can piece together the things he sees on his journeys and reconstruct the story of Britain's historic past, the changing pattern of social life through the ages and the character of the peoples who have made Britain what it is today. It is a wide canvas which can be covered only in outline within the scope of a single book. It must remain for the reader when he has grasped the essentials of the design to fill in the detail for himself with the heightened interest which knowledge inevitably brings and the keener perception which derives from knowing what to look for and where to find it.

The most obvious places for the traveller to discover links with the past are in the historic towns and the ruins of ancient abbeys and castles. Many a town such as York reveals to the practised eye links with every stage in its history from Roman days to the present. Though the old towns and especially the medieval walled towns are rich storehouses of interest as they are of ancient architecture, they are by no means the only sources from which knowledge of the past may be derived. The following pages suggest a number of other interesting fields for experiment and show how the present and the past are always inextricably woven together. The village of today is a natural development from the settlement of yesterday; the rural pattern of

field and hedge is the inevitable result of farming policy in the past and changing economic circumstances.

In a sense the countryside is every bit as much a part of historic Britain as the buildings in town and village, for the British countryside, at least as regards two-thirds of it, is man-made and reflects the story of the men who have made it what it is and whose handiwork is there before us all the time if only we can discern it. Whichever way we look at it there are links between landscape and history. Successive civilizations have put the stamp of their labour on every cultivated landscape, while the shape of the land and the nature of the soil have determined the course of history quite as much as the peoples whose joys and sorrows, successes and failures are the raw material of history.

From the earliest times the climate and the physical characteristics of the world's land masses have moulded history. At one time or another unusually vigorous peoples or unusually advanced civilizations have arisen above the limiting factors of climate and terrain, but that is the exception rather than the rule and such defiance of nature has always been shortlived. In the last hundred and fifty years—the age of invention, of power, of the dominance of man, the thinking being—people have become more independent of their environment, yet in spite of that the pattern set by history remains largely unchanged. Mankind makes a small advance here, a small gain there, but for every advance and every gain one can point to a retreat or a failure. Thus, for example, large areas of the arid belt of the United States of America have been brought under cultivation by means of irrigation. That is a remarkable gain at the expense of nature. By contrast, large-scale efforts to grow useful crops in the scrubby hinterland of East Africa have been a dismal failure in spite of millions of pounds worth of machinery and the labour of thousands of skilled men.

If we delve into the past, the direct influence of climatic changes can be seen in the rise and fall of ancient civilizations. Thus in the thousand years that ended with the dominance of Rome in the Mediterranean world the Sahara desert lay several hundred miles to the south of its present position. Thousands of square miles of what is now arid rock-strewn country, with scarcely a blade of grass to show, was then rich pasture-land sustaining herds and flocks, of importance enough to attract the envious eyes of the peoples who dwelt on, or near, the northern shores of the Mediterranean.

HISTORY AND THE LAND

Not only has climate been linked with the history of mankind, but the nature of the terrain has always determined, as it still does, the kind of life lived by the people. The steppes of Russia are traditionally the home of nomadic herdsmen. The mountainous regions of the world are inhabited only by shepherd communities. Islands breed fisher folk; lands endowed by nature with rich soil and a moderate climate are the home of wealthy peasant communities deriving enough from the land to satisfy their needs and to allow something over for the luxuries of their way of living.

What the world shows in broad outline Britain reveals in miniature. Nor is this surprising when we think of the vast difference in terrain between one part of Britain and another and the very considerable differences in climate. Average annual rainfall varies from little more than eighteen inches at the south-eastern tip of Essex (a figure which comes perilously near to the minimum required for successful agricultural development) to well over two hundred inches in parts of North Wales and Cumberland (a figure which if it were true of a large area instead of the very restricted one to which it applies would render agriculture impossible).

CLIMATE AND AGRICULTURE

There is a similar startling difference between sunshine figures for the north and south. Along the coast of Sussex and the Isle of Wight the average annual figure is nearly two thousand hours; in the far north round Cape Wrath and in the Orkneys and Shetlands the corresponding figure is only little over a thousand hours. If these extreme contrasts were paralleled by similar contrasts in temperature half of Britain would probably be uninhabited. In fact they are not, for the average temperature of the far north is not very different from that of the south. There is a mean annual range of only a few degrees, chiefly because the south-eastern half of England, which has the highest temperatures in summer, is also visited by some of the coldest weather in winter owing to its proximity to the reservoir of cold air which lies over the Eurasian continent between Christmas and Easter. But the contrasts in sunshine and rainfall have been sufficient to make the historic heritage of north and south entirely different and to make the pattern of husbandry today equally

HISTORICAL SITES IN ENGLAND AND WALES

✠ *Cathedrals*   ‡ *Famous Churches*
⚑ *Castles*   ■ *Other Places of Interest*

Berwick-on-Tweed
Norham
Lindisfarne
Bamburgh

SCOTLAND

Alnwick

NORTH

SEA

Roman Wall
Newcastle   Jarrow
Carlisle
Durham
Solway Firth
Dacre
Keswick   Staithes
Grasmere   Whitby
Richmond   Robin Hood's Bay
Castle   Rievaulx   Scarborough
Bolton   Abbey
Peel
Furness   Fountains
Isle of Man   Abbey   Lancaster   Abbey
Haworth   York
IRISH SEA   Beverley
Sandal   Pontefract
Epworth
Speke Hall   Bramhall Hall   Thorpe Hall,
Conway   Buxton   Chatsworth   Louth
Beaumaris   Chester   House   Lincoln
Caernarvon   Bangor St.Asaph   Matlock   Tattershall
Plas Newydd   Beeston   Moreton   Newstead
Llangollen   Old Hall   Nottingham
Chirk   Derby   Woolsthorpe   The Wash
Harlech   ENGLAND   Crowland   Castle Rising
Lichfield   Acre   Caister
Cardigan   Fotheringhay   Peterborough   Norwich
Bay   Maxstoke   Lutterworth   Ely   Grimes Graves,
Aberystwyth   Stokesay   Geddington   Thetford
Ludlow   Kenilworth   Huntingdon   Bury St.Edmunds
Warwick   Earls Barton
Leominster   Worcester   Northampton   Framlingham
Stratford-on-Avon   Cambridge   Lavenham
Hereford   Evesham   Elstow   Castle
Hedingham
Brecon   Kilpeck   Tewkesbury   Thaxted   Colchester
Tintern   Blenheim Palace
Kidwelly   Caerleon   Gloucester   Oxford   Hatfield   Bradwell
Berkeley   Hughenden   St.Albans   Greensted
Caerphilly   Malmesbury   Uffington   Manor   Bisham   LONDON
Pembroke   Cardiff   Windsor   Rochester
Bristol Channel   Bradford-   Avebury   Reading   Pilgrims Way
Lundy   on-Avon   Devizes   Guildford   Canterbury
Island   Wells   Stonehenge   Hever   Penshurst
Bridgwater   Glastonbury   Old Sarum   Place   Bodiam
Dover
Montacute House   Salisbury   Winchester   Battle   Lewes
Maiden Castle   Southampton   Porchester   Arundel   Rye
Exeter   Dorchester   Beaulieu   Chichester   Pevensey
Tintagel   Launceston   Portsmouth
Tavistock   Newton Abbot   Carisbrooke
St.Ives   Buckland Abbey   Corfe
Fowey   Plymouth
St.Michaels Mount   ENGLISH   CHANNEL

Scale of Miles
0   50   100

different between one part of the country and another.

East Anglia, which combines warmth of summer climate with comparative dryness, is the granary of the country; the cool and rainy west and north-west make up the cattle lands of Britain. The midlands of England, which lie between the two, share in the characters of both and are the home of mixed farming.

CLIMATE AND HISTORY

That is just one way in which climate affects rural life today. In the past it was a still more powerful influence. For instance, prehistoric man lived in the sunny south and it was only in the last thousand years or so B.C. that the civilizations of the Bronze and Iron Ages spread into northern England and southern Scotland.

That brings us inevitably to the other great factor which has influenced Britain's history, the nature of the land. The north and west are mountainous by comparison with the south and east. Anyone who has travelled in Wales, in Cumberland and Westmorland, or in the Highlands of Scotland, would appreciate just what this means in terms of human development and endeavour.

All southern England is like a garden on a vast scale. Wherever the wayfarer looks there is a pretty picture, of fields and hedges and woods and rivers; even where there are hills the slope of the land is gentle and the hills scarcely reach a thousand feet above sea-level. Intensive agriculture starts in the valleys and generally reaches to near the summit of the hills.

How very different are the look and the atmosphere of the hill regions of the west and north. In place of the trim pattern of hedge-girt fields there are tens of thousands of acres of unrelieved moorland backed by precipitous rock-strewn slopes which are good neither for man nor beast. There is notable beauty in the Highlands of Scotland, but there is no goodness in the land nor any hope of bringing the greater part of it into cultivation. Shooting parties make their way across the lonely roughs. There is walking for the hardy and climbing for the adventurous, but not enough rich land to sustain more than the needs of the tiny population which dwells among the mountains. The crofter has his patch of tilled land, but his living comes from his sheep as often as not, and a very precarious one at that, or from his fishing boat if he lives in a seaward village.

If this is a no-man's-land today, it was a no-man's-land a thousand years and five thousand years ago. You may walk ten, twenty, thirty miles across the treeless uplands of Ross and Sutherland, even farther south in Argyll, without seeing a single village or a single farmstead. It is only in the long, deep valleys that there is land fit for growing food for the people. In those long valleys the Highland clans grew from small beginnings in the Middle Ages into powerful communities, very jealous of their narrow strip of fertile land which they must protect at all costs from the predatory instincts of their neighbours in the next valley across the mountains.

MOUNTAINOUS REGIONS

The story is the same, though less well marked, in the whole of the mountainous north-west. In England's Lake District, in Wales and even in Cornwall the countryside is thinly peopled, the farms are mostly small and relatively poor, the husbandmen must work extra-hard in order to win a living from the land.

It is still more significant that in these mountainous regions there are no large towns. How could there be?

TANTALLON CASTLE, EAST LOTHIAN

The border country was the scene of intermittent fighting between the English and the Scots for many centuries from the time of the Norman occupation onwards, as it had been nearly a thousand years before when the Picts and Scots attacked the province of Roman Britain. In all the border country between Scotland's lowland belt and the line of Hadrian's Wall from Tyne to Solway there are the ruins of numerous castles. Tantallon was one of the strongholds of the Douglas family.

HISTORICAL SITES IN SCOTLAND

✝ Cathedrals   ♣ Famous Churches
♙ Castles   ■ Other Places of Interest

ORKNEY ISLANDS
Kirkwall

Cape Wrath
Duncansby Head

OUTER HEBRIDES

The Minch

Ardvreck
Dunbeath
Wick

NORTH SEA

Dunrobin
Dornoch

Dingwall
Elgin
Forres
Banff
Kingsburgh House
Beaufort
Auldearn
Dufftown
Huntly
Dunvegan
Portree
StromeFerry
Skye
Glen Moriston
Castle Grant

Barra
Kishmull
Invergarry
Corgarff
Balmoral
Glenfinnan
Braemar
Dunnottar

SCOTLAND

Blair Atholl
Cortachy
Mull
Glen Coe
Meggernie
Dunkeld
Glamis
Arbroath
Iona
Kilchurn
Balquhidder
Perth
Glen Gyle
Magus
St. Andrews
Loch Leven
Muir
ATLANTIC OCEAN
Inveraray
Doune
Stirling
Dunfermline
Tantallon
Firth of Forth
Culross
N. Berwick
Islay
Jura
Dunoon
Linlithgow
Dumbarton
EDINBURGH
Dunbar
Paisley
Haddington
Firth of Lorne
Rothesay
Largs
Glasgow
Blantyre
Duns
Strathaven
Neidpath
Melrose
Kelso
Burns Monument
Abbotsford
Dryburgh
Kilmarnock
Douglas
Jedburgh
North Channel
Alloway
Dunure
Drumlanrig
Hermitage
Firth of Clyde
Ballantrae
Loch Trool
Dumfries
Ecclefechan
Sweetheart Abbey
Caerlaverock
Dirk Hatteraick's
Cave
Dalbeattie
Wigtown
Threave
Solway Firth

ENGLAND

Scale of Miles
0   50

BETWEEN GLENCOE AND THE BRIDGE OF ORCHY

The narrow green valley is almost level between the encompassing mountains by the King's House, which is over the pass from Glencoe towards Bridge of Orchy. The photograph gives a vivid impression of the kind of countryside in which the medieval clans of Scotland rose to power, marred by constant discord. At Glencoe in 1692 part of the Macdonald clan was almost wiped out by supporters of William III whom they were entertaining, including as their commander a member of the Campbell clan.

Modern large towns have grown up as centres of commerce. London has been described as the world's emporium. Perhaps the description no longer holds good, but it certainly did until the growth of the great cities across the Atlantic. It remains one of the great ports of the world, one of the chief centres of commerce. So, too, Manchester and Liverpool, ports in their own rights, are commercial centres as well as centres of industry. The same is true of Scotland's Glasgow and to a lesser extent of Edinburgh, of Newcastle and Birmingham. The woollen towns of Yorkshire and the cotton towns of Lancashire have their own specialized history, but they, too, have to cope with the single problem that besets every big town—transport.

It is clearly true that without good facilities for transport no town can grow to any size today. It was equally true in every period of Britain's past. In this respect the present is only the past writ large. The problem of today is that in order to make things one must bring the raw materials to the factories and transport the finished products away from them. It is all very well to point to modern industrial towns like the pottery towns and say that they have

13

won their eminent position because of the district's wealth of mineral resources. It may come as a surprise to many to learn that some of the finest pottery made in the Five Towns is manufactured from Cornish china-clay. It may well be true that Bradford and Leeds and the other northern industrial towns would never have grown to their present size unless they had been on the fringe of the great Yorkshire coal measures, for it is indisputable that manufacturing towns are attracted to the site of the raw material of their industries and to the sources of fuel to feed the furnaces of their factories.

But that is only one part of the story. The Pennine sheep no longer give one-tenth of the wool necessary to feed the Yorkshire woollen mills, while cotton has never been cultivated in Britain, but from the beginning has had to be brought across the ocean to the Lancashire mills. As for London, the Thames Basin has no raw materials nor any fuel important enough to attract a single national industry. Its chief advantages are a navigable waterway and its position as a meeting-place of roads and later of railways.

Industrial towns, then, belong to the lowlands, to the river valleys. They

LANYON QUOIT, CORNWALL

This is one of the many prehistoric monuments of the south-western peninsula, an area particularly rich in remains of the later phases of the Stone Age in Britain. The quoit consists of three standing stones supporting a horizontal slab or table stone, with other large monoliths round the base. Originally, like all the so-called cromlechs which resemble it, it was a tomb dating from not later than 2,000 B.C. The whole structure was covered in earth in the characteristic elongated shape of the long barrow, but time and weather have combined to disintegrate the mound, leaving the stones exposed.

STONEHENGE

The most elaborate, though not the largest (a distinction which belongs to Avebury), of the prehistoric temples in the southern downlands, dating from 2,000 to 1,800 B.C., Stonehenge consisted of concentric circles of upright stones supporting horizontal slabs, and of so-called blue stones. The former were probably obtained from the immediate vicinity, the latter from the Prescelly Hills in Wales. The monument also included a horseshoe of giant trilithons (two uprights supporting a horizontal slab, one of which is shown in the photograph) and a number of detached stones.

could never exist in the wild uplands of the north-west. There the largest unit of population is the market town.

Thus the broad trends of local history are written in the landscapes of Britain for all to see. The fells and mountains, the towns and villages and farmhouses, cry aloud their story for the traveller to interpret if he has the necessary background of knowledge and understanding.

We have already noticed the way in which the distinct contrast between the mountainous north-west of Britain and the lowland south-east determines the way of life followed by the people who dwell in the two contrasting areas. This same contrast holds the answer to many other differences in the historic heritage. In ancient times the history of Britain was the history of a succession of invasions and migrations, moving eastward and north-eastward from the continent of Europe. Even the approximate dates of the early migrations are a matter of guesswork, but that they took place has definitely been established by the archaeologists. It is clear, too, that the

THE RIDGEWAY IN BERKSHIRE

The Ridgeway over the Berkshire Downs is one of the most ancient of the great pre-historic roads of Britain. These were at their busiest during the New Stone Age, when Salisbury Plain and the Marlborough Downs area were centres of Stone Age civiliza-tion and many trackways were blazed along the hills which radiate from the chalk plateau. The Ridgeway was still in use at the time of the Roman occupation, but thereafter was superseded by the Icknield Way, a trackway which runs along the side of the downs some three hundred feet lower. The Ridgeway is here photographed from a point looking east from Blowing Stone Hill, near Kingston Lisle.

story of these migrations can be summed up by saying that each successive wave of invaders drove previous ones before it.

Let us imagine that a race or tribe "A" migrated from the continent and established itself in the area of the southern downlands, there developing for a few hundred or maybe a thousand years. Then another tribe, "B," stronger and more vigorous and armed with better weapons, would appear in South-east England. Rather than do battle, or after a few skirmishes which showed that it was inferior in armour and war-like skill, tribe "A" elected to retreat,

ultimately coming up against the mountainous and unfertile regions of the north and west. Farther than that they could not go, so that successive cultures or civilizations tended to settle in the narrow valleys of the moun-tainous regions, feeling secure there from further attacks, while the new invaders were well satisfied with the living space they had won and could have no interest in a less fertile and climatically less suitable territory farther west or north.

Another thousand years would pass and the same process would be repeated, the remnants of tribe "B" coming as refugees into the mountain fastnesses of the west. As age followed age the north and west tended to be populated by the defeated or effete remnants of tribes which had previously flourished in the fertile south and east.

When a tribe or race settles in a country it leaves upon it the impress of its personality thousands of years after it has gone away or died out. It is in the nature of mankind to be builders and cultivators, the fulfilment of the two simplest needs of man, which are to have food to eat and shelter from the elements. Man the builder and man the cultivator have both set their impress on the land of Britain from the earliest times.

As civilization progressed man left many other traces of his occupation, such as fragments of pottery, weapons, and still later ornaments and other primitive expressions of the artistic

REMAINS OF THE ROMAN THEATRE NEAR ST. ALBANS

The Roman walled town of Verulamium was situated slightly to the south and west of modern St. Albans. It was one of the most prosperous towns of the Roman province of Britain, which is perhaps why alone among Roman towns in the province (with the possible exception of Canterbury) it possessed a theatre on the lines of the many similar sites in Italy and Provence. The remains of the stage and of the seating in tiers on banks surrounding the slightly oval amphitheatre can be seen here. The column, which is situated at the back of what was the stage, was erected in modern times.

instinct. But these in the story of pre-historic Britain at least are in the field of the archaeologist. They are not readily available for the traveller to see except in museums and art galleries.

There is one other phase of man's activity which appears at a very early date and has continued without pause, that of raising monuments, whether in honour of a dead chieftain or to mark the site of a victorious battle. These "monuments," ancient, medieval and modern, are a fascinating part of historic Britain as the wayfarer sees it today.

Four thousand B.C. is roughly the beginning of the first period which has left behind unmistakable reminders of the people who lived in Britain. From then onwards there is something representing every period of time,

ROMAN TOWN GATEWAY

The Newport Arch in Lincoln is the only remaining Roman city gateway in a comparatively good state of preservation, apart from the Balkerne Gate at Colchester, which was only a postern for travellers on foot. All the principal Roman towns in Britain were protected by walls which were pierced generally by at least four main gates. When in the Middle Ages the walls were rebuilt, much of the Roman building material was often used and the medieval walls frequently followed the course of the Roman ones, but in no other case except this was the Roman gateway maintained with little alteration. The remains of a postern gate is seen on the right.

DURHAM CATHEDRAL NAVE

The massive Norman piers which support the roof of the nave of Durham Cathedral represent better than any other building the rugged beauty of early Norman architecture. This massive quality is more apparent in the cathedrals and abbey churches of the north of England than in the corresponding churches of the south, such as Chichester. The moulding on the piers and round the margin of the semicircular arches above is the only form of ornamentation displayed.

THE CASTLE OF COLCHESTER

One of the largest and best-preserved of the Norman castle keeps in England, Colchester was completed before the end of the eleventh century as one of the chief Norman bulwarks in South-east England against possible Saxon resurgence. The fabric of the castle is partly composed of material taken from the ruins of Camulodunum, a city which had flourished in Roman Britain but had fallen into ruin after the Saxon invasions. The many "courses" of red Roman bricks are still clearly visible.

though until the birth of history proper, which in Britain is about the time of the Roman occupation, it is often difficult to date these things with any degree of precision.

A number of the long and remarkable list of ancient monuments which are widely distributed over southern England find a place in later chapters of this book. All we need do here is summarize the kind of monument associated with the different phases in the story of Britain from 4,000 B.C. onwards. The civilization which was centred on the Salisbury Plain area

between 4,000 B.C. and 2,000 B.C. was called Neolithic, which means "of the New Stone Age," to distinguish it from the many earlier cultures which belong to the Old Stone Age. The people whose work made New Stone Age culture the wonderful thing it was were members of a long-headed race. We know that from the skeletal remains which have been discovered in their burial mounds. The monuments by which this people are remembered fall into several categories, including stone circles, stone rows, single standing stones and the kind of monument which is variously known as a table stone or dolmen or cromlech. This last consists of several upright stones supporting roofing stones, though in most cases the structure has caved in and the stones have partially disintegrated. Dolmens were originally cists in which chieftains of the age were buried, one man to a tomb, the whole covered with a mound of earth usually longer than it was broad, whence the term "Long Barrow" was given to it.

In a very few cases has the earthen mound survived, while at Uley in Gloucestershire it has been reconstructed. All over the southern downlands, and in many of the upland regions of Devonshire, Cornwall and the West Country, there are examples of these ancient tombs, none of them less than four thousand, some of them possibly five thousand or six thousand years old.

It is only when man has a surplus of labour and wealth over and above the bare necessities of living that he turns to enriching his own home and to the refinements of living which belong to the more self-conscious and highly-developed civilizations. Stone Age man, so far as we know, lived in hollows scooped out of the ground and roofed with the branches of trees closely woven with smaller twigs in much the same way as some of the most primitive tribes of Africa do today, tribes which indeed have still not emerged fully from the

THE CASTLE AND TOWN OF CAERNARVON

Still closely resembling a medieval town, Caernarvon is built under the very shadow of the castle and partly surrounded by the strong walls which are contemporary with the castle itself. This was the largest and strongest of the Edwardian castles constructed to subdue the rebelling Welsh tribes before union with England was assured. It was built on the site of an earlier Norman fortress in which the first Prince of Wales, later Edward II, was born in 1284, about the time that the foundations of the present castle were being laid. The castle is now public property.

culture of the Stone Age. So nothing of Stone Age homes has survived except the rock shelters and caves which excavation has proved conclusively were inhabited in early prehistoric times.

The Stone Age civilization is known as Megalithic, the two parts of the word meaning "big" and "stone," a term which takes on fresh meaning when we come to look at the greatest of the prehistoric monuments of Britain, Stonehenge. The biggest of the stones which compose this most elaborate of circles weigh several tons each. Stonehenge, with Avebury and a number of the other fantastic reminders of Stone Age man's vigour and prodigious capacity for work, represent the end of one era and the beginning of the next, the end of the Stone Age and the beginning of the Bronze Age, between 2,000 and 1,800 B.C.

Again we know something of the people who made the Bronze Age what it was. In contrast with the long-headed Stone Age people they were round-headed people, a fact derived once more from the human remains left in their burial-chambers. The Bronze Age people are the peoples of the Round Barrows, which caused one early commentator to liken Salisbury Plain to a vast cemetery. The vast majority of the "barrows" belong to these people.

BRONZE AGE TRACKWAYS

The Bronze Age was a time, too, when the ancient trackways were being developed as means of internal commerce. The Pilgrims' Way, the Icknield Way, the Ridgeway, and many others are extraordinarily interesting parts of historic Britain, roads which in many cases have had a continuous history of usage for nearly four thousand years and probably began to develop as lines of communication during the New Stone

Age. A tour along any of them will bring the traveller near still-visible traces of many periods of civilization. The downland ridgeways in particular link together the fortress villages, the so-called "camps" which are the most spectacular memorials to the few centuries which preceded the birth of Christ, when an iron-using Celtic people was established in Britain.

THE ROMAN INVASION

Almost everyone has heard of Maiden Castle in Dorset. Exploring its complicated system of ramparts and ditches proved beyond a doubt the skill and highly organized activity of the men who built it. There are several score of these fortified sites, though none on so large a scale as Maiden Castle.

These peoples, the builders of Maiden Castle and the other hill towns, formed the population of Britain as the Romans found it. They were the woad-painted savages of which Caesar wrote so feelingly. They were the worshippers of the mistletoe, according to other Roman authorities. Woad-painted savages they certainly were not. Worshippers of mistletoe or Druids they may well have been, for Druidism was a religion which was well established across the Channel in what is now France and probably spread into Britain about this time.

History is often written in earth and brick and stone as vividly as it is in the pages of history books. The site of Verulamium by St. Albans, for instance, tells the story of two great eras of historic Britain. There are the ramparts and ditches of the Celtic tribal centre, and inside these prehistoric fortifications the stout wall of brick and stone which the Romans built when they founded Verulamium on the site of the British town and utilized with that economy for which they were justly famous the

THE HALL OF ST. CROSS

The foundation of St. Cross in Winchester includes a Norman church and this hall, which is the hall of a hospital founded early in the twelfth century by Henri de Blois, Bishop of Winchester. This was the earliest "hospital" founded for poor people exclusively and had an additional foundation to alleviate want among other poor people who were not resident. The charity is still in being.

YORK, THE SHAMBLES

York is a city which well illustrates the development of historic Britain from the earliest times to the present day. The Shambles is a narrow street lined with sixteenth- and seventeenth-century houses with projecting upper storeys almost meeting above the road. It owes its name to the fact that it was in medieval York the street of the butchers. The traditional conservatism of sites is well illustrated by the fact that the Shambles still contains several butchers' shops, as seen on the left of the picture.

defences of the earlier township to augment their own new wall.

If we go up the hill from Verulamium to where the great abbey of St. Alban dominates the scene we bridge another gap in the historic story. The abbey church and the poor fragments of the abbey itself represent the wealth of the Middle Ages as surely as the foundations of Verulamium, the Roman wall and the ramparts of the Celtic town represent Britain's story between 200 B.C. and A.D. 400.

There is a still further link, for much of the fabric of St. Albans Abbey today is composed of the red Roman bricks which the medieval builders took from the deserted site of Verulamium, sacked and razed to the ground by pagan tribes. As they did at Colchester and many other former Roman towns, the people of the Middle Ages built afresh to the glory of a new civilization from the useless fragments of an older one. That the modern market town of St. Albans grew up under the protection of the abbey is a fact that completes the story and provides a series of links which reveal in outline the whole chain of events that have shaped the destiny of this corner of old England through more than two thousand years.

ROMAN TOWNS

The Roman civilization is the first of which there are any written records, for Britain was a Roman province under the nominal government of Roman overlords and for four hundred years pursued a course of peace and increasing prosperity. The Roman civilization in Britain, too, was the first urban one.

Although the Roman towns were swept away when the imperial troops had to be withdrawn to defend their own country and the wild Saxon tribes began to overrun Britain, fragments of these Roman towns survive to the present day, chiefly in the form of walls where the site of the town has continued through the ages to be a centre of urban life, or in the form of more or less complete foundations which have been excavated thoroughly in places where after the Roman occupation there ceased to be a town, as at Verulamium and Silchester.

ROMAN YORK

Some towns now flourishing as modern cities reveal the story of the English town through nearly two thousand years. York is a splendid example which tells in outline the history of every important phase of English town planning, from Roman times onwards. First and earliest of its ancient monuments is the multangular tower, one of the very few examples of Roman mural defences almost perfectly preserved. A good deal of the rest of the walls of York date from the second or third century A.D., though the Roman material lies at the base of the walls now standing and is not readily discernible. It is enough, however, to remind us that York, then known as Eboracum (whence comes the traditional name Ebor, which attaches to the Archbishop), was a large and important town in Roman Britain.

That the multangular tower survives is a miracle. The destruction of the greater part of the strong walls which the Romans had built was the fate which overtook in some degree all the mural defences of Romano-British towns. The Saxon tribes brought fire and death to the peace-loving subjects of Roman Britain, rendered effete by four hundred years of peace and totally unequipped to defend themselves against a new and vigorous enemy. The Saxons had no respect for life or property and were

YORK, THE MINSTER AND CITY WALLS

York is still obviously a walled city, though the modern town has spread far outside the limit of the medieval walls. These never encircled the city entirely, but protected rather more than three-quarters of its circumference, the remaining sector being naturally protected by an expanse of swampy and treacherous ground. The first church on the site of the Minster was the see of St. Paulinus in the seventh century. The present building, which is a combination of all the architectural styles of four centuries, from the eleventh to the fifteenth, is one of the largest of the British cathedrals.

bent only on settling in a countryside which was rich and already well cultivated. The buildings which centuries of ordered government had produced were fired or pulled down and the site of York left empty and deserted for a hundred years or more.

The Minster, incidentally one of the most beautiful buildings in all Britain, forms the next link in the chain of history. It consists of many parts built over hundreds of years, but so cunningly welded together that it is hard for the untutored eye to separate them.

Together they tell the story of the resurgence of Britain in the Christian era. The wild Saxon settlers of the fourth and fifth centuries A.D. were transformed within three hundred years into a confederation, loosely knit it is true, but of a rapidly increasing civilization into which a swift acceptance of the Christian religion induced new life.

Hand in hand with this resurgence of civilization went a resurgence of town life. York, like many other towns all over Britain, began a new era under the

IN YORK CASTLE MUSEUM

York Castle, as well as being the modern assize court and one of the seats of York's local government, also houses a collection of old shop-fronts and accessories. This picture represents an apothecary's shop; its gracious façade with shop windows recalls York as it was towards the end of the eighteenth century.

RUINS OF CORFE

*Corfe Castle, situated in the Purbeck peninsula, was once one of the strongest fortresses
in Britain. The most famous siege of Corfe was in 1645, when it was held for the
Royalists against the Parliamentary army. For a time the garrison was commanded
by the lady of the manor, a certain Lady Bankes, who was honoured by friend and foe
alike for her gallant defence even though, like all the sieges of the Civil War, it ended
finally in the surrender of the castle to the Roundheads. At the close of the war the
battlements were destroyed by its captors. The ruins today include most of the outer
wall and fragments of the keep, seen here silhouetted against the sky.*

28

auspices of a monastery, the church of which has become the Minster and Cathedral Church of today. Though it has been rebuilt many times, York Minster remains essentially an early medieval church. Little that is definitely Saxon remains, but enough to prove the point, while of the other great periods of architecture there is ample evidence in the fabric of today. There are the round arches and solid masonry which characterized the Norman builders. There is the delicate sculptural quality of additions made in the thirteenth century, the flamboyance of the fourteenth and the severity of the fifteenth.

THE TOWN WALLS

The other link with pre-Reformation England in York is the circuit of the walls. These are Roman, as we have seen, in conception, although when they came to be rebuilt their line was altered in many places to make room for the precincts of the abbey and the growing town which was thriving under its protection.

York continued to be huddled within the protective barrier of the walls for hundreds of years. Even in the eighteenth century there was little or no building outside the walls. At that time England was still predominantly a farming country, its industry chiefly a farmhouse industry, as it had been since the woollen boom of the fifteenth century that made every farmer's wife in the sheep-rearing districts of England a woollen manufacturer. The towns were still chiefly market centres and centres of social life, the strongholds of the clergy and of the administrative officers of the central government.

There are many other sidelights on the history of a great city which can be garnered from walking about the streets of modern York. The old houses in the Shambles and other ancient thoroughfares which have survived centuries of change, the trim Georgian frontages of the many fine houses near the Minster, the riverside with its mixture of industry and "amenities," the latter in the form of riverside promenades and boats for hire—all these reflect the change and progress in the last few centuries.

The nineteenth- and twentieth-century expansion of the city is illustrated by the canal (or rather the canalized river) which runs through a gap in the walls where formerly there was a strip of protective marshland. The marshes, now drained, are covered in rows of nineteenth-century dwelling-houses, drab and uninteresting by comparison with the older homes in the centre of the city or with the more recent blocks of offices and flats which are the contribution of the twentieth century. Along the canal side, because of the ease of transport which this great new invention brought, there are many flourishing industrial plants, ugly perhaps but vigorous and forming now an essential ingredient in the mixture which determines the life of a city.

FAMOUS HISTORIC TOWNS

York earns this full treatment only because it is unusually characteristic of the many phases of Britain's historic story. Dozens of other towns and cities show a similar cycle of historic happenings reflected in the bricks and stones of today, though not perhaps in so complete a sequence.

Winchester, the capital of all England before London attained that dignity, the centre from which King Alfred sought to bring learning to the English people as well as independence, is a place which well illustrates most of the episodes in the English story. So it is with Canterbury and Chichester in the south, with

Like Caernarvon Castle in Wales, Herstmonceux gives a remarkable impression when seen across the moat of being a complete medieval stronghold. In fact it was never intended as a stronghold, and apart from the walls has a comparatively modern house within. These latter buildings are now the permanent home of the Royal Observatory, transferred here from Greenwich so as to make astronomical observation easier in the comparatively pure air of Sussex. When first built in the middle of the fifteenth century Herstmonceux ranked as one of the earliest brick-built residences since Roman

Exeter in the west and Chester in the north. So to a lesser extent it is with Salisbury (though its story starts later) and Southampton, Dover and Rochester, Leicester and Nottingham, and literally dozens of others. In fact, of course, none of the cathedrals of the old foundation was established in open country. Inevitably they were built in important places, unlike the medieval abbeys for which sites were often chosen on virgin soil. Inevitably, therefore, the cathedral city from Norman times

onwards was the centre of learning and of social life in its district. It needed to be fortified in the Middle Ages, and as time went on and industry bulked larger in the British economy it attracted its own industries and enjoyed corresponding expansion.

Again industrial cities are often the traditional county towns. Thus Norwich has always been the chief town of East Anglia, a vital centre of communications and commerce, and incidentally a medieval corn market and cattle market

HERSTMONCEUX

times. It was a castellated manor-house rather than a defensive castle, its moat and drawbridge and elaborate gatehouse intended for display rather than to ward off enemies. Internal peace was confidently expected in England at the time the building was started, while the English kings had by then discovered that the indiscriminate building of castles by their followers might result in points of defence for rebels. The elaborate gatehouse and moat, characteristics of the medieval castle, were retained in many manor-houses built in the fifteenth and early part of the sixteenth centuries.

as well as a cathedral city. In the west, Worcester and Hereford and Gloucester have similar histories relative to their own local activities and histories.

There are many towns, too, which have history written in their highways and byways, but which have never won the distinction of being the see of a bishopric. King's Lynn and Colchester are two which spring to mind, the former the very prototype of a medieval port, the latter showing in the fabric of its castle, of a ruined priory and several

churches, the red bricks seized from the ruins of Roman Camulodunum in just the same way as we have seen that the abbey of St. Albans is built partly from the ruins of Verulamium.

The distinction between town and country is an age-old one, not merely one that has arisen since the industrial revolution and the consequent migration in mass of the people from the fields to the tenements. From 1800, of course, the development of the towns has been rapid beyond all possible expectation,

THE CHURCH OF GREENSTED-JUXTA-ONGAR

*Apart from the miraculously preserved Saxon parish church in Bradford-on-Avon
and the equally remarkable one at Bradwell-on-Sea, Greensted Church is the most
fascinating of the many still-present links with Anglo-Saxon England. It is unique
in that the walls of its nave are composed of the split trunks of oak trees, now reinforced
with metal or stone fillings but still largely unimpaired. Most of the earliest Saxon
churches were built of wood, but all others which have survived were rebuilt in stone
in the years immediately preceding the Norman Conquest.*

though it is interesting to remember
that agriculture remains the most
important single industry of Britain.
Before that nation-wide migration
began, however, life in the country was
very different from life in the market
towns. So that villages and the country
houses of Britain make up an entirely
different facet of historic Britain from
that revealed by the towns. Through
them we can trace the story of changing
social life and manners in the countryside for more than a thousand years.

We can trace the influences which have
moulded the character of the people,
the agricultural booms and slumps which
century after century have enhanced or
depressed the standard of living. We can
see the changing tastes of the wealthy
reflected in revolutions of design
expressed in their houses and we can
visualize the unique relationships which
existed in the feudal era and observe
how they developed.

Just as some old towns reveal far
more of their story than others, so some

INSIDE THAXTED CHURCH

*Thaxted Church is a notable example of the late Gothic style of architecture asso-
ciated with the fifteenth century and known as Perpendicular. In Essex, and also in
the counties of Suffolk and Norfolk, Kent and Gloucestershire, this style is associated
with churches which were enlarged or built afresh during the period of the late medieval
woollen boom in those areas. In contrast with the rather grim and gloomy interiors of
early Gothic churches, those of the Perpendicular style were airy and light.*

THE VILLAGE OF CHIDDINGSTONE

Chiddingstone is the centre of a part of Kent which was especially flourishing in Tudor times. The village is unique in that it retains a whole row of Tudor and Elizabethan half-timbered houses, the earliest of which dates from the reign of Henry VII. This was a time at which landlords were first becoming conscious of the need to rehouse their workers and were building trim villages at a short distance from the manor-house, and were using more substantial materials for the cottages than the wattle and daub which before then had been customary in the countryside.

rural districts of Britain have a more interesting and a longer story to tell than others. Yet there are very few districts indeed where the chief elements of the story through the ages cannot be pieced together from the buildings and monuments and ruins which are there today.

In most rural communities the church is the oldest building standing today. Some few of these churches date back to Saxon times; not the early period of Saxon infiltration when the villages were being founded, but the later period of Saxon rule when Christianity swept across the country and Norman influence was beginning to make itself felt, especially in the reign of Edward the Confessor. It may be only a tower or an arch or, as in the case of Greensted, a nave of timber, or it may be the whole church, as at Bradford-on-Avon. Whatever it is, it is a link with the earliest period of real civilization in Britain after the time of the Roman occupation.

BRAMHALL HALL, CHESHIRE

This picturesque half-timbered building which dates in part from the fifteenth century illustrates one of the most interesting facets of historic Britain—the tendency for special localities to develop specialized forms of architecture in the Later Middle Ages. So in Cheshire and neighbouring counties, which at that time formed part of a well-wooded area, it became fashionable during the reign of the Tudor kings for wealthy landowners to vie with each other in building half-timbered houses of this unusual design and decoration. This fashion never spread beyond a small area.

HATFIELD HOUSE

The noble façade of this fine classical mansion, the ancestral seat of the Cecil family, has changed little since the beginning of the seventeenth century. It was James I who was the last royal resident at Hatfield and who exchanged it for near-by Theobalds Park. Then the old palace of Hatfield, where the young Princess Elizabeth was living when news of her accession was brought, was superseded by the brand-new classical mansion which dominates the extensive buildings of modern Hatfield House. Some parts of the original Tudor and Elizabethan house also remain.

Whether the parish church of today shows any signs of Saxon workmanship or not, it is most often on the site of a Saxon church. The unalterable elements of a Saxon village were the church, the home of the lord of the manor, or the thane as he was called then, the common-fields in which the people worked and, of course, the homes of the people themselves, though these were mere hovels, none of which have survived. None of the Saxon thanes' homes has survived either, because they were built of timber, a building material far from imperishable. The earlier Saxon churches were of timber also, but Greensted is the only one of these which has survived even in part—and that only because there the nave is fashioned from trunks of oak trees split in half, an unusually massive type of building.

It is significant that when once Christianity was firmly established the church was always the most pretentious building in the parish, and for several hundreds of years the only building commonly of stone, except in those few areas of the country, as the Cotswolds, where stone suitable for building is ready to hand and easy to obtain.

ST. PAUL'S CATHEDRAL, LONDON

*Damage from enemy bombardment during the Second World War opened out this
new view of London's St. Paul's Cathedral, which is generally recognized as the masterpiece of Sir Christopher Wren, himself the supreme master in Britain of Renaissance
building (1632–1723). The great dome is one of the finest of its kind in existence.
Wren is buried in the cathedral, with this inscription on his tomb:* Si monumentum
requiris, circumspice *(If you wish to see his monument, look around you). The
cathedral, known for long as the new St. Paul's, was built on the site of a Gothic
cathedral which was utterly destroyed in the Great Fire of 1666.*

THE ROYAL CRESCENT, BATH

Bath is often quoted as one of the earliest examples of modern town-planning. Roman towns in Britain were obviously planned with care; but at no time thereafter was any consciousness of design apparent in the growth of towns until the eighteenth century, when the architects Woods, father and son, were engaged in expanding the town at the time of its greatest fame. Rapid expansion was necessary because more and more people were settling in what had become an important centre of fashion. The Royal Crescent in Georgian style is one of the many handsome blocks of buildings erected. Other fine architectural features include Queen Square and the North and South Parades.

The village church is an eloquent witness to the varying fortunes of the parish from Saxon times until the Reformation. Whenever the parish was exceptionally prosperous the church was rebuilt or enlarged. When the land was held in the grip of poverty, as happened all too often in the Middle Ages, the church inevitably was allowed to decay.

There are literally hundreds of churches which show the work of successive centuries from the twelfth to the fifteenth, with perhaps a round-headed Norman window representing the twelfth century, early Gothic lancets in the chancel representing the thirteenth century, some ornamental tracery in the windows of one of the aisles representing the fourteenth century, and a tall tower added in the fifteenth. Not every church shows all these changes, but many do retain something from each century.

Apart from village churches the castles and abbeys are the signposts to the nature of rural life in the Middle Ages. They represent the two facets of life open to younger sons of gentle birth. The squire's eldest son always followed in his father's footsteps, but the many younger sons had virtually to choose between a military and a religious life. In rural England, before Tudor times, professional occupations as we understand them had not attained maturity or dignity. The vast majority chose a military career. Those who rebelled against the idea of violence frequently joined one or other of the monastic orders.

The castles in England started as a chain of fortresses built by the Normans to hold the Anglo-Saxons in check, many of them on the sites of Saxon castles. By the thirteenth century they

MARSTON MOOR

This monument beside a minor road which traverses the fertile Vale of York, a few miles from the city, commemorates the site of the battle of 1644 which proved the crowning victory of Oliver Cromwell's forces over the army of Prince Rupert. The site is level and now intensively cultivated. Not a hillock breaks the level expanse for miles around. In the seventeenth century, of course, the scene was entirely different, with many square miles of marshes, reed-choked and spongy, hampering movement and providing natural defence against the attack of an enemy.

GATEWAY OF BATTLE ABBEY

Battle Abbey in Sussex commemorates the site of the most famous of battles on British soil—Senlac, commonly known as the battle of Hastings. The story is that William the Conqueror, on gaining his victory, swore a vow that he would build an abbey on the site. The abbey he subsequently founded, a place of importance in medieval times, became known as Battle Abbey. The entrance gateway is seen here.

40

had outlived this purpose and became the centres of law and order and the administration of local justice. They were often the strongholds of barons who were by no means firm in their allegiance to the Crown, the undisputed overlords of petty "kingdoms," whose power over the people was very nearly absolute and whom the people were compelled by feudal precedent to follow into battle. There was, of course, another side to the coin. The forces at the disposal of the baron were useful in protecting the people of the neighbouring countryside against the bands of robbers and brigands which even then were beginning to infest the land.

If the castles may be regarded as the centres of law and order, the abbeys became the centres of good works, initiating whatever charity there was in a land where right still tended to be measured by might and where old people were few and far between, because the expectation of life was less than thirty years at birth and where the man or woman who could not work was regarded as a burden on the community.

ABBEYS AND PRIORIES

The earliest of the monastic orders which had widespread influence was the Benedictine. Another order which built a large number of houses in England and achieved a very wide influence was a breakaway order which rebelled against the growing affluence of the Benedictine abbots and restored some of the early ideals of monasticism. This order was known as the Cistercian Order. The majority of the rural abbeys belonged to it, for it was a cardinal point of Cistercian policy to find sites for their new abbeys far from the temptations and growing affluence of the towns. The monks are said to have built with their own hands the very

fine buildings of which generally only the ruins can be seen today. They tilled the land, fostered learning and looked after the spiritual needs of neighbouring communities with rather more singleness of purpose than the parish priest, who was usually a nominee of the lord of the manor.

Meanwhile the castle was merging into the manor-house. The two types of dwellings went on being built side by side for a time, but the later castles are more aptly called castellated manor-houses, their battlements unequal to even a day's siege. That fact reflects the changing spirit of the age and the changing nature of rural life in England. The risk of violence was no longer paramount. The need for castles was thought to have ceased to exist.

FORTIFIED MANORS

The earliest of the fortified manor-houses which have survived date from about the end of the fourteenth century. There are a number of dwelling places of this kind in Yorkshire and one or two in most counties. They are specially numerous in Kent, where life was particularly prosperous from the fourteenth to the sixteenth centuries. The manor-houses, like the churches and castles, were rebuilt again and again or enlarged at the whim of successive owners. Thus in the case of a manor-house such as Penshurst Place, the ancestral home of the Sidney family, we can trace the development of the Englishman's home from the early part of the fifteenth century to the present day. Ightham Mote is another house in Kent which was occupied as a manor-house before Tudor days and has been enlarged and rebuilt several times.

The early manor-house was a hall home, a house occupied almost entirely by a single large chamber, in line with the living quarters of the Norman castle, which were usually on the second or third floor so as to be out of the range of "fire" from attacking bowmen, but often confined to a single storey.

By the sixteenth century the manor-house had become a mansion and the number of rooms increased apace. Wealth and prosperity allowed the lord of the manor to keep large retinues of personal servants so that there grew up a hierarchy on the domestic side of the house as rigid as that in the squire's family. This, too, was the time when an increasing consciousness of the needs of the common people persuaded the great landowners to build substantial homes for the village people. The village as we know it today began to take shape. There are several examples of Tudor villages, especially in Kent, where Chiddingstone, for instance, remains today essentially in the shape and form of the early sixteenth century.

GREAT HOUSES

From the Tudor period onwards the interest of the wayfarer in search of historic Britain is not confined to the perception of changing social life, but includes recognition of the changing forms of architecture in the great houses as described in a later chapter in this book. We pass from the Elizabethan houses and the vast Jacobean mansions like Knole and Hatfield to the Renaissance palace and the birth of Georgian England, which is really the beginning of modern times. A new look in town and country alike has kept pace with the changing social order. It has developed briskly, but has never undergone a radical or sudden variation. Almost every village numbers a few sedate and dignified Georgian houses among its dwellings. Every old town, too, retains some Georgian façades.

The latter part of the eighteenth century was a great time for expansion in village and town alike. Modern ideas of town planning came into their own. Nash's design for Regent Street and Regent's Park is one example, the building of Bath and Cheltenham are two others where the tasteful styles of old building still dominate the town.

VICTORIAN HOUSES

It is not until we come to the nineteenth century, especially the second half of it, that development runs riot. This was an age of rapid town expansion and prosperity, with the accent on industry rather than agriculture. The Victorian stamp is on all the industrial towns, with their rows of ugly or at any rate monotonous small houses alternating with a few pretentious mansions on the outskirts of the towns where the industrialists made their homes.

The countryside escaped. There are, of course, Victorian villages, especially where the railway opened up new areas for development. This modest development in the countryside was matched by the decline of villages on or near the coach roads where the pleasant Georgian cottages remained the last word in up-to-dateness. That is why the landscape of the average village is today so much more attractive than that of the average town.

So finally in our everyday journeys, wherever they are, we can trace the story of town and village to the twentieth century, with its accent on experiment and its recoil from the Victorian tradition. A new era of prosperity in the countryside, added to a growing sense of responsibility in the minds of farmers and landowners, have produced a revolution in rural housing.

The chapters that follow reveal many other phases of historic Britain, and

ROBIN LYTHE'S CAVE, FLAMBOROUGH

Named after a notorious smuggler, this cave is one of many in Yorkshire's chalk headland of Flamborough Head. Whether any or all of these caverns were used by smugglers as temporary refuges or dumps for contraband goods is not known for certain, but the tradition that they were is strong. Certainly the Yorkshire coast was one of the most notorious areas in which smuggling was carried on profitably and with comparative immunity for a large part of the eighteenth century.

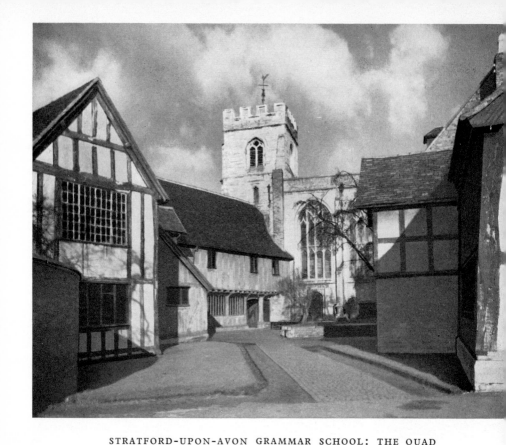

STRATFORD-UPON-AVON GRAMMAR SCHOOL: THE QUAD

There is a tradition that William Shakespeare was educated at the Grammar School of Stratford-upon-Avon, a tradition which is quite likely to represent the truth, for the school was founded at least as early as the fifteenth century. The building seen on the left in front of the chapel was originally the Hall of the Guild of Holy Cross, which was founded in the thirteenth century. The church was the chapel of the Guild and was rebuilt in the fifteenth century. The elaborate half-timber work is characteristic of the Stratford-upon-Avon district, which was exceptionally well wooded in medieval times.

especially the mark which great events and great men and women have set on the land. The literary pilgrim can follow in the footsteps of a Wordsworth or a Thomas Hardy, visiting the places that come to life in his favourite author's work and perceiving something of the spirit that moved those many great authors and authoresses who have been responsive to the countryside. One can visit the sites on which the great events of British history have taken place and recapture the atmosphere of a vital battle or an important event. At Runnymede, for instance, and on Magna Carta Island, we can envisage the scene as it was when King John met his barons and consented to sign the Briton's first charter of rights.

Sometimes there is a monument to remind us of a great event, as there is on the site of the battle of Marston Moor outside York, and on the sites of many other famous battles of the Civil

44

War and other troubled times. But monuments are poor things, of interest to the sightseer who collects snapshots rather than to the country lover interested in history. The latter's preoccupation must be with the atmosphere of the place, and in the case of battlefields with the nature of the terrain which often determined the course of the battle. Glencoe, the battlefield of Flodden, even the site of the battle of Hastings on which William of Normandy built the abbey which carries the name of Battle to this day, the fields of Bosworth, Edgehill and Naseby, Culloden Moor and Prestonpans—all these have their place in the historic story and all reveal to the wayfarer more of the nature of the country over which the great battles were fought than can be gleaned from any description, however detailed.

There are many houses, inns and cottages up and down the country which are associated with men and women who have inscribed their names, as it were, on the roll of fame. So numerous are the places associated with some of the most famous that imagination boggles at the number. It comes as no surprise to find that legend often improves on fact, sometimes for

THOMAS HARDY'S BIRTHPLACE

Thomas Hardy is known the world over as the novelist of Wessex, an Anglo-Saxon kingdom which has corresponded with no recognized geographical boundaries since the end of Saxon days. Many places in Dorset and neighbouring counties are recognizable, only thinly disguised, in Hardy's works. Hardy was himself a shrewd observer of Wessex country folk, just as he had an appreciative eye for the scenery in which they lived. Here is his birthplace in Higher Bockhampton, Dorset.

THE PARSONAGE AT HAWORTH

The parsonage at Haworth in the West Riding of Yorkshire was the home of the Brontë sisters from 1820 onwards, when their father, Patrick Brontë, was appointed to the living of the parish and took over the old parsonage. Here the three sisters, Charlotte, Emily and Anne, passed most of their lives. Charlotte was four when she came to Haworth, Emily was two, while Anne, the least successful of the three, was actually born in the parsonage. Charlotte and Emily both died here. Later the house was enlarged and is used as the headquarters of the Brontë Society.

wholly commercial reasons. If Queen Elizabeth had slept in all the beds that are claimed for her by optimistic inn-keepers she must indeed have been a lady of many more years than her life actually spanned.

However much imagination improves on fact, the facts do remain and there are a number of places given genuine added interest by their associations with the kings and queens of the realm and the famous through the ages. There is no doubt, for instance, about the royal visits to Kenilworth, and no doubt about the fantastic court which was once held in Berkhamsted Castle, nor any real doubt about the long line of early kings and queens who lived and stayed for a time in Windsor Castle and the other royal homes.

History and places and people are linked together, each the complement of the other, each making the under-standing of the other and its appreci-ation the easier to achieve. It would take a whole series of volumes and many millions of words to tell even in brief the historic story of all the ancient homes and the castles and the churches of Britain, but in the pages of this book there is a grand selection of the most romantic tales and the most interesting happenings associated with people and with places.

The fascinating hobby of discovering and interpreting the associations of the countryside does not end there. Almost every facet of country and town reflects the changing pattern of life. The inns, for instance, reflect in full the pageant of five centuries of change, starting from the pilgrims' inns, such as "The George" at Glastonbury, to the ultra-modern inns such as "The Battle of Britain" in Kent, which take their names from near-contemporary events.

There is a natural link between the old inns of Britain and the story of travel through the ages. The village pub is one thing, the roadside inn is something quite different, although often the two perform the same functions today. But the village pub away from the main roads is usually a cottage inn, if it is old, or a four-square rather uninteresting place if it is new. The roadside inns, by contrast, are often interesting in their architecture as well as in their story. On the trunk roads the largest of the old inns are usually those

KENILWORTH CASTLE FROM THE AIR

Norman fortress, Tudor palace, Kenilworth in its ruins spans eight hundred years of history. This photograph from the air shows the square Norman keep, the strong medieval encircling wall and the ruins of the palace in which Robert Dudley, Earl of Leicester, entertained Queen Elizabeth, as related in Sir Walter Scott's Kenilworth. After the Battle of Evesham in 1265 the son of Simon de Montfort held out in the castle for some months. The palatial buildings were largely destroyed by the Parliamentarians under Cromwell at the end of the great Civil War.

THE GEORGE INN AT GLASTONBURY

England has several inns which have continuous history as hostelries since the Middle Ages. The George Inn at Glastonbury is one of the most notable of these. It was originally a guest-house built in the fifteenth century to receive pilgrims to Glastonbury Abbey. When the monasteries were dissolved and Glastonbury Abbey along with the rest despoiled by order of Henry VIII, the inn continued in secular use.

which won fame and wealth for their landlords in the great coaching era, which reached its peak just before the competition of the railways ended it for ever.

Through the wayside inns we can recapture another absorbing tale of old England, the story of the roads and associated with them that of the vagabonds and highwaymen who from the first days of travel on the king's highway have plundered and robbed and made a precarious living from their violent deeds. It is a strange commentary on the unpredictable vagaries of memory that though the majority of highwaymen in every period paid for their misdeeds with their lives, after only a few years of brigandage, the names of some of them have been whitewashed by posterity until their owners are almost legendary heroes.

The story of travel in Britain starts in prehistoric times when the downland trackways were blazed and long roads stretching for hundreds of miles were

ROMAN ROAD NEAR MONMOUTH

Although the Romans were not the first road builders in Britain (that distinction belongs to a much earlier civilization), they were the first to engineer an outline system of main paved roads which could carry traffic at all seasons of the year. Although the course of many of the Roman roads remains the course of modern roads, as in the case of Watling Street, the actual paving of Roman roads has disappeared except in a few places, such as here near Monmouth, where much Roman paving has been laid bare.

engineered along the lower slopes of the hills, well above the tangled undergrowth of the valleys, but avoiding the steepest inclines and the exposed position of the tracks on the summit of the downs. These latter include the Pilgrims' Way and the Icknield Way, the former extending parallel with the North Downs from Salisbury Plain to Dover, the latter also starting at Salisbury Plain and following the line of the Berkshire Downs, the Chiltern Hills and the East Anglian Heights to the coast near Hunstanton.

The Romans, who were great road engineers, improved these earlier highways. That is why many parts of them are still metalled roads today; for once a highway is established, however much it falls into decay there is the likelihood that at some future time it will be revived or rebuilt. In other parts these ancient roads are grassy tracks.

As well as renewing the older roads, the Romans built a complex series of new roads linking in straight lines all the chief centres of population in the south. Although after the Roman era in Britain there were several hundred years of anarchy, these Roman roads still form the basis of our modern network of highways, among them the Roman road from London to York and the straightest road in all Britain for a comparable number of miles, the great Watling Street, linking London with the midlands and the north-west in one direction and with Dover in the other.

LITTLE JOHN'S GRAVE AT HATHERSAGE

The legends surrounding Robin Hood and his Merrie Men are among the most persistent and widespread in Britain and cover a wide area which includes Sherwood Forest, and extends as far north as the coast of Yorkshire and as far west as the Welsh Marches. A national hero by all accounts as typifying the resistance of the indigenous people to conquerors from abroad, Robin Hood achieved for his exploits a respect greater than that accruing inevitably to the daring deeds of every adventurer. Here in the churchyard of Hathersage, Derbyshire, is the reputed grave of Little John.

"THE ROSE AND CROWN," HEMPSTEAD, ESSEX

Several houses, including more than one inn, claim the "privilege" of having been the birthplace of Dick Turpin, the most notorious of English highwaymen. "The Rose and Crown" at Hempstead has strong claims, for the parish register records the baptism on 21 September, 1705, of Richard, the son of John and Mary Turpin. It is said the young Dick, as a boy, listened to the exploits of the highwaymen and robbers, who frequented his father's inn, through a hole in the floor of one of the upper rooms. These tales fired his imagination and led him to become in later life a highwayman himself.

In early Saxon days organized travel on the roads ceased, for every man's hand was against every other man and there was no normal trade or commerce to take people far from their homes. By the time the crown of England passed to the Normans life in most of the country was once more settled and travel once again a natural concomitant of life. Inevitably the state of unrest which followed the change of government produced its own group of brigands and highwaymen, especially since the roads were mostly rough and difficult tracks and provided many opportunities for staging an ambush. The roads at that time were chiefly the remains of the Roman system of highways which had been allowed to fall into disrepair for hundreds of years and which neither the Saxons nor the Normans had had the labour nor the opportunity to set in order again.

Legend has sanctified these highwaymen of the eleventh and twelfth centuries and transformed them into heroes quite different from what they really were. The legends of Robin Hood and his Merrie Men are widespread and varied. Above all, the other Robin Hood has become a national hero, the subject of countless stories, numerous books and more than one film. His exploits were centred on Sherwood Forest, and he is always pictured as a man incredibly daring, incredibly skilled and incredibly good.

THE REAL ROBIN HOOD

Robin Hood's character is based without a doubt on a genuine historical outlaw who lived in defiance of Norman authority, carrying on the Saxon tradition in barely accessible parts of the country during the early part of the twelfth century. There is an actual reference to Robin Hood in fourteenth-century literature, by which time he had assumed many of his legendary characteristics. He is the embodiment of all the sturdy Anglo-Saxon virtues, the enemy of the Norman-controlled church, the stern opponent of tyranny, the robber of the rich to succour the poor.

As the civilization of Britain increased and its internal commerce became more and more important, travel along its roads was an inescapable risk which merchants and private people, too, had no option but to accept. New roads were built, but even when the first of the regular stage-coach services were in operation many of the main roads were still little more than tracks—hollow ways, as some of them came to be called, because literally the repeated passage of coaches over them dug deeper and deeper into the mud until very often all that could be seen of a passing coach from the near-by fields was its upper deck or its roof. After heavy rain coaches would become hopelessly stuck in the mud, especially on hills, and that was one of the times when the highwaymen could strike successfully.

THE LAST OF THE HIGHWAYMEN

Claude Duval was one of the most famous or infamous of highwaymen of the seventeenth-century Restoration days. He was a Frenchman who came to England at the time of the Restoration in the service of one of the King's friends and soon found that he could make a more profitable living from a career of lawlessness.

Dick Turpin is the best known of all highwaymen, a man who was born within a few years of the beginning of the eighteenth century and was hanged with due pomp and circumstance in 1739, a short life and not so far as can be seen a very merry one. In any age Dick Turpin would have been an outlaw. He was horse-stealer, smuggler and burglar, as well as a specialist in holding up coaches and robbing travellers. Yet such is fame that more than one house in Essex claims to be the place of his birth—he was born at an inn at Hempstead—while the exploits of himself and his horse, Black Bess, and his legendary ride from London to York are the subject matter of Harrison Ainsworth's best-selling and well-loved novel called *Black Bess*.

Highwaymen had almost died out by the time the railways came. The birth of the railways sounded their death-knell, for robbing the traffic that was left to the roads was no longer a profitable investment if it involved the possibility of the highwayman being hanged.

CHAPTER 1
INVADERS THROUGH THE AGES

FROM earliest times, long before recorded history began, a succession of invaders has overrun Britain. Britain stands on the very edge of the Continent, a land of promise to peoples living across the broad moat of the English Channel, a place of refuge when they are threatened from the rear, a place of hope when their numbers are multiplying or their crops failing.

Such are the things that cause invasion in modern times and in ancient times alike. Go where you will in southern England you will never be far from some tell-tale sign of invaders who have passed over the land, some of them six thousand years ago, some of them less than one thousand. We now know that peoples migrated from the Continent to Britain scores of thousands of years ago, but the traces they left have been erased.

It is said that when the earliest invaders came to Britain the Strait of Dover was less wide than it is today, indeed that Britain was once linked to the Continent by an isthmus. This is now accepted by many scientists as a fact. We can at any rate be certain that some of the monuments of ancient races who peopled Britain and who won their new living-space by invasion are five or six thousand years old.

Have you ever walked along the Ridgeway on the summit of the Berkshire Downs, a magnificent walk from near the Thames at Goring, right on as far as the Marlborough Downs? If you have you will almost certainly have noticed a clump of trees on the hilltop a few miles from Wantage and have seen some large stones in the shelter of the trees, though the purpose and meaning of the stones may have escaped you at first glance. This is Wayland's Smithy and it is a link with the Stone Age in Britain. The stones which you see today are part of a burial-chamber built by Stone Age man about five thousand years ago. The stones are called megaliths, which literally means "big stones," and in this sense all Stone Age stones are megalithic. They represent the work of an invading people known to be a long-headed race. This is known because fragments of skulls which have been discovered in several burial-chambers like Wayland's Smithy have proved to be those of a long-headed people.

It is assumed that Wayland's Smithy was the tomb of a famous chieftain or warrior because, although a few long barrows (as these burial-places are called) may have disappeared entirely, aerial surveys have brought to light a number which were not previously suspected, and the relatively small number of them suggests that this form of burial must have been reserved for very special members of the tribe.

A barrow means a mound of earth. You may find that surprising when you see Wayland's Smithy and find no trace of an earthen barrow. Actually when they were constructed all the Stone

Age burial-chambers were covered over with earth, which has disappeared in the intervening thousands of years, partly by natural erosion (that is, the normal wearing away of raised parts of the earth's surface by weather) and partly through cultivation and the instinctive tendency of agriculturalists, the world over and at all times, to level out small irregularities in the land.

If you would like to see what a long barrow looked like three thousand years ago you must go to Gloucestershire, where the Belas Knap Long Barrow has been restored with meticulous care to something like its original appearance.

Burial-chambers are not the only stone monuments which these races of invaders have bequeathed to us. Have you ever driven along the road from Oxford to Stratford-upon-Avon ? If you have you will have seen the signpost pointing to the Rollright Stones. Here within a hundred yards of each other are three different kinds of Stone Age monument. There is a burial-chamber called the Whispering Knights, a circle of standing stones called the King's Men and a single large upright stone called the King Stone. Single stones like this are called monoliths. They occur in all parts of Great Britain to

A PREHISTORIC TOMB ON ANGLESEY

This megalithic tomb, known as Bryn-celli-ddu, is in the island of Anglesey. The type of burial-place it represents, consisting essentially of a chamber walled and roofed with large stones with a more or less elaborate entrance, is associated in England with the late Stone Age. The chamber was covered by an earthen mound usually long in shape, but sometimes round. The tomb, seen here, has been restored and has an earth covering. In the case of many tombs the mound has disappeared owing to the action of the weather or other causes leaving the stones exposed (see page 55).

TRETHEVY QUOIT

Trethevy Quoit is near St. Cleer, in Cornwall. Like most of the Cornish quoits (the word being a Celtic variation of cromlech), Trethevy is all that remains of a late Stone Age burial-place, and was originally capped with an elongated mound of earth (see page 54). Such barrows are attributed to the latter part of the Stone Age. Confirmation has been given by human remains found in many of them, the barrows revealing remains of the long-headed megalithic race then found in Britain.

which the long-headed Stone Age people penetrated, all over the southern downlands, along the Pennine Chain, on the moors of the south-west and in the Lake District. Yet no one can say with certainty for what purpose they were set up. All that can be said is that they are monuments, perhaps in memory of a successful battle or of a great hero.

A little more is known about the stone circles. They are thought to have been temples to the worship of the sun god, for it is almost certain that Stone Age man was an actual worshipper of the sun.

Like the single standing stones, stone circles are widely distributed in Britain. There is a famous one near Keswick, in the Lake District, several on Dartmoor, at least two in Derbyshire, and a number of others of which only fragments remain.

There is one thing that all the monuments to this race of long ago have in common. Every one of them is near the prehistoric trackways which comprised the first road system in Great Britain, along which in fact successive waves of invaders advanced through Britain.

THE DRUIDS' CIRCLE AT KESWICK

This is a stone circle on the fringe of Lakeland, also known as Castlerigg. The association with the Druid religion presupposed by its popular name is imaginary. It belongs in fact to the large family of stone circles of which Stonehenge is the most elaborate in Britain (also popularly but wrongly associated with the Druids). Most probably these stone circles were temples at which the people worshipped in the last few centuries of the Stone Age (about 2,000 to 1,800 B.C.). Many, partly by inference from their form, regard them as temples to a sun god.

Many of the ancient trackways are traceable today. In fact so well were they sited that many of them have continued in use throughout the four or five thousand years since they were constructed. The two most famous are the Pilgrims' Way and the Icknield Way.

The Pilgrims' Way, which follows the lower slopes of the chalk downs from Salisbury Plain to the sea at Dover, takes its modern name from the thought that it was used by pilgrims to the shrine of St. Thomas à Becket at Canterbury. It is, however, known for certain that it is very much older than the pilgrimages to Canterbury. It always avoids the low ground of the valley, which in prehistoric times was boggy and forest-covered, yet it rarely rises to the summit of the downs and has remained through the ages an ideal road linking the points at which the rivers cutting through the chalk downs can be most easily forded. So it passes through Guildford at the traditional ford over the Wey, through Burford Bridge over the traditional ford at the Mole, and so on.

It is itself part of the longer road that is called the Hard Way and which goes on by the Dorset Downs from Salisbury Plain into the south-west corner of England, the trackway that once linked the populous districts of the plain with the Dartmoor country, also an important centre of prehistoric civilization.

The Icknield Way bears the same relation to the northern spur of the chalk as the Pilgrims' Way does to the southern spur. It runs through Berkshire and Buckinghamshire, following the line of the Berkshire Downs and the Chiltern Hills, continuing by the borders of Cambridgeshire and Essex and along the line of high ground which borders East Anglia, ending at the chalk cliffs at Hunstanton in Norfolk. For its last few miles it is called the Peddar Way, a name derived, like the Pilgrims' Way, from a misapprehension. Peddar means "pilgrim" and the name originates from the erroneous belief that the road was made by pilgrims to the shrine of Our Lady of Walsingham.

If you stand on any high point in the area of Salisbury Plain on a clear day and scan the land around you with the help of a pair of field-glasses you will be struck by the numbers of little hills or irregularities in the surface of the plain. These are round barrows, the burial-places of the invading races which followed Stone Age man. These races had mastered the use of bronze.

STONE AGE DWELLINGS IN THE ORKNEYS

Skara Brae is the name of the place in which excavation has revealed these well-marked foundations of human dwelling places. These were used by a Stone Age people of the same stage of civilization as the builders of the many Stone Age monuments in southern England. The date of these dwellings, however, is probably much later than 2,000 B.C. when Stone Age civilization was at its height in the south. As fresh hordes of invaders swept across southern England the indigenous population migrated northward and their descendants, the Picts, were later harrying Roman Britain.

The age in which they lived in Britain, from about 1,800 B.C. for at least a thousand years, is called the Bronze Age.

An interesting thing about the Bronze Age people is that they were a round-headed race buried in round barrows, in contrast with the long-headed Neolithic race who were buried in long barrows. It is possible only to surmise how they came to Britain, but it seems fairly certain that they advanced from the south-east coast along the trackways which have been constructed by Stone Age man, and with the help of their superior bronze weapons defeated their predecessors. They may well have absorbed a good deal of the Stone Age culture, including their religious worship; there is evidence for that at the great temple of Stonehenge.

STONEHENGE

Stonehenge is one of the most remarkable prehistoric monuments in the world. Excavation on the site by archaeologists has proved almost beyond doubt that it was built at the extreme end of the Stone Age and was in active use well into the Bronze Age. This suggests that the method of worship did not change suddenly with the coming of the bronze-using people, though it may be that bronze was introduced by way of commerce even in advance of the round-headed race who used it for all purposes.

Stonehenge consists of two concentric stone circles and a number of other stones outside the circles proper. One of the stone circles consists of blocks of sandstone set perpendicularly, with horizontal slabs resting upon them and adhering to them by toggle joints. The composition of these vast stones is the same as that of the other standing stones and stone circles of the downland country, that is to say, sandstone, which was found locally and was part of a covering of sandstone which hundreds of thousands of years ago lay over the chalk.

The smaller circle of Stonehenge, the circle of blue stones, as they are called, is composed of stones which the geologists maintain could not have been found nearer than the Prescelly Hills in Pembrokeshire. So here we have an example of prehistoric people taking enormous pains to procure for their greatest temple stones which must have had some sacred properties. To transport these stones from Pembrokeshire to the centre of Salisbury Plain was a feat of communications which presupposes a high degree of civilization and tribal organization. How it was done is one of those mysteries which still defy scientists. Whether the stones were brought overland along the trackways or brought by sea round Land's End and up the Wiltshire Avon is a problem which can never be solved.

EARLY IRON AGE

The next wave of invasions into Britain was associated with the early Iron Age. We have seen how bronze superseded stone as the raw material of weapons and implements and made possible the widespread incursions of bronze-using people. Much the same happened with iron. How or when it was invented no man knows. Iron weapons proved vastly superior to weapons of bronze. Consequently a people equipped with them were able to defeat any people equipped only with the earlier weapons.

Iron was probably introduced into Britain along the trackway trade-routes before this next conquest, but the Bronze Age people were not able to arm themselves effectively with the new

THE ENTRANCE TO MAIDEN CASTLE

Maiden Castle in Dorset is the largest and the most elaborate of prehistoric earthworks in Britain. It is defended by triple earthen ramparts and ditches, still much in evidence. The fortified east entrance is shown in this picture, which also gives an idea of the nature of the defences. These originally had vertical sides, each bank and ditch forming a real obstacle to an attacking enemy. Maiden Castle was a tribal centre and was at the height of its power in the centuries immediately preceding the Christian era. It continued to be occupied during part at least of the Roman domination of Britain.

material before waves of invaders burst out from the continent of Europe, following much the same routes of invasion as had their predecessors. There were in fact invasions by several races of iron-armed warriors between the end of the first millennium B.C. and the beginning of the Roman occupation in the first century A.D.

By comparison with the stone monuments of the New Stone Age and the round barrows of the Bronze Age there are comparatively few memorials to the Iron Age peoples, though the few that do exist are spectacular and fascinating.

If you have ever been to the loveliest of all English racecourses, Goodwood, on a race day you will have seen hundreds of people posted on a conspicuous near-by hill. This is the Trundle Hill. If you look more carefully you will see that its summit rises, as it were, in tiers. These tiers are the entrenchments of an Iron Age village.

The Trundle is one of many similar fortified positions belonging to about the same age. They vary in size and in the complexity of their defences. Some have a single rampart and ditch to protect them. Others have two or three concentric ramparts. They all have one thing in common: they are set on high ground, usually in the chalk country and nearly always occupying a dominating position from which to look out and watch for the advance of any attacking forces.

Maiden Castle in Dorset is one of the finest of them all. Here there are triple lines of entrenchments with most cunningly concealed entrances. The ramparts enclose a space which even by modern standards would hold a sizable village or small town. Maiden Castle was a tribal capital in the Iron Age.

From this time dates the first lowland civilization of Britain which had previously been colonized only on the high ground away from the swamps and the impenetrable forests which covered the valleys. Iron has a very special significance because the use of iron tools allowed the Britons to make a start on the enormous work of clearing the valleys, and so make available for cultivation vast areas which had previously produced nothing. The clearing of the valleys necessitated valley settlements. Towns began to arise at strategic points in the valleys, especially where rivers could be forded and at points which were suitable for the defence of some pass through the hills.

That brings us to the next phase in Britain's story of invasions—the Roman occupation. The Romans often adopted

ON THE ARAN ISLANDS

Research by archaeologists is discovering more and more information about prehistoric civilization in Scotland and Ireland. Dun Aengus in the Aran Islands, one of the many prehistoric forts of Ireland, encloses an area of eleven acres on the edge of the cliffs. The outer defences of this vast encampment are shown below. They consist of well-built dry-stone walls in the same tradition as the walls, for instance, of the dwelling places (shown on page 57) in the Orkney Islands.

THE ROMAN WALL, NEAR HOUSESTEADS

This is one of the finest parts of the great Roman military wall which formed the boundary of the Roman province of Britain from the reign of Hadrian onwards and linked the estuary of the Tyne with the Solway Firth. The wall is here well preserved and is about four feet high and five feet thick, consisting of the usual filling of rubble faced with locally quarried stone. Originally the wall was considerably higher, its foundations having subsided in the many centuries since it was built.

pre-Roman towns, re-fortified them and made them their own. At St. Albans, for instance, you will see the whole story spread before you. You will find the ruins of a Roman city which was a proud place for hundreds of years before it was swept away and destroyed in the Anglo-Saxon invasions. You will find substantial remnants of the Roman wall which defended the city and outside it parts of the ditch and bank which were the fortifications of the British town, itself, like Maiden Castle, a tribal centre long before the Romans came.

You will see how the Romans wisely retained the defences of the town that already existed and strengthened them by adding a wall of rubble and stone.

Many and varied are the traces left of the Roman occupation, which after its warlike opening of invasion and battle settled down into four hundred years of almost continuous peace and unbroken development.

The first invasions of the Romans were under the leadership of Julius Caesar in 55 and 54 B.C., but they were no more than large-scale raids. They

THE BALKERNE GATE AT COLCHESTER

This gateway, one of the oldest surviving in Britain, was a postern gate for the entry of foot passengers only into the Roman walled city of Camulodunum. The Balkerne Gate and the fragments of the Roman walls recall the capture of the town by the Iceni led by their queen, Boadicea. It was after this that the Roman engineers surrounded the town with walls which proved impregnable until the Saxon invasions.

left no mark on the British countryside. When the Romans came again, almost a hundred years after these raids, they came in greater strength and with the full determination to conquer. This they did with little difficulty, for the ground was prepared before them by a fifth column and the only decisive battle which it was necessary to fight took place in the hills on either side of the Medway, near where the city of Rochester stands today.

Just outside London, Epping Forest is a sure bulwark against the further extension of the metropolis. Among its leafy glades are two ancient encampments, both of them undoubtedly fortified positions of the Iron Age Britons. One of them, Ambresbury Banks, is still recognizable by its deep trench and well-preserved earthen ramparts. It recalls memories of a most successful rebellion against the Roman invaders, a rebellion organized and carried out with great military skill by a tribal queen known in legend as Boadicea. It was here, tradition relates, that Boadicea made her last stand against the Romans, when they had collected their forces and turned their whole army against the revolting Britons.

The majority of present-day links with Roman Britain derive from the two hundred or so years during which Roman civilization was at its height, and the province of Britannia was organized and productive not only of the first urban civilization that Britain had known, but also of many great works of art, especially in architecture.

FIRST URBAN CIVILIZATION

Perhaps the most significant monuments to the skill and persistence of the Romans are the walled towns which they established. The outline plan of these is still often visible in the layout of modern cities. Substantial fragments of the walls are still standing nearly two thousand years after they were built. St. Albans, which has been mentioned before, is unusual because the site of the medieval and modern town is different from that of the Roman. The Roman town was called Verulamium, and the centre of the modern city of St. Albans is about a mile away from the nearest part of the Roman walls. This has made it possible to reconstruct the ground plan of Verulamium with far more certainty than is possible in most places where the original site has been built over.

In every Roman town there were four main streets, running roughly north, south, east and west, and crossing at a central crossroads. There were gates at the four extremities of the main roads. The civic centre, which included administrative offices, the public baths and the market, was situated near the central crossroads, while the villas in which the citizens lived were built along the main roads and along subsidiary roads which led off the main ones at right-angles. Many of the houses facing the main roads had shops for their lower stories, where the craftsmen who were the most important people of the Roman town offered their wares for sale.

ROMAN TOWN-PLANNING

Chichester is a famous example of a place which was first built by the Romans and has survived as far as the ground plan is concerned to the present time. The four main streets of Chichester which meet at the medieval market-cross close to the cathedral are sited on precisely the same ground as the four main streets of the Roman town.

There are many other examples up and down Britain. Take London, for example. You might not expect to find anything belonging to Roman London in the modern metropolis, but as in many other cases the medieval city of London grew up on the site of Roman Londinium, and the medieval walls were raised on the remains of the Roman walls and used much of the same masonry and nearly always the same foundations. At Tower Hill and several other places you can see the fragments of the Roman wall, usually built into the wall of some relatively modern building, but still exhibiting the same courses of Roman tiles as does the wall of Verulamium.

Some of London's main roads are, as at Chichester, on the same sites as the roads which the Romans built. This is not strictly true within the old city of London, for the rebuilding after the

Great Fire changed the lay-out of the whole beyond recognition. It is true, however, of some parts of the West End and of the near suburbs which have grown up in the last two or three hundred years and where no great catastrophe has necessitated re-planning. Thus the Old Kent Road, leading from New Cross Gate to London Bridge, is a Roman road, a part of Watling Street, of which we shall have more to say later. The Edgware Road is part of the same road, which originally led from Dover through London to the Midlands. In other words, the Old Kent Road is Watling Street before it entered the Roman town of Londinium, the Edgware Road is Watling Street after it had left the town. Oxford Street is largely on the site of a Roman road.

CHEDWORTH ROMAN VILLA EXCAVATED

The Romans were the first builders in stone and brick on a large scale in Britain. They brought to their far-distant province all the artistry and skill which made their own Italian homes famous throughout the civilized world. Inevitably most of what they achieved in Britain has perished, but excavation has brought to light parts of many of the country houses which they built in the south. The Chedworth Roman villa which was buried for some centuries under a landslide is unusually well preserved. Here is the interior of the bathing chamber, showing the tessellated floor of the larger room and the elaborate heating arrangement beneath.

BURGH CASTLE, NEAR YARMOUTH

One of the more substantial Roman remains in Britain, Burgh Castle belongs to the group of defences known as forts of the Saxon Shore built during the fourth century as a last despairing effort by the Romans in Britain to hold off the attacks of the invading Saxons. The fortress encloses about five acres of land. On one side there is no wall, nor any signs of there having been one. It is thought that this may have been occupied by a quay, the fortress itself affording a safe anchorage and unloading facilities for supply vessels coming to Britain from the Continent.

So we might go on almost indefinitely giving examples to show how the influence of the Roman invaders on modern town-planning is real and definite. Wherever you find four straight roads meeting at a cross in a city which is known to have been a Roman town, the probability is that these modern streets are sited on the lines of the original Roman roads.

There are many other towns, too, where you can see parts of the original Roman walls. York is one of them. Here the Roman remains include a multangular tower, the only one of its kind left in Britain, part of the supporting defences of the main wall.

At Colchester there is the Balkerne gateway, hard by the castle, one of the original entrances into the Roman town. Indeed, the whole of Colchester cries aloud its association with the Roman invaders. It is not so much that any Roman buildings survive. They do not. But almost all the old buildings (and there are many in Colchester) are built partly or entirely from Roman materials, including the Norman castle and the ruins of the Norman abbey of St. Botolph.

One part of England is often referred to as the country of the Roman Wall. This is the expanse of wild country just south of the Scottish border reaching from the North Sea to the Solway Firth. It was here that the Romans finally set the boundary of their province and constructed a wall, one of the greatest engineering feats of the ancient world, to act as a protection against the incursions of the hostile Picts and Scots who lived in what is today Scotland.

ROMAN ROADS

There are many Roman roads in Britain still in use. One of the finest is probably that which runs from Cirencester to Gloucester. It has all the qualities by which you can recognize the hand of the Roman engineers. It is straight, so straight that one wonders immediately how it was possible to drive such a road through untrodden country. That is one of the wonders of the Roman road system which is a complete system linking all the centres of population of those days. It was a system so well surveyed that where the old centres of population are still cities or towns the roads linking them today are generally on the same course as those constructed by the Romans.

If you travel from London to Dover through Chatham you will be on the Roman road almost all the time. If you travel from London to Huntingdon you will follow the line of the Roman road all the way beyond Puckeridge, more than half the total distance. It is rather odd when you come to think of it that the shortest way from London to Alconbury Hill (where the Roman road meets the Great North Road) is by way of Huntingdon, that is to say, by the old Roman road rather than by the

newer Great North Road, which actually takes about two miles more to reach the same place. The Romans, indeed, knew the truth of the geometrical proposition that the shortest distance between two points is a straight line joining them, an axiom which medieval road-builders completely forgot and modern ones often choose to neglect in order to avoid a difficult crossing of a river or a steep gradient.

Bignor is a tiny village nestling under the northern slopes of the Sussex Downs. If you have travelled along the road that connects Bignor with the main road at Bury Hill you will have seen a signpost which says: "To the Roman Villa." Here is to be found the ground-plan and fragments of a house, large even by modern standards, which was inhabited about the second and third centuries by a merchant-farmer.

ROMAN VILLAS

A tremendous amount about the way the people lived in Roman Britain can be learnt by looking at this and other ruined villas and by studying the reconstructions and reading the guide-books. The finest of them all is generally conceded to be the one at Chedworth in Gloucestershire. This, the story goes, was buried by a landslide soon after the end of the Roman occupation and so remained more intact than any others have done. You will be surprised at the luxury of the tessellated pavements which Romano-British builders used for floors. You will be amazed at the elaborate system of baths which almost every villa contains—not just a bath in the modern sense of the term, but a series of chambers which were heated with hot air and gave something very like a modern Turkish bath.

It is often said that British people are Anglo-Saxons. That like so many other

66

THE CHURCH OF WING, BUCKINGHAMSHIRE

Before the Norman occupation there were many hundreds of churches in England,
most of the older ones being made from timber, the newer ones built near the beginning
of the eleventh century in stone. Less than a dozen have survived in anything like an
intact condition, but many, like the parish church of Wing above, have substantial
parts of the original Saxon church overlaid by later medieval additions. Here the apse,
part of the nave and the crypt are all attributed with some certainty to Saxon builders,
though, as the picture shows, the apse has been pierced by a later window.
The shallow arcades of the apse are typically Saxon in design.

DONAGHMORE CROSS,
COUNTY DOWN

This perfect example of a Celtic cross is one of many thousands in Ireland, Scotland, Wales and the northern districts of England. Many of them are beautifully carved in traditional Celtic style, others are plain and unadorned. They vary in date from the middle Saxon period until the end of the Middle Ages. Crosses were sometimes erected in villages and small settlements where there was no church as a constant reminder to the people of the need to worship God. In late medieval times many were erected at crossroads.

general statements is only partly true, as can be seen when it is remembered that all the invading peoples we have so far mentioned have no Saxon blood, and indeed the Saxons had not yet appeared in Britain. The Saxon invasions began as the Roman occupation ended. The Saxons were barbarians by Romano-British standards and laid waste the civilization of Britain.

The earliest monuments to them are the Roman castles called the forts of the Saxon shore, which were built in South-east England at the end of the fourth century, when the Saxon tribes were showing signs of becoming dangerous. Amazingly strong buildings these are and amazingly intact are the walls of at least one of them, the great fort at Pevensey called Anderida, a particularly interesting ruin today because inside it later invaders, the Normans, built one of their own castles, so that here at this one site you have the fortifications of two separate periods nearly seven hundred years apart.

THE SAXON INVASIONS

Tradition has a great deal to say about the early Saxon invaders. Ebbs-fleet, near Ramsgate, in Thanet, is the place where legend has it Hengist and Horsa landed at the head of the earliest Saxon invasions. The same spot is also the supposed site of the landing of St. Augustine, who introduced Christianity into the south of England. Such links with the Anglo-Saxons are tenuous in the extreme, but they left a far more solid memorial to themselves, a memorial that consists of no less than the very shape and character of the British countryside. The Angles, the Saxons and the Jutes founded by far the greater number of the villages of Britain. They founded them most commonly by the side of rivers, where they obtained a

68

OFFA'S DYKE

Offa's Dyke is now a discontinuous earthwork and ditch which originally extended in an unbroken line from the estuary of the Wye to that of the Dee. It shows little sign of having been an important defence, and is more likely to have been a treaty line or line of demarcation between the land of the Welsh tribes and Saxon England. It is named after Offa, King of Mercia (died 796). We have not sufficient evidence to say whether it was actually constructed during the reign of that king or not, though the author of an early life of Alfred ascribes it to the king. A small section of the earthwork is seen here.

constant supply of fresh water. They made clearings in the forests where the Romans had failed to do so and extended the clearings which the Romans themselves had begun.

The Saxons gave their name also to many of the counties. Sussex is the land of the South Saxons, Essex of the East Saxons. Norfolk and Suffolk are distinguished as being the country of the North Folk and the South Folk, and so on. Nor is that surprising when it is remembered that the Saxon invaders virtually gave to Britain its language.

Just as the Saxon invaders, or rather their descendants, were beginning to build a stable state, the next wave of invaders arrived on the scene—this time the Vikings or Northmen, who, coming from Denmark and Scandinavia, sailed in their longboats into the Saxon realms of eastern England. Like the Saxons before them they were successful in establishing themselves; at one time almost half of England was under the government of the Northmen.

When Christianity had swept Britain after St. Augustine's conversion of

THE HERITAGE OF SAXON CARVING IN STONE

Although Saxon workmanship was generally rude by comparison with the refined beauty of Norman and later medieval building, Saxon art in the form of stone carving was well in advance of the achievements in architecture. Probably most of the few existing Saxon stone carvings were carried out under the supervision of Norman master-masons. This carved coffin lid is in Wirksworth Church. It depicts several interesting episodes from the life of Christ arranged in two strips above and below the narrow projecting ridge seen in the centre of the piece of sculpture.

Kent the village churches began to be built. The history of the typical village church is that the first building was erected during the latter part of the Saxon period and was then rebuilt and enlarged again and again through the Middle Ages, so that many churches show a mixture of building styles ranging over five hundred years. That is the reason why there are so few Saxon churches left intact. They were solidly built enough and many would probably have survived to the present day had it not been for the necessity of enlarging them for the growing population.

Greensted Church in Essex is one of the most remarkable Saxon monuments in Great Britain. Here the walls of the nave are made up of trunks of oak trees cut in half down the middle, with the smooth face innermost and the rounded face forming the outer wall. Greensted Church goes back to the time before stone had begun to be widely used for building, and in the forest country timber was the commonest, and perhaps the only, building material.

There is no other church in Britain which quite rivals Greensted in antiquarian interest, but there are a number scattered over the country in which you can see substantial parts of the Saxon church—churches such as Bradford-on-Avon and Earls Barton.

There is one other memorial to Saxon times which few wayfarers notice. We have seen already how many roads derive from the Roman road-system. What is not so well known is that there is still a number of roads which derive from Saxon rights of way. It is really quite simple to distinguish them. If you are travelling on a road (it will usually be a by-way, because the main roads have been straightened) and find you go straight for about a quarter of a mile, then turn sharply to the right or to the left, then after a hundred yards find that the road makes another sharp turn and resumes its original direction, you can be pretty sure that this is a road first coming into existence in Saxon times. The reason is that under the Saxons Britain followed the feudal system. One facet of this system was that the land was cultivated in strips, long and narrow, with rights of way going down the length of each strip and along the bottom of it. The twisting road is thus a combination of rights of way down two strips of cultivated land.

The last of the great invasions of Britain was the Norman invasion in 1066. The Normans landed at Pevensey. The battle of Hastings was fought at Senlac. On the site of the battle an abbey was founded to commemorate the Norman victory. This abbey is

THE CASTLE OF CARDIFF

Norman suzerainty was never recognized by the Welsh tribes. In the north and central districts indeed the Normans made little progress, but in the south they made a real effort to subdue the Celtic people and bring the fertile Vale of Glamorgan into the English economy. Cardiff Castle, of which the Norman mound and part of the keep survive (clearly seen near the centre of the photograph), was their most elaborate fortress in this part of Wales. Part of the outer walls was added in the nineteenth century.

THE SOUTH DOORWAY OF BARFRESTON

Unique in the beauty of its late Norman carving, the church at Barfreston, Kent, is remarkable also for the perfection of its Norman design and the absence of important later additions or alterations. The south doorway, pictured here, is the most elaborately carved part of the whole church. Classical columns support recessed and carved semi-circular arches, each delicately moulded, while above the door the tympanum contains a carving of Christ with added foliation and scroll-work.

known to us today as Battle Abbey. After the battle of Hastings there was little apparent resistance to the Normans. The Norman king, William, brought over a number of his barons to hold the country in security. Each of the barons built for himself a castle. Therein lies the origin of the string of Norman castles which is such an important and even exciting feature of the medieval architecture of Britain.

There are many other links with the Norman invaders, such as the Rufus Stone in the New Forest, which marks the place where William Rufus was shot by a stray arrow while hunting. The New Forest itself was created by the Normans as a reserve for sport. Yet the castles are the most vivid links with the last armed conquerors of Britain— Rochester, the Tower of London, Colchester, and dozens of others.

THE CASTLE OF DOVER

Nearly two thousand years of defence are represented on the castle hill of Dover. The earthworks are Roman and possibly earlier in origin, while the whole hill was one of the key points in the defence of the Roman province against the invading Saxons. The church of St. Mary-in-Castro in the background contains much Saxon work, while the lighthouse in front of it dates from the time when Dover was a port for commerce between Britain and the Roman Empire. The keep of the castle in the foreground is Norman, the encircling walls a mixture of medieval and modern.

BATTLEFIELDS
IN BRITAIN

Scale of Miles

0   50   100

Cape Wrath
Duncansby Head
L.Shin
Moray Firth
Inverness
Culloden Moor 1746
Harlaw 1411
R.Don
Aberdeen
R.Spey
L.Ness
R.Dee
Inverlochy 1645
Killiecrankie 1689
Brechin, 1452
SCOTLAND
Dundee
R.Tay
R.Earn
Loch Lomond
Stirling Bridge 1297
Bannockburn, 1314
Firth of Forth
Falkirk, 1298
Glasgow
EDINBURGH
Prestonpans, 1745
Pinkie 1547
Dunbar, 1296, 1650
Largs, 1263
Ayr
R.Clyde
Berwick
Halidon Hill, 1333
R.Tweed
Flodden Field, 1513
Firth of Clyde
R.Nith
Alnwick 1093, 1174
NORTH SEA
Solway Moss 1542
R.Tyne
Sunderland
Carlisle
Neville's Cross 1346
R.Eden
R.Tees
Solway Firth
Middlesbrough
Standard Hill 1138
Boroughbridge 1322
York
Flamborough Head
Marston Moor, 1644
Stamford Bridge 1066
IRISH SEA
Preston, 1648
Towton 1461
Hull
Wakefield 1460
Atherton Moor 1643
Liverpool
R.Don
Spurn Head
R.Humber
Lincoln 1141, 1217
R.Trent
R.Witham
The Wash
ENGLAND
Nottingham
WALES
R.Severn
Shrewsbury 1403
Bosworth Field 1485
Leicester
Norwich
Cardigan Bay
Birmingham
Naseby, 1645
R.Ouse
Orewyn Bridge 1282
Worcester 1651
R.Wye
Northampton 1460
Edge Hill, 1642
Assington 1016
Ipswich
Evesham, 1265
Tewkesbury 1471
Oxford
Chalgrove 1643
Barnet 1471
St.Albans, 1455
Colchester 1648
St. George's Channel
Cardiff
Ashdown 1871
Newbury 1643
Brentford 1016
LONDON
R.Thames
Bristol Channel
Edington 878
Roundway Down, 1643
Sevenoaks 1450
Dover
Sedgemoor 1685
Lewes 1264
Hastings, 1066
Southampton
Exeter
Brighton
Hastings
Portsmouth
Plymouth
Lands End
ENGLISH CHANNEL

CHAPTER 2

THE BATTLEFIELDS OF BRITAIN

TRAVELLING about the peaceful countryside of Britain today it is difficult to realize that battles which have changed the whole course of history were once fought where there are now rolling fields and quiet cottages. Yet such was indeed the case.

It is little more than two centuries since the last battle was fought on British soil. This was at Culloden Moor, east of Inverness. On this bleak, windswept heath in April, 1746, five thousand Highlanders were cut to pieces by the nine thousand regular troops of the Duke of Cumberland. Twelve hundred Highlanders died that day, and half that number were taken prisoner. The English lost only three hundred men. And as the Highland irregulars were mown down by grape-shot and musket fire, the last hopes that the Stuarts would ever regain the throne finally faded.

Culloden Moor is one of the few battlefields in Britain that still looks like a battlefield. With few exceptions —the road across the moor is one of them—it looks now as it did then. Mounds and a cairn mark where the dead are buried. It is a wild, lonely spot—a grim place where grim deeds ran their course. Not the least of these was the massacre carried out by Cumberland's troops when the battle had been lost and won.

The Highlanders, under the leadership of Bonnie Prince Charlie, whose uniform is in the Scottish National Military and Naval Museum at Edinburgh, formed up for battle to the skirl of the pipes. They were ill equipped and exhausted after a fruitless attempt to surprise the enemy the night before. They were hungry, too—so hungry that some of the gunners deserted their posts to forage for food. The English gunners commanded by Colonel Bedford, one of the best artillery officers of the day, began to cut the Highland lines to pieces with grapeshot. To this Highlanders knew only one answer. Across the moor they charged with claymore and broadsword, while the English artillery continued to pump grapeshot into their ranks and the infantry withered them with musket fire. The Highlanders fought with the desperation of men who knew that only the breaking of the English line could stave off defeat. But the English line stood firm.

It was the Highlanders who finally broke, and Prince Charlie's bid for the crown was over. Then came the massacre. On the pretext that Prince Charles had issued an instruction of "No quarter," Cumberland, son of George II, urged his men on to a series of atrocities which have linked his name for all time with the epithet "Butcher."

The atrocities which followed Culloden Moor stand out in awful contrast to the splendid action of Bonnie Prince Charlie when he set at liberty the English taken prisoner at Prestonpans. At Prestonpans, nine miles from Edinburgh, the Highlanders, guided

75

across a marsh during the night, fell upon the Government troops in a surprise attack just as the morning mists were breaking. Their furious charge gave them victory in less than ten minutes. The English army, four thousand strong, under Sir John Cope, ran "like rabets," as Charles himself wrote to his father afterwards. Four hundred English lay dead on the field when the battle was over, while the Scots lost only thirty men.

BATTLES NEAR FALKIRK

Between his victory at Prestonpans and the tragedy of Culloden Moor, Charles won another victory over the English at the battle of Falkirk, fought about a mile from the town, where he defeated the Government troops commanded by General Hawley. It was the last victory Charles was to gain, and the long retreat of which it formed part was to end at Culloden Moor.

This was the second time the Scots had taken the field against the English in the vicinity of Falkirk. The first battle, fought midway between Falkirk and Carron nearly five centuries before, marked the end of Wallace's bid to give Scotland independence. Like Prince Charles, he was retreating at the time, his small force being hopelessly inadequate to pit against the great army with which Edward marched into Scotland to oppose him. Wallace laid waste the countryside as he retreated—tactics which might well have proved successful, for the difficulty of maintaining so large an English force in rugged, hostile country can easily be imagined. But near Falkirk Edward caught up with him and Wallace had no alternative but to turn and fight. The result was never in doubt. Hopelessly outnumbered, the Scots were completely defeated by the English forces.

A year earlier Wallace had won a brilliant victory at Stirling—a victory which showed his inventive genius as a military commander at its best. He took up his position in a loop of the Forth. From Abbey Craig, a hill near the abbey of Cambuskenneth, he watched the English army crossing the river by means of a wooden bridge which stood about a mile upstream of the "Old Bridge" of today. When the English army was half on one side of the river and half on the other Wallace launched his attack. A detachment of his men captured and held the bridge. The rest swooped down on that part of the English army which had already made the crossing. His victory was complete. Abbey Craig today is crowned by the Wallace Monument commemorating the victory.

From the top of the Wallace Memorial and from the ramparts of Stirling Castle may be seen several of the battlefields on which Scotsmen have fought and died. It was on the wild heath northeast of Stirling that the indecisive battle of Sheriffmuir brought the rising of 1715 virtually to an end. And not far away, between Bannockburn and St. Ninians, Robert Bruce fought what was perhaps the most momentous battle in Scotland's turbulent history.

AN INDECISIVE BATTLE

Sheriffmuir, for all that it decided the rising of 1715, cannot be described as a momentous battle. The Jacobite army under the Earl of Mar was drawn up against the army of the Duke of Argyll, who had been sent to quell the rising. About five hundred men were killed on either side during a battle in which both left wings broke and ran. Neither side could possibly lay claim to victory, but when the muddle was finally sorted out it was Mar who retreated—not Argyll.

ON CULLODEN MOOR

Culloden Moor is a bleak and almost treeless expanse about five miles from Inverness. Here the Duke of Cumberland won final victory over the army raised by Prince Charles Edward on 16 April, 1746. Several monuments commemorate the great battle, at which the loss of life was exceptionally heavy. These include some which commemorate the graves of clansmen and individual chieftains who fell in the battle. Above, by the Well of the Dead, a monument marks the spot where the chief of the MacGillivrays fell.

True, the rebellion was to linger on a little longer, but Mar's retreat from Sheriffmuir marked the beginning of the end.

Bannockburn was something quite different. The site of the battlefield is today hidden by cultivated fields, but on an eminence at St. Ninians is the Bore Stone where Bruce planted his standard. Bruce's forces were much smaller than those of the English, but by a wise choice of position he turned what at one time looked like almost certain defeat into complete victory. The English cavalry floundered helplessly among the iron caltrops and concealed pits with which Bruce protected his position. Horses went lame as their

77

feet were impaled on the caltrops—iron frames on which spikes were arranged in such a way that three of the spikes bit into the earth while the fourth projected wickedly upwards. Other horses were ripped open as they plunged on to the pointed stakes planted in concealed pits.

Edward II, who personally commanded the English army, had a narrow escape from death. Four Scots knights seized the trappings of his horse. Edward vanquished them with a battle-axe, but the horse was slain and only

the timely arrival of a fresh mount enabled him to escape to Dunbar Castle and then to Berwick. Despite the failure of their cavalry, the English obstinately stood their ground until a group of Scottish camp-followers appeared over a distant ridge. To the English the camp-followers appeared as a new army. Weary and dispirited, the English broke. Edward is said to have fled all the way to Dunbar Castle without drawing rein.

Just over the border into England, on the banks of the Till, is Flodden Field, one of the most tragic battlefields on

THE BATTLEFIELD OF STIRLING, FROM STIRLING CASTLE
The battle of Stirling Bridge was fought in 1297. Its result was to bring temporary triumph to Sir William Wallace, who, after gathering a band of outlaws to defy the suzerainty of Edward I (who was seeking to establish by force his claim as King of Scotland), led a revolt against the English. Only a year afterwards Wallace was defeated by the forces of Edward I at Falkirk, later being taken prisoner and executed in London in 1305. The Wallace monument is seen on a wooded hill.

BANNOCKBURN BORE STONE

The defeat of the Wallace rebellion in no way discouraged the Scots in their struggle for independence of the English crown. The exploits of Robert Bruce once again reaffirmed Scottish determination. At Bannockburn in June of 1314 that great leader defeated the army of Edward II, inflicting heavy losses and driving the remnants of the English forces back towards the border. Thereafter Scottish independence was unchallenged for a long time. The Bore Stone, pictured here, is traditionally supposed to be the very stone on which the Scottish standard was unfurled before the battle.

which Scottish manhood has ever fought. Sir Walter Scott has written that there was scarcely a Scottish family of note which did not have at least one of its number killed at Flodden.

Although the flower of English manhood was fighting in France at the time, the battle of Flodden Field was one which proved fatal to James IV, who led the Scots, and disastrous to his kingdom. The two armies were evenly matched—there were about thirty thousand men on each side—and for a time there was little to choose between them. Both sides had to throw in all available

reserves, the Earl of Surrey, who commanded the English army, and his personal bodyguard moving into action, and James and his bodyguard moving to intercept them.

Then, unable to restrain themselves, the Highlanders threw caution—and their shields—to the wind, and charged with battle-axe and broadsword. The English stood firm until the first charge had spent itself and then counterattacked before the Highlanders could re-form their ranks. When darkness fell, over nine thousand Scots lay dead on the field. James died near the standard

WILD SHERIFFMUIR

The battle of Sheriffmuir was fought during the ill-conceived Scottish rebellion of 1715. Sheriffmuir, in Perthshire, is a moor which falls away to the north of the Ochil Hills north-east of Stirling. During the battle the Jacobite revolutionaries were led by the Earl of Mar and the King's forces by the Duke of Argyll. The result of the battle was inconclusive, which is surprising because the contemporary accounts estimate that the Jacobites outnumbered the Royalists by nearly three to one.

of the English commander, towards whom he had been hewing his way to engage in personal combat. Around him lay the bodies of twelve Scottish earls, the Archbishop of St. Andrews, three bishops and fifteen clan chieftains.

Twizel Bridge, over which the English army crossed to give battle, still exists. It has the longest span of any medieval bridge in England, and is certainly one of the most picturesque. On a hill near Branxton Church, where James probably fell, stands a fine monument "to the brave of both nations."

England's battles were not by any means confined to conflicts with Scotland. There were battles between English and English, and battles against the Welsh. Near Builth, Llewelyn, the last native Prince of Wales, was killed in a skirmish with the English at almost the same time as the main body of his troops was being defeated at Orewyn Bridge.

At Worcester an English army under Henry IV and a combined French and Welsh army under the great Welsh patriot, Owen Glendower, were drawn up facing each other for three days and nights, neither side being willing to forsake a strong defensive position by being the first to attack. Finally, their provisions running short, Glendower's troops were forced to retreat.

Many a bloody battle was fought on English soil in the long struggle for the throne which history has handed down to us as the Wars of the Roses. The struggle lasted for thirty years, and during the course of it something like a hundred thousand men fell in battle. The conflicting sides were the Lancastrians, with the red rose as their emblem, and the Yorkists, who favoured the white rose.

WARS OF THE ROSES

The first engagement of this long struggle took place at St. Albans. It was a minor battle, about a hundred men falling on the two sides. Victory went to the Yorkists, who took Henry VI prisoner. In the second battle of St. Albans, six years later, the victory went to the Lancastrians led by Queen Margaret.

Margaret was for a long time the main driving force behind the Lancastrians, her weak-minded husband being but a pawn in this game of internal power politics. More than once Henry was captured by the enemy, but it made no difference to the continuance of the conflict. How different things might have been if Margaret instead of Henry had been captured in the battle fought at Hardingstone Fields, Northampton, in 1460! But it was Henry who was captured again, while Margaret and the young Prince of Wales just managed to escape from the field. Victory went to the Earl of March, who afterwards became Edward IV, and to the "king-making" Earl of Warwick, ten thousand of the enemy being slain. But Margaret

ON FLODDEN FIELD

The battle of Flodden Field was decided on Flodden Hill, Northumberland, in 1513. The English troops were under the command of the Earl of Surrey, the Scottish army was led by James IV in person, who, with many thousands of his troops, was slain. This monument commemorates the site of the battle.

escaped to fight again another day, and the result was her striking victory at Wakefield on the last day of the same year. The small army of York was lured from behind the defences of Sandal Castle by Margaret's taunts, ambushed and overwhelmed. York was killed in the battle, and his head, with a paper crown on it, was afterwards exposed on the walls at York.

The tide of conflict was again turned in favour of the Yorkists, however, by the victory which Edward, who had now taken his father's title of Duke of York, gained at Mortimer's Cross. At Hereford, after the battle, Owen Tudor

This tall monumental stone, which stands on a common beside the main road just beyond the northern outskirts of London, commemorates the battle of Barnet. This battle was fought in 1471, when the army of the Earl of Warwick, popularly called the Kingmaker, was defeated by the forces of Edward IV, and Warwick himself was killed on the field of battle.

Following the battle of Towton the course of this prolonged conflict took a curious turn. Margaret escaped to the Continent. The Earl of Warwick, at loggerheads with the young king of his own choice, replaced Henry on the throne, and Edward too was forced to flee the country. But he returned soon afterwards to defeat Warwick at Barnet on the very day that Margaret landed back in England with her eighteen-year-old son.

The battle of Barnet was fought in a thick fog, which caused the centre and left flank of the Lancastrian forces to attack each other. This blunder decided the day, and Warwick, who led the Lancastrians, was slain on the field.

LANCASTRIAN DEFEAT

Then came Margaret's defeat at Tewkesbury, marking the end of the second stage of the Wars of the Roses. The "Bloody Meadow" at Tewkesbury received its name because of the slaughter of the fugitives which took place there after the battle. This meadow was in the rear of the Lancastrian position, and the battle was fought in a field on rising ground close to the first milestone on the road from Tewkesbury which runs through Tredington to Cheltenham. The Lancastrians, who had made a forced march of forty-four miles to reach the spot, were defending a well-chosen position surrounded by dykes and hedges. Their defeat was due largely to the strategy adopted by the Duke of Gloucester, who commanded the van of the opposing army. Direct frontal attack on such a natural defensive position being out of the question, Gloucester feigned an attack followed by a retreat. The time-honoured trick came off yet again. The Lancastrians were lured from behind their defences. Immediately Gloucester's

was beheaded, while in London Edward became Edward IV.

So events marched their dramatic course to Towton, in Yorkshire, which has come down to us with the reputation of being the fiercest and bloodiest battle ever fought in Britain. From four o'clock in the afternoon, all through the hours of darkness—an unusual thing for those days—until noon the following day the battle raged. Nearly sixty thousand Lancastrians were routed with tremendous slaughter for those times.

THE ABBEY OF TEWKESBURY

Edward, Prince of Wales, who was killed at the battle of Tewkesbury in 1471, is buried beneath the central tower of the abbey. The actual battle, the last of the critical engagements in the Wars of the Roses, was fought about one mile to the south of the town. After the battle the Duke of Somerset, Lord St. John and a dozen other Lancastrians were dragged from the abbey and beheaded at the town cross.

THE BATTLE OF EDGEHILL

Edgehill is a spur of the extension of the Cotswold range which overlooks the Midland Plain. This photograph from the summit shows the countryside over which the battle of Edgehill was fought in 1642, partly in the plain and partly on the slopes of the downs. The battle was the first of the many engagements in the great Civil War. On this occasion the army under the command of Charles I was opposed by a Parliamentary force under the Earl of Essex. The conclusion of the battle was indecisive.

troops turned on them, driving them back and penetrating their defences.

Right through the town of Tewkesbury and into the sacred precincts of the great abbey flowed the battle. The Duke of Somerset, Lord St. John, and a dozen others, were dragged bodily from the church to be beheaded at Tewkesbury Cross. Because of this the abbey was afterwards re-dedicated. The Earl of Devonshire, Lord Beaufort, nine Lancastrian knights and over three thousand men died on the field. The young Prince Edward was killed while flying from the scene of battle. Margaret herself was taken prisoner, and her long struggle for the throne was over.

BOSWORTH FIELD

But there was another phase of the Wars of the Roses still to come—a phase which opened when Henry Tudor, Earl of Richmond, landed at Milford Haven and ended with the battle of Bosworth, which was fought some three miles south of Market Bosworth. Richard III, who had come to the throne after the murder of the young princes in the Tower, was killed at Bosworth and Henry was crowned Henry VII on the actual battlefield.

Richard took the field with by far the larger army—he had fifteen thousand men; Henry had only six thousand—but it was an army in which many of the commanding lords were of doubtful allegiance. Henry, in fact, had been promised by Lord Stanley, who was in Richard's army, that he could be sure of help from him during the course of the conflict. It was this help which largely decided the final course of the battle, for Stanley and his troops suddenly switched sides and attacked the royal flank.

One of the most dramatic incidents of the battle was Richard's personal attempt to attack Henry. It was no tempestuous attempt. On the contrary, it was deliberately planned in the hope that Henry's death might create confusion in the ranks of his troops and turn the tide of battle in Richard's favour. Richard on his milk-white steed, White Surrey, a gold crown worn as a crest over his helmet, rode first to some high ground on the flank in order to catch a glimpse of Henry, whom he did not know by sight. Then, supported by a handful of chosen knights, he made his gallant charge. He himself as he charged unhorsed Sir John Cheney, and cleft the skull of Sir William Brandon, Henry's standard-bearer, snatching the standard from his grasp and trampling it under his horse's hooves. Then as he was on the point of attacking Henry himself, the sudden arrival on the scene of the traitorous Lord Stanley and his men brought Richard's gallant attempt to its unhappy end. Their attack on Richard was so fierce that his armour was dented and broken beneath the rain of blows he received. They inflicted enough wounds on him to have killed a dozen men, so mutilating his features that he was scarcely recognizable when the battle was over. And it was Lord Stanley who, when Richard lay dead, picked up his fallen crown and placed it on Henry's head. The long conflict was over.

DEFEAT OF DE MONTFORT

In the vicinity of Lewes in 1264 the army of the barons, under Simon de Montfort, defeated the royal army under Henry III. Henry's eldest son, who afterwards became Edward I, made the same blunder at Lewes that Prince Rupert was to make during the Civil War four centuries later. Having swept away the right wing of de Montfort's army with a magnificent

CHALGROVE MONUMENT

This obelisk recalls the battle of Chalgrove, near Watlington, Oxfordshire. Fought in 1643, the engagement was a skirmish rather than a battle and arose from the attempt of a small Parliamentary force to intercept a body of Royalist troops led by Prince Rupert. It was here that John Hampden, one of the chief organizers of the Parliamentary forces, received a fatal wound. The obelisk marks the traditional spot where John Hampden himself fell.

cavalry charge, he permitted his men to dash on in reckless pursuit, and finally returned to the field to find the battle lost. But Edward learnt his lesson well. A year later at the battle of Evesham he annihilated de Montfort's army. De Montfort had placed the captive Henry III in the van of his army, hoping that he would be killed by the very troops who were fighting for his release. At the first onset, however, Edward recognized his father and hastened through the thick of the battle to release him. Both de Montfort and his son were killed in the battle and they were afterwards buried in the abbey.

THE CIVIL WAR

The most important civil war in British history started on Standard Hill, close to Nottingham Castle, when Charles I raised his standard there in August, 1642, and the first engagement took place at Edgehill, in Warwickshire, two months later. It was at Edgehill that Prince Rupert made the same mistake that Edward had made in the thirteenth century. The cavalry charge which he led swept the wing of the Parliamentary army right off the field of battle—not altogether unexpectedly, for the Royalists were the better horsemen, and a cavalry charge was the type of fighting which found them in their element. But Rupert, instead of re-forming his men at once for a fresh charge, allowed them to sweep on in pursuit of the fleeing foe. In his absence the Parliamentary foot-soldiers, stubbornly holding their ground, enabled those cavalry regiments which had not been swept away with the rest to recover formation and charge the Royalist flank. Rupert's cavalry reappeared on the scene only just in time to prevent a complete rout. All in all, Edgehill was an indecisive engagement, though

86

CHESTER, KING CHARLES'S TOWER

This is the best-preserved of the towers along the medieval walls of Chester, more commonly known as the Phoenix Tower and now used as a museum. Its connexion with King Charles I is that there is a tradition that the King watched the battle of Rowton Moor in 1645 from this vantage-point, the site of the battle at which the Royalist troops were defeated being two or three miles to the east. Chester was stoutly Royalist throughout the Civil War and suffered a long siege in the Royalist cause.

87

CAER CARADOC, SHROPSHIRE

The summit of Caer Caradoc, a hill near Church Stretton, is surrounded by the earthen ramparts and ditches of an ancient fortress camp. It is associated in legend with the last struggles of Caratacus, King of the Silures, against the Romans. It is at least possible that Caratacus, who was captured in A.D. 50 by the Romans and taken to Rome, where his gallant mien won him a reprieve from death at the hands of the Emperor Claudius, had led the Britons in their final resistance before they were forced to retreat into the Welsh mountains by the Roman forces.

honours were undoubtedly on the Royalist side.

It was at Chalgrove Field, a skirmish rather than a battle, that the celebrated John Hampden received the wound from which he died six days later. Although Hampden was fighting for the enemy, it is said that Charles respected him so much that he sent his own physician to attend the wound. Only a few miles from the battlefield at Chalgrove is the quiet town of Thame, where John Hampden was educated.

At the battle of Winceby the Royalists had their first taste of Cromwell's famous Ironsides. In the early days of the war Cromwell had been quick to mark the spirit and fire of those who fought for the Royalist cause. The Parliamentary troops he considered courageous enough, but lacking in audacity and inspiration. So he set about building up those picked regiments which under his leadership were to become the best in Europe. Enthusiasm, self-discipline, moral austerity and physical fitness were the qualities he demanded. When he had finished his work, the Ironsides had not only the dash of Rupert's cavalry, but something else that Rupert and his men could never learn—discipline. How well Cromwell picked and trained his men is shown from the fact that at Marston Moor his Ironsides routed Rupert's own troopers in a cavalry engagement.

From the viewpoint of numbers alone Marston Moor was the biggest engagement of the Civil War, the Parliamentary army of twenty-seven thousand men considerably outnumbering the Royalists. Marston Moor not only shattered the King's northern army, but established Cromwell as a general.

King Charles's Tower at Chester is so named because from it Charles watched the defeat of his army on Rowton Moor on that misty morning in September, 1645, when Sir Marmaduke Langdale and the Royalists broke and fled.

PARLIAMENTARY VICTORY

Rowton Moor followed upon the resounding Parliamentary victory at Naseby, in Northamptonshire, where all the King's artillery and baggage were captured. Probably no finer body of troops has ever taken the field than the Parliamentary forces at Naseby, for the fine spirit and iron discipline which Cromwell instilled into his Roundheads had by then spread throughout the whole Parliamentary army. Cromwell made good use of the hills and trees to screen the movements of his men. He had possession of the village of Naseby and the Royalists were forced to advance across rising ground in order to attack. The right wing of each army, the Royalists under Rupert and the Roundheads under Cromwell, were both victorious; but while Rupert again flung victory away by fruitless pursuit, Cromwell made his troops wheel to charge the Royalist centre.

It was at Dunbar in 1650, after Charles II had been proclaimed king, that "the Lord delivered the Scottish army into Cromwell's hands." The phrase is said to have been Cromwell's own. Harried by the Scots, he had been forced to fall back on Dunbar, where, with supplies running low, it seemed almost certain that he would have to attempt to escape by sea. Then the Scots left their positions in an attempt to cut him off from the sea. Cromwell immediately hurled his troops upon the centre of the straggling columns and advanced to occupy Edinburgh. It was not until the following year at Worcester that he finally defeated the Scots.

EARLY INVASIONS

Among the earliest recorded battles fought in Britain were those in A.D. 43, when the Emperor Claudius decided to add Britain to the Roman Empire. Four Roman legions landed on the coast of Kent, fighting two actions in their advance on Colchester, from where Cunobelinus ruled his kingdom of South-east England. One of these actions was fought on the line of the Medway and the other on the Thames.

After the withdrawal of the Roman legions came the series of battles involving the Picts, Scots, Jutes, Angles and Saxons. At Aylesford, on the Medway, the Jute pirate chieftains, Hengist and Horsa, defeated Vortigern, the king at whose invitation they had originally landed in Britain. Somewhere between A.D. 493 and 516 was fought the famous battle of Mount Badon in which the victorious army, according to the seventh-century *History of the Britons*, was led by King Arthur. In A.D. 552 Cerdic, who had landed a number of years before near Totton, at the head of Southampton Water, defeated the Britons at the battle of Searabyrg. Now known as Old Sarum, a prominent landmark with its surrounding ditches and ramparts, Searabyrg stands a little north of Salisbury, overlooking the valley of the Wiltshire Avon. It was a place of some importance until abandoned in the thirteenth century in favour of Salisbury.

Other battles resulted in the Britons being defeated at Barbury, a few miles south of Swindon, and at Dyrham, a few miles from Bath. The victory at Dyrham enabled the King of the West Saxons to split the Celts of Devon and Cornwall from those of Wales and to establish the kingdom of Wessex. Similarly, in the north, the King of Northumbria split Wales from Cumbria when he shattered the allied forces of the Celts at the Battle of Chester.

For a century or more there was battle after battle between the minor Anglo-Saxon kingdoms until the King of Wessex inflicted a defeat on the Mercians at Ellandune, in Wiltshire—the first victory of a campaign which was to unite almost the whole of England under one king for the first time. Then came the Danes in their longships, defeating the King of Wessex in a battle fought near Charmouth, and being themselves defeated by him at the battle of Hengston Down two years later.

But the defeat did not stop the Danish incursions into Britain. On the contrary, they became more persistent and more formidable, being made not in small isolated detachments, but in great armies which needed a fleet of six hundred ships to convey them. At Aclea, which would seem to be either

THE WHITE HORSE OF UFFINGTON

That King Alfred, first king of a united England in Saxon times, won a great victory in Berkshire over the Norse invaders is certain. The traditional name of the battle is Ashdown, its date about 871. It may well be that the battle was fought near modern Uffington, which lies beneath the downs on which this impressionistic horse is cut in the chalk. Popular belief that it was cut by order of King Alfred to commemorate the victory is almost certainly false. It is likely that the horse is a prehistoric sacred emblem.

AYLESFORD BRIDGE OVER THE MEDWAY

Dating from the fourteenth century and only partly modernized, this bridge, which consists of a large central arch and six smaller ones, still carries the road across the Medway at Aylesford. This is the legendary scene of another of the decisive battles fought during the dark ages of British history. When the Roman legionaries were withdrawn, Britain was exposed to sporadic attacks on the coasts from Angles and Saxons, with the Picts and Scots attacking on the northern frontier. Vortigern, a native chieftain, is said to have rallied the people of Britain to resist the invaders and to have been defeated at Aylesford by Saxon warriors led by the legendary heroes, Hengist and Horsa. The church chiefly dates from the fifteenth century. At the White Horse Stone, near the village, the invaders are said to have set up a standard.

SUENO'S STONE, FORRES

This beautifully carved stone, twenty-three feet high, is a mile from Forres (North-east Scotland). There is a local tradition that it was erected in the eleventh century to celebrate a victory gained by the Viking invaders under Sweyn over the Scottish forces under Malcolm II, King of Scotland from 1005 to 1034. The carving is certainly consistent with an eleventh-century origin, but little else supports the legend. The pillar is of sandstone, and is carved with figures of men and animals.

92

Oakley, near Basingstoke, or Ockley, in Surrey, the Danes were again defeated, but their onslaughts continued.

It was left to Alfred the Great finally to check the inroads of the Danish invaders. Somewhere on the Berkshire Downs, south of Wantage—where a statue commemorates the fact that Alfred was born there—was fought the battle of Ashdown, a great Saxon victory which forced the Danes back into their fortified camp at Reading. Thousands, including the Danish king, were slain in the battle, but it did not prevent them from defeating Ethelred, Alfred's brother, at Basing, a fortnight later. The curious white horse carved in the chalk near Uffington, though now considered a prehistoric monument, was for long thought to commemorate Alfred's victory over the Danes.

TRIUMPH OF ALFRED

The Danish capture of Chippenham forced Alfred to take refuge in the marsh-surrounded Isle of Athelney, from where he rallied his men, and at the battle of Ethandun, which is believed to have been fought where the picturesque little village of Edington now stands on the northern edge of Salisbury Plain, the banner of Wessex flew victorious at the end of the day.

Somewhere in the north of England, possibly at Bromborough, on the main Chester–Birkenhead road, was fought the unlocated battle of Brunanburh, where five kings and seven of the earls of Anlaf, leader of the Norsemen from Ireland, were slain. Anlaf and his Norsemen had joined with the Scots to challenge the right of Athelstan to style himself "King of All-Britain." But Athelstan's victory was complete, and the enemy forces, some thirty thousand men, were put to rout. Legend has it that before the battle Athelstan visited

Beverley Minster and placed on the altar the sword given to him by his famous grandfather, Alfred, vowing to redeem it with gifts to the church if he was granted victory. The privileges he granted Beverley after the battle included the right of sanctuary which persisted for centuries, and the stone Saxon sanctuary chair which he is said to have given at the same time is still to be seen in the north transept.

ELEVENTH-CENTURY BATTLES

Near Forres a sandstone monolith, twenty-three feet high and over nine hundred years old, carved with the figures of warriors and animals, commemorates Sweyn's victory over Malcolm II in 1008, while bones found on the heath east of Ipswich are believed to be those of soldiers killed in a great battle which was fought there in 1010 between the Danes and Ulfketel.

And so history hastened on towards the decisive battle which took place near Hastings in 1066. Crowned King of England by the Archbishop of York, Harold was in the south, awaiting the invasion of William of Normandy, when news reached him that Harold Hardrada, who also had eyes on the English Crown, had landed in the north. Taking the pick of his troops with him, Harold marched north and defeated the Norsemen at Stamford Bridge.

Within a week of the battle of Stamford Bridge William of Normandy had landed at Pevensey, where the ruins of the old Roman fort, the first place they occupied, are still to be seen. Harold raced south again at full speed, reaching London in ten days. Collecting what reinforcements he could, he pushed on into Sussex, where he took his stand on the hill of Senlac, overlooking the Hastings plain, his troops lining the whole ridge. William at first attempted to take the position by frontal assault, but neither his foot-soldiers nor his mailed horsemen could break the wall of English shields. But when his own horsemen broke, some of the English abandoned their lines and rushed in pursuit. William was quick to note this and ordered his men to feign flight. The English, with the exception of Harold's own bodyguard, streamed down the hill in pursuit. The Normans turned in a fresh charge and the English were cut to pieces.

The splendid pile of Battle Abbey, founded by William to commemorate his victory in accordance with a vow he made before the battle, now stands where the battle probably took place.

THE LEGEND OF BEVERLEY FRID STOOL

The Frid Stool in Beverley Minster is an ancient stone seat of unknown age. The meaning of its name is " chair of peace." As such it is associated with the right of sanctuary which was the privilege of Beverley Minster from Saxon times. Legend has it that before the famous battle of Brunanburh, King Athelstan visited the Minster and placed a sword on the altar, vowing if victory was his he would redeem the sword by gifts to the church. After the battle was won the Minster received from the King among other privileges the right of sanctuary. According to the legend the King himself is said to have presented the stool to the Minster.

CHAPTER 3

BUILDING THROUGH THE AGES

MUCH of the story of Britain's historic past is written in the bricks and stone which make up the fabric of buildings through the ages. By looking at these buildings and noting the significant differences between them you can re-create a great deal of the romance and realism of the peoples who built them.

The study of buildings is, too, the open door to the appreciation of the way in which British people have lived at different times. Houses of every century from the fourteenth to the twentieth reflect the tastes of the people who lived in them. The castles, churches and abbeys of the Middle Ages are the key to the understanding of the times in which they were built.

Buildings in fact do more than all this. They will tell you (if you know how to interpret them) the story of the changing ideals, the growth of civilization and the very essence of the will to progress which has characterized the people of Britain from the earliest times. Whether you are looking at a magnificent essay in church-building such as Salisbury Cathedral or at modest Tudor dwelling-places such as the row of cottages in Chiddingstone, Kent, you have before you the most fascinating evidence of the progress of history and at the same time some of the most beautiful facets of historic Britain.

First let us go to St. Albans and find the abbey church which dominates the valley in which are the ruins of the Roman town of Verulamium. Here is a true link between the Romans, who were the first to build in the modern sense of building, and the Normans, who re-created the art and brought it to perfection.

Verulamium, of which only a few sections of the wall, the foundations of some of its villas and parts of its theatre remain, was one of the wealthiest and most flourishing of the towns of Roman Britain, with a vigorous life which extended from the first to the fourth century.

When the protection of the Roman soldiers was removed and the wild Saxon warriors destroyed most of what the Romans had built, Verulamium was laid waste, remaining ruined and almost deserted for close on five hundred years. By then the Saxon tribes had become united and civilized. Christianity, which came to Britain in Roman times, was carried to the Saxons by missionaries and swept away the pagan Saxon religions. So the Saxons turned to building churches. They built first in wood and used stone only in the centuries immediately preceding the Norman invasion.

Because wood is less durable than stone very little early Saxon building has come down to us, though the wooden walls of Greensted Church in Essex are a forceful reminder of the times when the early Saxon builders were at work. Mostly, however, the early wooden buildings were rebuilt in stone. That is what happened in the case of St. Albans

ROMAN WALL AT RICHBOROUGH
Richborough was one of the forts of the Saxon Shore, strongly fortified at a time when there was a threat of Saxon invasions. It was also in Roman times an important port for trading with Gaul. This photograph shows the characteristic rubble and flint of the interior of the wall, with the trimmed stone facing broken up by courses of the thin red bricks.

as in hundreds of other churches, great and small, up and down the country.

The Saxons founded a church on the spot where St. Alban, the first of Britain's martyrs, was put to death by the Romans for proclaiming his faith in Christ in the town of Verulamium. The Normans rebuilt the Saxon church and gave us much of the building which stands on the hill today. The link between the Romans and Normans is at once apparent if you look at the massive square tower. You will see that a large

part of its fabric is made up of thin red bricks or tiles which contrast with the grey stone of the rest of the church. These red bricks are Roman tiles which the Normans salvaged from the ruins of Verulamium and put to this use.

NORMAN CHURCHES

You will find the same kind of link between Romans and Normans in many other towns of Britain, particularly in southern England, where the Roman towns were most numerous and Roman buildings most magnificent. Colchester Castle, for instance, one of the greatest of the Norman fortresses, has a large number of these same red bricks in its fabric, in this case taken by the Norman builders from the ruins of the Roman town of Camulodunum which stood on the site of modern Colchester. The castle is not the only building in Colchester which shows these telltale signs. The ruins of St. Botolph's Priory are equally striking, whilst there are a few courses of Roman brick in the fabric of several old churches in the town, as there are in the churches of all parts of the country where there were Roman settlements. This is especially true of Essex, because the absence in that county of local building stone compelled medieval builders to put their hands to whatever they could find.

Most of the great Norman buildings were enlarged and embellished in the Later Middle Ages. St. Albans is no exception to this rule. Even so, if you go inside the church and look at the nave you will have before you some of the chief features of Norman buildings and at the same time an impression of the artistry and magnificence of Norman architecture.

The style is called Romanesque, for like the work of the Saxons in the centuries before it is modelled on

THE SAXON TOWER OF BARTON UPON HUMBER

This is another genuine example of Saxon building, with the additional interest that it may date from the end of the tenth century, a very early date for Saxon stonework. Its most interesting feature is that its whole design is strongly reminiscent of a timber-framed tower which it almost certainly superseded. Commonly the Saxons built their earliest churches of wood and then rebuilt in stone when opportunity offered.

solid and strong. Yet somehow in spite of their comparatively rude craftsmanship and their lack of ornamentation they fit in perfectly with the predominant theme of all Norman buildings.

The repetition of the semicircular arch is a feature of Norman work which gives it its greatest attraction. In some cathedral churches, as at Chichester, you will see the theme of the rounded arch carried farther by subdivision into groups of smaller arches.

This symmetrical style appears in all the great Norman churches of Britain, perhaps with greatest effect in the churches of the south, but with equal grace if a more severe effect in some of the north, such as Durham, where the severity of design is lessened by the use of chevron and dog-tooth moulding.

SAXON ARCHITECTURE

There is Norman work dating from some time between the Conquest and the middle of the twelfth century in most (though not all) of the cathedrals of the old foundation, but extraordinarily little of the earlier Saxon work. In order to find surviving examples of the period of building between 900 and 1066 we must look at some of the small village churches. We shall not, it is true, find a whole church surviving intact in the Saxon style, but we shall find quite a large number which show unmistakably the handiwork of the Saxons. If we go to Earls Barton, Northamptonshire, we shall be struck by the square-towered parish church, one of the most significant examples of Saxon work in Britain. The tower is squat and solid like the Norman towers, but is distinguished from them by raised strips of stone encircling it which give the tower when viewed from a distance the appearance of being built of wood. This is no accident, for the earliest builders

---

THE TOWER DOORWAY OF
BARNACK CHURCH

The tower of Barnack Church in Northamptonshire is one of the finest examples of Saxon stonework. Some of the rough untrimmed stones of which the lower part of the tower is composed are seen in the photograph, which also shows the rude Saxon arch which may have been repaired after the Norman occupation but remains essentially Saxon in character, with its rudimentary columns and arch raised on corresponding slabs of stone.

Roman ideas. The first thing that strikes you is the immense size and girth of the columns which support the roof of the nave—that and the repetition of the semicircular arch form. The columns are very different indeed from the columns of the classical temples of ancient Rome, as different as they are from those of later Gothic churches. They are round and pier-like, immensely

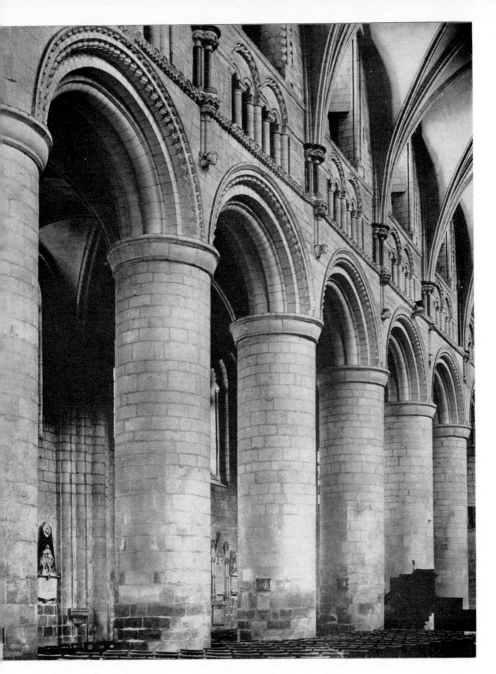

THE NAVE OF GLOUCESTER CATHEDRAL

The grandeur and simplicity of this Norman design deserves comparison with the picture of the nave of Durham (see page 19). Although nearly contemporary with Durham, Gloucester shows more lightness of touch. The columns of the nave are more finely proportioned, while the moulding in the arches is more delicate and finely chiselled.

in stone imitated consciously the styles which had evolved in the period of timber building.

Saxon houses were all of timber. The lower orders in the feudal system lived in hovels, but the Saxon thanes had fine timber dwelling-places, though not a single one of them exists today. It is inferred that they were lofty hall homes rather like medieval timber barns, of which there are, even now, a few surviving from the thirteenth and fourteenth centuries.

In Norman times a few of the leading citizens lived in stone-built houses, and at least two of these have been handed down to us, the Jew's House of Lincoln and Moyse's House at Bury St. Edmunds. These were solid stone-built structures, each with a round-arched

THE JEW'S HOUSE, LINCOLN

Although Britain retains so many splendid links with the religious and military architecture of Norman times, there are few surviving fragments of private houses built during the eleventh and twelfth centuries. This obviously Norman building in Lincoln (notice the round-headed openings of the windows on the upper floor) and a rather similar building known as Moyse's House at Bury St. Edmunds are two fine examples of Norman secular building. It is possible that they were originally built for merchants who began to infiltrate into town life soon after the Norman occupation and were later identified with the Jewish element which bulked largely in the merchant class.

THE HALL OF OAKHAM CASTLE

The castle of the little market-town of Oakham, Rutland, has a long history as manor-house and latterly as court of law. The hall, pictured above, shows clearly the fine Norman workmanship with its foliated columns and moulded arches. Oakham is unusual among English castles in that it seems to have been built primarily for residence as a mansion and scarcely at all for serious defence. In this respect it was at least two hundred years before its time. The horseshoes hanging on the wall are part of a collection originating from the custom that a horseshoe should be given by royalty and peers who passed through Oakham. Many of the horseshoes are surmounted by crowns.

doorway and round-arched windows, very much after the style of church windows of the time.

The Norman barons, in contrast with the majority of the people, lived in stone-built castles which combined the functions of dwelling-places and fort-resses. These reflect in their structure the twin ideals of utility and beauty. Go to any of the great Norman castles, to Rochester or Castle Hedingham in the south, to Richmond or Bolton in the north, all of them substantial ruins which have been preserved almost intact

since the time when their battlements were dismantled after the great Civil War. Or go to one of the castles which have been reconstructed and now serve other purposes—to Norwich or to the White Tower of the Tower of London, or to Colchester, which is midway between the two in that its exterior has not been rebuilt but has been roofed over and now is used as a museum. They will all tell the same story.

There is in all of them masonry several feet thick, great stone slabs used as facing for a core of rubble and

A GLOUCESTERSHIRE COTTAGE

Two facets of medieval village architecture are illustrated by this photograph. One is the half-timbered style which was a development from the early "wattle and daub" (timber and clay). It was superseded by stone in some areas (and by brick in a few large manor-houses). The other facet is what is known as the cruck style, in which the whole weight of a building is sustained by two large beams meeting at a sharp angle.

WELLS CATHEDRAL, THE WEST FRONT

This is the most elaborate and highly decorated façade of the Early English period of Gothic building in Britain. The tall, narrow lancet window openings are typical of the period, but the numerous niches for statuary are not paralleled by any other church. Bishop Jocelin inspired the building of the west front, which was the last part of the cathedral consecrated in 1239. The three hundred and fifty sculptures represent scenes from the Bible, both the Old Testament and the New, including a fine treatment of the coronation of the Virgin and another of the resurrection of the dead.

cement. In the large, high chamber which made up the hall of the castle the baron and all his family and some of his servants, too, spent their leisure. The hall combined the functions of modern sitting-room, bedroom and dining-room. Meals were taken at long wooden tables, and when the food was cleared away the stone floor was covered with straw and the people laid themselves down to rest, warmed by the wood fire burning in the central hearth, from which the smoke escaped through a vent in the roof.

In times of peace many of the retainers and the troops who were in attendance lived in temporary buildings in the forecourt, which was in turn surrounded by a strong curtain wall with battlements as at Rochester. In other places, such as Windsor and Arundel, the keep is much less elaborate, nothing more than a round tower-like structure which was designed to be used only as a place of refuge in time of attack. In these cases the permanent quarters of the Norman baron as well as of the soldiers and retainers were in the outer ward.

About 1175 a new conception of architecture was appearing. You can see the forerunners of this in many of the great churches of Britain in the style called Transitional, that is to say, between Norman and Gothic. In short it represents a breakaway from the round arch. It takes the form of a pointing of the arch, particularly a pointing of the arch of the chancel and of the arch above the pillars supporting the roof, though the pointed arch later spread to every part of the building, including the arch over the doorway.

There is no certain knowledge of the reasons which led medieval builders away from the traditional forms of the Romanesque style. It is thought, however, that experience showed that the semicircular arch had definite limitations in that its width determined its height, so the height of the roof was determined by the width of the church.

EARLY ENGLISH STYLE

The Transitional stage did not last for long. Within fifty years the first phase of Gothic architecture was at its peak, the phase known as Early English, a style which flourished throughout almost the whole of the thirteenth century.

Salisbury Cathedral is the most perfect example in Britain of the Early English style. It is unique in that it was started and finished, apart from some very small additions, within forty years. The first stones were laid in 1220, the last had been put in position by 1260. So, unlike most of the other great cathedrals, Salisbury is not a rebuilding

or enlargement of a Norman church, but a building complete in itself, designed and executed to a plan and showing none of the contrasts of style which are a feature of interest as well as a defect of most of the great churches.

By the thirteenth century, as shown in this lovely building, the pointed arch had entirely superseded the round one. From whatever angle you look at the interior of the cathedral you will see a succession of very fine pointed arches receding into the distance.

LANCET WINDOWS

The typical window-opening in the Early English style is the lancet, a window tall in relation to its width and often arranged in threes or fives, the centre one being taller than those flanking it. The lancet window is in fact the feature of Early English Gothic which distinguishes it most sharply from the later styles of Gothic, in which the several lights or windows are grouped under an encircling arch.

Many critics of architecture find in this Early English style the full flowering of Gothic architecture and regard later variations as something in the nature of an anticlimax. That is one thing which the individual student of old buildings must judge for himself. Certainly Salisbury as a full expression of the new style is wonderfully satisfying. The absence of ornament in the façade and interior is absolutely in keeping with the simplicity of the conception. Elaborate carving and tracery are almost entirely absent. In the façade of the west front, however, the architects of the Early English churches allowed themselves a degree of elaboration. Here at Salisbury, and still more in the west front of Wells Cathedral, which is approximately of the same date, the rich effect is obtained by a great number

YORK MINSTER

This photograph shows the central tower and south transept of York Minster, the cathedral church of the Archbishop of York, who is also Primate of England and ranks second only to the Archbishop of Canterbury (Primate of all England) in ecclesiastical precedence and authority. The fine lantern tower was built under the supervision of William of Colchester, master mason of Henry IV, in the early fifteenth century, when the Decorated and Perpendicular styles of Gothic were merging.

of niches cut in the stonework in which were placed the carved figures of saints and holy men.

The picture is very different in the fourteenth century. This was the age of the Decorated style of Gothic architecture, expressed like the Early English one chiefly in church building. There are extraordinarily few churches which are mainly in the Decorated style, for it was a century of enlargement and enrichment rather than of new foundations. It is in a window here, a doorway there, a tower in another place, that we shall find the best examples.

DECORATED STYLE

The extravagant tracery of the windows in the Decorated churches was probably a conscious reaction against the plain lines of the early Gothic and of the Romanesque style which had preceded it. The effects were obtained by filling the space between the top of the various lights of the window and the top of the pointed arch surrounding them with carved stone. The patterns of the carving or tracery were at first quite simple geometrical forms, but in the later churches of the period full rein was given to the imagination and some beautiful effects were achieved by means of intricate designs of a more elaborate kind.

Whereas the Decorated Gothic of the fourteenth century does not appear to very good effect in complete churches, the case is very different with the last period of Gothic which is known as Perpendicular and reached its full expression towards the middle of the fifteenth century. At Lavenham, in Suffolk, or Northleach, in Gloucestershire, to name only two examples of surpassing beauty, are churches which though they were not founded at that time were so extensively remodelled as

to become almost new churches and remain as permanent monuments to the builders of one of the greatest and most prolific eras of architecture in Britain.

If you look carefully at Lavenham Church (or Thaxted Church, in Essex), or at any other of the larger Perpendicular churches, the first thing that is bound to strike you is the great height of the building in relation to its breadth and the tall straight lines of every part of the church. The windows are even larger than in the Decorated churches. By contrast with the fanciful tracery of the latter the Perpendicular windows are without any decoration at all, the several lights of the window being divided by straight stone strips which are carried up to the top of the arch.

The same reaction in every part of the church, except perhaps in the towers, is noticeable. The nave is lofty, so lofty that the walls are nearly always supported by external flying-buttresses to help bear the weight and outward thrust of the roof. The chancel arch is high so that you can get a clear view from one end of the church to the other. The church is a fine place for preaching, as bare as a stone barn, its beauty (and many late Gothic churches are extremely beautiful) is the beauty of line and light added to the sheer attraction of spaciousness and stone unadorned.

MEDIEVAL ABBEYS

The medieval abbey ruins are as important a commentary on the life of the Middle Ages as are the parish churches and cathedrals. In many cases you will find that the church of the medieval abbey has been restored and still serves as a parish church, while the abbey itself has fallen into ruins.

In every abbey the church was the most important part of the whole group of buildings; the grandeur of even some

INSIDE LAVENHAM CHURCH

Lavenham Church, Suffolk, is a fine example of the type of church built during the fourteenth- and fifteenth-century woollen boom. The considerable access of wealth in the countryside, particularly in East Anglia, coincided with a great period of preaching, and many lofty naves suitable for preaching were erected. The great height of the nave, the fine timber roof, the straight perpendicular lines of the features of the church (except the window, which is earlier) are characteristic of this period.

IGHTHAM MOTE IN KENT

Ightham Mote has two separate links with historic Britain. First, it is one of the best-preserved of medieval manor-houses: the stonework of the lower storey was certainly standing at the beginning of the fifteenth century, while the upper storey is Tudor. The manor's second link with the story of Britain is its legendary association with the Gunpowder Plot of 1605. One of the ladies who resided in the house, Dame Dorothy Selby, is said to have helped in the discovery of the plot.

BODIAM CASTLE, SUSSEX

Bodiam is one of the last of the genuine medieval castles built for defence rather than residence. It was, in fact, being built about the same time as the castellated brick-built manor-house of Herstmonceux, a few miles away (page 30). Begun in about 1385, it was not completed until the first decade of the following century and was erected by Sir Edward Dalyngrigge, a soldier who had performed distinguished services in the French wars, by special licence from the King. The moat, which is fed by a tributary stream of the River Rother, is still well filled. The gatehouse, walls and angle towers are admirably preserved, but the interior was destroyed by fire and has not been rebuilt.

of the smaller ones is well illustrated by the parish church of Tewkesbury, which was originally the church of Tewkesbury Abbey. In almost every county are to be found interesting ruins of abbey or priory buildings. Some of them are set in such romantic situations that they have a beauty greater perhaps than the intrinsic beauty of the buildings themselves. Tintern, in Monmouthshire, Rievaulx and Fountains, in Yorkshire, are three very famous ones.

The medieval monastery was a self-contained community of priests or lay brethren who took the vows of their particular order and lived their entire life within the confines of the abbey buildings. There were a number of abbeys in towns, including those attached to the cathedral churches, but the majority of the ones which have survived were in rural districts. They were established deliberately in remote parts of the country far from the towns and by implication from the temptations of town life. That is why so many of the ruins today are in picturesque surroundings. All that the monks needed was drinking water and a fairly level expanse of land on which they could build.

When you are looking at abbey ruins you are seeing all that remains of a very interesting phase in medieval British history. The abbeys were oases of quiet and culture in a desert of uncivilized life. Britain in the Middle Ages was a good country to live in for the higher orders in the feudal system, but life was miserable and harassed for the poorer people. For them there was little sympathy, seeing that a social conscience had not developed, and the feudal lords and their lieutenants took for granted everything they could grasp.

MONASTIC LIFE

The monastic movement represented a revolt on the part of religious thinkers against these conditions. The abbeys and priories offered a retreat where men could escape from the world and do good work in the ways of charity and the arts without the need to fight. The monasteries naturally became centres of good works and goodwill which the heads of the feudal system were too wise to disturb.

Conditions in the abbeys were rigorous. How difficult they often were is illustrated by the manner in which many of the great abbeys were founded and built. From the magnificent ruins of Tintern or Rievaulx it will seem scarcely credible that the splendid stone structures were raised almost entirely by the labour of the monks. Yet such was the case.

Whichever of the abbeys is visited you will find that the buildings were arranged in rather similar fashion. The cloisters were always constructed round a square, one side of this being against the south wall of the church. If you want to see cloisters perfectly preserved

you must go to one of the ancient cathedrals such as Norwich or Gloucester, which were originally monastic foundations. In the case of most of the abbeys which are now ruined only fragments of the cloisters remain.

The other abbey buildings included a dormitory and a dining hall, for the life of the monks was communal except in the case of one small order in which each monk had his own cell in which he worked and ate and slept alone.

During the thirteenth and fourteenth centuries as we have seen many new churches were built and many others were enlarged and beautified. There was no corresponding development in the building of castles which were such a noble monument to the architects of Norman days. The power of the baron entrenched in his castle moat was found to be a boomerang as far as the kings of England were concerned. The castle certainly enabled the baron to keep order over the countryside. It also enabled him to revolt against his king, as many of the barons did.

LATE MEDIEVAL CASTLES

By order of the Crown, therefore, few new castles were built except in the outlying areas of the west and north. We must go to Wales to see the finest examples of Gothic castles in Britain. Caernarvon is the most magnificent of the Edwardian castles, as mighty a stronghold as many of the Norman-built ones, but constructed on an entirely different principle. Here it is the strength of the outer walls which must bear the brunt of attack, and not as in the Norman castles the strength of an inner fortress to which the garrison could retire when the outer walls were breached.

In spite of the absence of castles in the greater part of England, or perhaps

THE GUILDHALL, LEICESTER

Leicester's Guildhall is one of the few surviving links with the flourishing medieval town which grew up on the site of a Roman town laid waste by the Saxons in the fifth century. Originally the Hall of the Guild of Corpus Christi, the most powerful of Leicester's medieval guilds, it was built at the end of the fourteenth or beginning of the fifteenth century and is notable for the "minstrels' gallery" and for the simplicity of its timber-work. It was used as a town hall until the late nineteenth century.

SHOPS OF TUDOR ENGLAND

Lavenham (the church is illustrated on page 107) was one of the most flourishing towns of eastern England in Tudor times. Its prosperity was derived from the woollen trade, of which it was one of the chief commercial centres. Many of its houses were originally built as dwelling-places for the merchants. The wool hall and the inn are of similar origin, while this fine half-timbered row of shops with its overhanging upper storey is one of the earliest groups of its kind found in England.

because of it, there was great development in the building of homes or mansions, which were the forerunners of the Tudor and Elizabethan manor-houses. At Penshurst Place in Kent is to be seen one of the earliest of them, though here as elsewhere many new buildings have been added to the original ones.

The single characteristic of all early dwelling-places was that they were what are called "hall homes"—that is to say, the great hall handed down from the

Norman architects was retained as the main part of the house, where the lord of the manor, his family and in the earlier ones his servants, too, spent the greater part of their lives. Other apartments were entirely subsidiary.

Some of these almost entirely "domestic" homes are called castles, though the battlements were for show and tradition rather than for prospective use. The castle had become a castellated manor-house. Herstmonceux Castle is an admirable example of this tendency.

There were still a few castles built in special circumstances under licence from the Crown. Bodiam Castle, for instance, in Sussex, was begun about 1385. This was a castle proper. It is today one of the most beautiful castle ruins in Britain, still surrounded by a well-filled moat and from the outside looking to be almost intact, though only the shell of the fabric remains, as you will see immediately you cross the drawbridge and enter the inner ward. How the two periods—of castle building and of manor-house building—overlapped is illustrated by the fact that only a few miles away from Bodiam the brick-built manor-house of Herstmonceux was being constructed at the same time. Though Herstmonceux, now the home of the Greenwich Observatory, was called a castle, its battlements could not have stood up to a single day's siege.

Now we come to a time when building materials were changing. Herstmonceux was one of the earliest brick-built

IN HADDON HALL

Haddon Hall, Derbyshire, has been the home for nearly a thousand years of two of the north country's most famous families. After the Norman conquest it descended from the Avenells to the Vernons. Then in the sixteenth century, when the Vernon male line died out, the marriage of Dorothy Vernon to Sir John Manners brought it into the possession of the family who became Dukes of Rutland. Much of the house dates from medieval times. The long gallery pictured here is one of the later additions, and shows the influence of classical ideas from the sixteenth century onwards.

residences in the country (if we exclude Roman building). Layer Marney in Essex is another of the early brick-built residences. Previously all the great buildings had been of stone, and the smaller houses, all of which have disappeared, were of lath and plaster.

From the fifteenth century onwards there is greater and greater variety of building materials. Stone continued to be used in areas where it was easily quarried and proved durable for building, as in the Cotswold country. Cotswold stone has in fact been used for building right through the ages, and is even now being used in the area side by side with the more common brick. Timber also began to come into its own. Many fine houses dating from the fifteenth and sixteenth centuries are half-timbered, especially in the country bordering on Wales and in other areas where timber was abundant and easily felled. The effect was to produce an entirely new kind of architecture, in which the black-and-white pattern of the partly timber-built houses formed a design of beauty and distinction. This is a style of building best seen in Cheshire. Brick tended to be used where

HARDWICK HALL

This is the most spectacular of the many large country houses built in the last quarter of the sixteenth century when the noble families of Britain were divided on the question of whether to follow traditional precedent in building new houses (the characteristic "Elizabethan" house) or to strike out along new and uncharted paths, following the newly-introduced fashions of the classical Renaissance. Hardwick, which was built for the Countess of Shrewsbury, carries the neo-classicism to an extreme degree and set a new standard of lighting with its symmetrical rows of rectangular windows.

MASTERPIECE OF SIR CHRISTOPHER WREN

Sir Christopher Wren, the most famous of British architects, brought fresh impetus to the art of building and has had great influence on architecture in Britain. He himself was very deeply influenced by the classical styles of Greece and Rome. Above is seen Fountain Court, Hampton Court Palace, one of his masterpieces. The ground level is built as a delightful cloister with small rounded arches on the square pillars.

there was neither a local stone nor a reserve of timber to draw upon, as in many parts of the Midlands and eastern England.

Another fascinating change took place at the end of the fifteenth century, marking the end of the long period of Gothic architecture. There was a spread of culture and a renewed interest in classical learning, a movement which is often called the Renaissance. The interest in classical culture generally was reflected in architecture.

The Renaissance style marks a complete breakaway from the Gothic forms and a modified return to the classical forms which had last been seen in Romanesque building. The pointed arch was seen no more except when there was a conscious revival of the Gothic style. Its place was taken by the rounded arch and a great symmetry in every part of the building.

Like every other movement in English building the change was a gradual one. Though late Tudor and Elizabethan manor-houses are classical in design they reveal a real British adaptation of the style which makes them among the most British things in Britain. There are very many of them, several in almost every county, and

LATE SEVENTEENTH-CENTURY CUSTOM HOUSE

King's Lynn, Norfolk, possesses many fine old houses, and the Custom House is a particularly pleasing example of urban architecture of the late seventeenth century. The interesting pyramid roof with its dormer windows is topped by an elegant cupola, a popular architectural feature of the time. The town was once one of the chief English ports and even today has a considerable trade. The Custom House is situated by the river.

many cottages and smaller houses, too, of about the same date. In all of them, though the magnificence of the hall remains, it ceases to be the main part of the house.

Old Moreton Hall in Cheshire is a fine example dating from about 1580. It makes the fullest use of timber both in construction and for decoration. By contrast Wollaton Hall in Nottinghamshire illustrates perfectly the style as interpreted in stone. These two and others of about the same period contrast in a most interesting way with the earlier Tudor work of buildings such as Hampton Court Palace and some of the Oxford colleges, in particular Wolsey's Christ Church. They contrast equally strongly with the early seventeenth century, when first Inigo Jones and then Sir Christopher Wren brought a fresh impetus to the art of building and represented also the beginning of a long line of master architects in a more professional sense than any before them.

WORK OF CHRISTOPHER WREN

Many of the buildings of this period were based on the work of the Italian Palladio and are known after him as Palladian. Sir Christopher Wren, however, revolted against the formality of Palladian architecture. His work is characterized by a greater freedom and decoration which verges on the Baroque, a fanciful style which was popular on the Continent but had no real expression in Britain. After the time of Sir Christopher Wren there was another reaction against the freedom of his imagination. Architects returned once more to the formality of the Palladian style.

It is quite impossible to list the very large number of buildings which represent these transitions. Inigo Jones is best known for two buildings which approach very near the perfection of the style in which he worked, the Banqueting Hall at Whitehall and the Queen's House at Greenwich. Similarly, Sir Christopher Wren is best known for the building of the new St. Paul's Cathedral (1675–1700), and for the number of smaller churches which were erected under his supervision in London after the Great Fire. Yet scores of big houses, including a particularly fine one in Chichester, were attributed rightly or wrongly to the architecture of Christopher Wren.

THE ENGLISH RENAISSANCE

Go to Hampton Court Palace, not only because it is one of the noblest of all the buildings of Britain, but because there you can compare the two most spectacular periods of the English Renaissance. One half of the palace is Tudor, the other half, including the Fountains Court and the Garden Front, was designed by Sir Christopher Wren. The junction of the two makes an amazing contrast; yet it is not one which jars on those seeing it for the first time, but rather leaves them wondering at the ease with which two distinct styles are fused into an integrated whole.

Similarly, if you visit Oxford or Cambridge you will see endless examples of " Renaissance " architecture from the very earliest Tudor to eighteenth-century Georgian. Those two towns are the greatest storehouses in Britain of historic architecture. Blickling Hall in Norfolk, now the property of the National Trust, is a good example of pure classicism dating from about 1620. Blenheim Palace, the work of the architect Vanbrugh, and Chiswick House are two which illustrate the return to Palladian simplicity which took place at the beginning of the eighteenth century.

The rest of the eighteenth century in architecture is largely the story of a few great architects, each of whom impressed his skill and his genius on a single part of the country. There were the brothers Adam who were responsible for the Adelphi in London about 1770. There were the Woods who laid out Bath in the classical style; the Royal Crescent remains a monument to their unsurpassed vigour of imagination. There was Chambers who designed Somerset House in 1780. This distinctive building makes an interesting contrast with the more florid architecture current in other parts of the country, as for instance in Harewood House in Yorkshire, built about 1760. Finally there was Sir John Nash, the last of a long line of great architects, who between 1810 and 1830 introduced town planning on the grand scale to a part of London which was previously derelict. Nash was the man who created Regent's Park and the Regent's Park Terraces as well as the Marble Arch and the old Regent Street. It seems likely that some of the best of his work,

BLENHEIM PALACE FROM THE AIR

A grateful nation rewarded the services of the Duke of Marlborough with the presentation of Blenheim Park and a sum of money with which to build the vast mansion which forms its centre-piece. The selection of the architect and style of house was left to the Duke, who chose Sir John Vanbrugh, the foremost name in classical architecture of the times. The great mansion took nearly twenty years to complete. An artificial lake is seen in the background. This, together with the lay-out of the park, was the work of a famous landscape gardener, "Capability" Brown.

PARK CRESCENT, REGENT'S PARK

As Christopher Wren embodied the spirit of the full-fledged Renaissance, so John Nash represents all that is finest in the Regency style of architecture current at the beginning of the nineteenth century. Nash was the designer of old Regent Street and was responsible for the major scheme of town planning which included Regent's Park and many of the streets in the district between the park and the line of Oxford Street. Park Crescent is one of the finest of his creations. Before engaging in town planning in London, Nash had gained a great reputation as a designer of country houses.

badly bombed as it was during the Second World War, will be preserved indefinitely after restoration, a monument to the work of John Nash as signal as is Bath to the work of the Woods.

The gracious early nineteenth-century town house is a conspicuous feature of many country towns today. The guide-books usually call them Georgian and leave it at that, but in fact if you look carefully you will see small but significant differences between the houses of one county and those of another and between the houses which are built of stone and those which are of brick or half-timbered. That is a facet of architecture which exploration of the countryside will impress on you.

In the larger towns, too, you will see many imposing buildings erected during the nineteenth century and for that matter during the present century. They are varied in the extreme and some consciously strive toward a completely new style of architecture which is not yet fully developed. In general, however, the largest buildings fall into two groups. Most of the town halls and other secular buildings remain in the classical style, like the mighty St. George's Hall in Liverpool, which was built in 1839. Some of the largest of the modern churches have reverted to the Gothic style, including the Anglican cathedral at Liverpool.

It remains to be seen what new forms will emerge from the present age of steel and concrete, and whether these new forms will cause the disappearance of classical and Gothic forms alike.

A MODERN RESIDENTIAL SUBURB

The story of building in Britain is brought down to date by the rapid expansion of industrial and commercial towns since the middle of the nineteenth century. Critics find little to commend in the typical Victorian terraces and rows, but the half-century since 1900 has brought into prominence ideas of town planning which may revolutionize the lay-out of towns in the future. This view of a residential area in South London illustrates the dominant style of treating such areas during the period of most rapid expansion. Identical villas were built in great numbers in extended rows back to back and front to front often with exact correspondence.

CHAPTER 4
PLOTS, INTRIGUES AND EXPLOITS

TODAY we regard the Crown as an assured part of the British constitution, and it is difficult to realize that such was not always the case. Yet there has been many a time in British history when the head that wore the crown has lain uneasily indeed, and when it has been as dangerous to be too close to the throne as to be too much opposed to it. Mary, Queen of Scots, Lady Jane Grey, James I of Scotland, Edward II, Roger Mortimer, Piers Gaveston— these are only a few of those who found, to their cost, the danger that lurked in high places.

Many were the plots and intrigues which centred around the tragic personality of Mary, Queen of Scots. Most notorious was the plot which resulted in the murder of Mary's Italian favourite, Rizzio. In Holyrood Palace is the small panelled room where Mary, Rizzio and the Countess of Argyll were at supper when the conspirators burst in upon them.

Darnley, Mary's weak and worthless husband, was among those who crept up the narrow spiral staircase which gives direct access to this tiny room. More of the conspirators came up the main staircase, striding across the audience chamber and through the Queen's bedroom. It must have been a tense, dramatic moment when the conspirators burst into that tiny room. Rizzio, terrified, tried to screen himself behind Mary. But Darnley seized his wife with ungentle hands, while even rougher hands gripped the Italian, half dragging him through the bedroom and the audience chamber to the head of the staircase. A brass plate marks the spot where he died.

The old university at Edinburgh stands partly on ground which once belonged to the collegiate church of Kirk o' Field, and it was here in a house close to the city wall that another of the intrigues associated with the Queen of Scots reached its grim climax. After the murder of Rizzio, Darnley, weak and vacillating as ever, was won back to Mary's side, and the following year found them at Kirk o' Field, Darnley ill with smallpox and Mary nursing him. Early one morning, while Mary was at Holyrood attending the wedding of a favourite servant, the house was blown up, Darnley and his page afterwards being found dead in an adjoining garden with marks of strangulation on their throats. How far Mary was implicated in the plot will never be known, but in little more than three months she had married Bothwell after he and his men had intercepted her near Edinburgh, and carried her off to his castle at Dunbar, the ruins of which still stand on a rock dominating the harbour.

Even after Mary's long imprisonment had begun, plotting and intrigue continued around her. There were many plots to effect her escape, and perhaps the most romantic of these was that which took place at Lochleven Castle.

THE SCENE OF RIZZIO'S MURDER

The palace of Holyroodhouse is the official residence of the Sovereign in Edinburgh.
It stands on the site of an abbey founded by David I in the twelfth century, and there-
after frequently visited by the kings and queens of Scotland. Mary, Queen of Scots
was resident here when her former counsellor, David Rizzio, was murdered in 1566.
A plate let into the floor here at the entrance to the Queen's private room recalls the
traditional spot at which Rizzio was slain, after being dragged from the Queen's
presence by a group of Scottish nobles, including Lord Darnley.

CRAIGMILLAR CASTLE

This is another of the historic residences associated with the troubled reign of Mary, Queen of Scots. When Bothwell was scheming to remove Darnley in order that Mary might be free to marry him (Mary married Lord Darnley in 1565), he and several other conspirators inimical to Darnley signed at Craigmillar Castle what is known as the Bond of Craigmillar. This bound the signatories, it is said with Mary's connivance, to murder Darnley. Darnley was in fact murdered in February, 1567, and the Queen and Bothwell were married in May of the same year.

It was a plot in the best Ruritanian tradition, with messages written on a handkerchief in soot and water, and with a pearl ear-ring as a sign that preparations were complete. It was an eighteen-year-old youth, William Douglas, who obtained the keys which enabled Mary to escape. It was young Douglas, too, who tampered with the boats on the loch so that they could not be launched in pursuit as he rowed Mary to the mainland where men and

horses were waiting. The plot succeeded, but eleven days later Mary was to see her forces routed at Langside.

Chartley Manor, eighteen years later, was the setting for the last of the long series of intrigues in which this tragic queen figured. Francis Walsingham, Elizabeth's principal secretary-of-state, deliberately contrived things so that Mary should have easy communication with the world outside her prison. Mary fell into the trap. Young Anthony

Babington, who headed the group of conspirators planning to place Mary on the throne, hoped, like others before him, to be rewarded with Mary's hand in marriage. But one of the conspirators was in Walsingham's pay, and the plot ended, for both Babington and Mary, with the headsman's block. The scanty remains of Fotheringhay Castle, where Mary was executed, may still be seen about nine miles from Peterborough.

The galleried courtyard of the fifteenth-century New Inn at Gloucester witnessed the proclamation of Lady Jane Grey, Queen for only nine days and a tragic victim of another's plotting. Even after her brief reign had ended, Jane might have escaped the supreme penalty had not her father, the Duke of Suffolk, participated in a further plot led by Sir Thomas Wyatt. Wyatt attempted to march on London, but his

NEW INN, GLOUCESTER

Though still called the New Inn, this hostelry in Gloucester's Northgate Street is one of England's oldest, its traditional foundation date being 1457. The New Inn reached the pinnacle of its fame during the coaching era, from which most of the present buildings date. It is said this old courtyard saw the proclamation of Lady Jane Grey as Queen during the famous conspiracy to prevent Mary ascending the throne of England on the death of the latter's brother, Edward VI, in 1553.

CENTRE OF THE RYE HOUSE PLOT

The Rye House at Hoddesdon, Hertfordshire, is the traditional centre of the plot to assassinate Charles II and his brother James, then Duke of York, in 1683. The plotters were members of the Whig party, including the notorious Ferguson and Colonel Ramsey. The plan was for the regicides to lie in wait at the Rye House, which was then a farmhouse adjoining the main road, and lay an ambush for the royal party during its return journey to London from a visit to Newmarket. In the event the King was warned, left Newmarket early on his way to London and escaped unscathed. Many of the conspirators, however, were executed.

forces were split in two between Kingston and Ludgate, and overcome.

Wyatt, Suffolk, Lady Jane Grey and her husband were among those—the total was over a hundred—who were executed as a result of the plot. Among the many inscriptions on the walls of the Beauchamp Tower is the name "Jane," carved there, it is believed, by her husband, young Guilford Dudley, as he waited to go to the block.

It was while Jane was already a prisoner in the Tower of London that Wyatt hatched the plot which was to seal her doom, and it is with the Tower that many of the darkest deeds in our history are associated. On Tower Hill and Tower Green many plotters have paid the penalty for their scheming.

It was in the Tower that the horrible plot to poison Sir Thomas Overbury, secretary to James I, ran its grim course. The plot followed a sordid intrigue between James's favourite, Viscount Rochester, and the shameless Countess of Essex. When the countess

HUDDINGTON COURT, WORCESTERSHIRE

This fine old half-timbered manor-house is a link with the Gunpowder Plot, for it was here that one of the leading conspirators, R. Winter, lived. The Gunpowder Plot, or the Guy Fawkes' Plot, as it has come to be known, was a conspiracy of Roman Catholics pledged to destroy the government of James I. Its plan was to blow up the Houses of Parliament on 5 November, 1605, when the King would be opening Parliament and the Lords and Commons would be together in the Chamber. The plot was denounced, Guy Fawkes and many of the others were arrested and executed.

finally divorced her husband after a series of shameless proceedings Overbury advised Rochester not to marry her. What followed is proof of the old adage that hell hath no fury like a woman scorned. She not only married Rochester, but persuaded him to have Overbury confined to the Tower and supplied daily with poisoned food. Even the very salt and pepper supplied to Overbury during his period of confinement were poisoned. But Overbury had a sturdy constitution, and before he

finally succumbed to this fiendish treatment he seems to have absorbed enough poison to have killed a score of men.

When the truth of the plot leaked out, James, who himself had a constant fear of being poisoned, ordered an investigation. Those who had been accessories to the plot, including Sir Jervis Elwes, Lieutenant of the Tower, were executed, but Rochester and his terrible wife—they were now the Earl and Countess of Somerset—were only imprisoned in the Tower. They had originally been condemned to death, but James for reasons known only to himself refused to sign the death warrant. And five years later he not only issued them with a royal pardon, but also settled £4,000 a year on them. His motives are one of the mysteries of history.

Revolution House at Whittington, in Derbyshire—once an inn—witnessed the hatching of the plot which placed William of Orange on the throne instead of James II, while Bidston Hall, in Cheshire, was the meeting-place of those who planned the insurrection of the Duke of Monmouth. The actual meeting-place was a curiously shaped summer-house in the grounds of the hall, where the plotters gathered on the pretext of attending Wallasey races.

Some of those who planned the insurrection were also concerned in an earlier plot to assassinate Charles II and the Duke of York, afterwards

A PRIEST'S HOLE

The historical background of "priests' holes" is that during the several periods of Catholic persecution in Protestant England, as during the Protectorate of Oliver Cromwell and in the reign of James I, Roman Catholic priests were given succour by the faithful, and were concealed in hidden chambers or within the thickness of the walls of houses until such time as they could emerge with safety. This picture of such a hiding-place is in an upper bedroom of Huddington Court, a house which was one of the centres of the Catholic intrigues against the Government which culminated in the Gunpowder Plot (see page 126). A whole section of the panelling in the wall swings aside to disclose the entrance to the hiding-place.

James II, a plot which has gained historical fame because its detection brought about the deaths of three prominent men who appear to have been in no way involved in it—Lord William Russell, the Earl of Essex and Algernon Sydney. The plot was hatched at Rye House, Hoddesdon, the conspirators planning to overturn a cart on a near-by highway and then shoot the King and the Duke of York from behind a hedge. That the plot went astray was largely due to the fact that the King returned to London from Newmarket three days earlier than had been expected. The plotters were betrayed, and in the subsequent investigation Russell, Essex and Sydney became involved on the flimsiest of evidence. Russell and Sydney were executed, and a tablet in Lincoln's Inn Fields indicates the place where Russell died. Essex was found dead in his cell in the Tower of London, and no one will ever know whether he was murdered or committed suicide.

GUNPOWDER PLOT

Most famous of all plots in British history was that which is still celebrated with bonfires and fireworks each November. The Gunpowder Plot was hatched in a room in the half-timbered gate-house of the old manor-house at Ashby St. Ledgers and in a house at Dunchurch which in those days was the Lion Inn. Had the plot succeeded Dunsmore Heath was to have been the scene of a Roman Catholic rising planned to follow the destruction of Parliament. The manor-house at Ashby St. Ledgers was the home of Catesby, one of the conspirators, and it was there that five of them, including Guy Fawkes, a soldier of fortune, met for the first time. Their number eventually rose to thirteen and their first plan was to undermine the Houses of Parliament

by digging through from an adjoining house. The task proved slow and tedious, however, and before it was completed the conspirators had managed to rent a cellar directly under Parliament itself.

In the Public Record Office in London is the curiously worded warning letter received by Lord Mounteagle which resulted in a search of the vaults. Barrels of gunpowder were found hidden under stacks of wood, and Fawkes, who was in the cellar at the time of the search, was arrested.

FATE OF THE CONSPIRATORS

Five of the conspirators, including Catesby, fled to Holbeach, and were killed while trying to hold out against those sent to arrest them. Two more— the priests, Garnett and Hall—were captured at Hindlip Hall, Worcester. The present building, now the county police headquarters, stands on the site of an older one riddled with trapdoors, hiding-places and secret entrances. Garnett and Hall were hidden in a secret compartment off one of the main bedrooms. They remained undiscovered even after the building had been searched from top to bottom, and it was only the confession of another conspirator that kept the search going. Eventually after remaining hidden for ten days, and unable to breathe properly in their small hiding-place, though they were well supplied with food, the two priests gave themselves up. Some of the conspirators, including Fawkes, were tried at Westminster and afterwards executed.

A loft in London's Cato Street was the headquarters, in 1820, of a plot very similar to the Gunpowder Plot. It was led by a man named Thistlewood who planned to blow up the Cabinet. The Home Secretary, Viscount Sidmouth,

CATO STREET

This quiet street off the Edgware Road was the meeting place of a number of discontents in 1820, when the policy and government of Prime Minister Castlereagh was awakening much resentment in certain sections of the community. The plot was devised in the first instance by a politically insignificant person by the name of Thistlewood, who planned to assassinate Castlereagh and other members of the Government. The plot misfired and had no important consequences, but it has always been known as the Cato Street Conspiracy, after the street where the conspirators met.

IN ST. MARY'S CHURCH, WARWICK

The lovely fifteenth-century Beauchamp Chapel in St. Mary's Church, Warwick, recalls some of the plots and intrigues centring round various Earls of Warwick. In the centre is the monument of Richard de Beauchamp, the Earl of Warwick who endowed the chapel. A monument to the Earl of Leicester, the courtier of Queen Elizabeth, is also here. The most famous intriguer of all the Warwicks was Richard Neville, known as the Kingmaker, who died at the Battle of Barnet, 1471 (see page 82).

was informed of the plot, however, and there was a raid on Cato Street which resulted in fierce fighting between the conspirators and the police. The conspirators were imprisoned in the Tower, and five of them, including Thistlewood, were eventually hanged.

London has associations, too, with the so-called Popish Plot of the seventeenth century—a plot which seems to have existed only in the imagination of Titus Oates. For two years Oates deceived the country with his tales of this plot to murder the King, burn London and massacre the Protestants. While the tales were believed Oates was rewarded with a pension and lodged in the Palace of Whitehall for safety, while numerous Catholics were arrested and executed. But the day of reckoning was to come. Oates eventually found himself pilloried in Palace Yard, again in front of the Royal Exchange, and whipped very severely from Aldgate to Newgate and from Newgate to Tyburn.

GOWRIE CONSPIRACY

The Gowrie Conspiracy of 1600 is as well known in Scotland as the Gunpowder Plot is in England. The County Buildings at Perth stand on the site of Gowrie House, where these strange happenings took place. A bronze tablet in one of the blind windows bears a representation of the picturesque old mansion to which James VI was lured. What really happened in that small turret room at the head of the narrow, winding staircase will never be known. But the King's followers certainly thought he was being assassinated. In the struggle which followed the Earl of Gowrie and his brother were killed, and afterwards three of the earl's servants were executed and the Gowrie estates confiscated. What was the motive behind this attempt at assassination? It

has been suggested that there was no motive and no conspiracy, that the plot was one hatched by the King to rid himself of the two brothers.

The castles at Berkeley, Nottingham, Hertford and Castle Rising all come into the grim intrigue which wove itself around Queen Isabella, "the She-Wolf of France." At Berkeley her husband, Edward II, was foully murdered. At Nottingham Isabella and the proud Roger Mortimer were taken by the supporters of the young Edward III, and at Castle Rising and Hertford Queen Isabella was to spend the rest of her life in enforced idleness.

DEATH OF GAVESTON

In another castle, Scarborough, the last act was begun of the long intrigue which brought about the death of Piers Gaveston, hated favourite of Edward II. At Scarborough Piers Gaveston surrendered to the Earl of Pembroke, who pledged his word that his prisoner should be kept unharmed in the castle at Wallingford. At Deddington, a village between Warwick and Oxford, however, Gaveston was roused from sleep and ordered to dress, and he descended into the courtyard to find himself confronted by his bitterest enemy, the Earl of Warwick. Seated on a mule, the wretched favourite was taken thirty miles to Warwick's great fortress-palace overlooking the Avon, where an ironic fanfare of martial music heralded his arrival. In the great hall, its floor strewn with rushes, the darkness broken by the flames of a great leaping fire and the flickering light of sconces, Gaveston was tried by the chief barons. Two miles away, on a wooded rise at Blacklow, a stone monument marks the spot where his head was struck off in the hollow of a crag which formed the headsman's block.

TRAQUAIR HOUSE, NEAR PEEBLES

This baronial mansion is certainly one of the oldest inhabited houses in Scotland; some of the stonework may date from the twelfth century. It is the original of Sir Walter Scott's Tully Veolan in the historical novel Waverley, *and is traditionally associated with many generations of Jacobite intrigue. In 1715 and 1745 attempts were made to restore the dynasty of James II, the last Stuart king. These were unsuccessful, and Jacobitism ceased to be an important political force. Several of the great families of the Tweed valley in which Traquair House is situated supported these rebellions. The old house stands on the banks of the River Tweed.*

Perhaps the most audacious exploit in British history was Colonel Blood's attempt to steal the Crown jewels, and this brings the story back—as any recital of plots and exploits must inevitably be brought back—to the Tower of London. The Crown jewels at the time were housed in the Martin Tower. Blood, posing as a parson, made friends with the custodian to such good purpose that there was talk of a match between the custodian's daughter and the colonel's nephew. A meeting between the young couple was arranged —a meeting for which the colonel turned up accompanied by his "nephew" and two companions. The colonel's wife was supposed to be joining them later,

and it was suggested by Blood that while they were waiting for her the "nephew" should be shown the jewels. No sooner were they in the jewel-room, however, than the unfortunate custodian was felled with a mallet. Blood seized the crown, one of his companions seized the orb, while another began filing through the sceptre which was too large to be concealed in one piece.

The unexpected arrival of the custodian's son interrupted the theft, but even then Blood made an attempt to get away with at least part of the spoils. Abandoning the sceptre, he and his accomplices made off with the crown and the orb, themselves pretending to

DUNNOTTAR, KINCARDINESHIRE

Dunnottar Castle changed hands many times in medieval times during the struggle between England and Scotland. During the Civil War, when Dunnottar was besieged by the Parliamentary army, the royal regalia of Scotland, which were held in the castle, were brought to safety before the place yielded to the besiegers. One story recounts that the regalia were brought out of the castle hidden in a fish-wife's creel, another that they were concealed under bundles of flax. The castle is seen above.

SCARBOROUGH CASTLE

The keep and great encircling walls of Scarborough Castle were built by the Normans, and much of the present fabric dates from the twelfth century. This photograph shows part of the walls, as well as the still existing fragments of the keep. A notable exploit took place here during the rebellion of Sir Thomas Wyatt in 1553, when the castle was surprised and taken by the Earl of Stafford, by the stratagem of introducing within the walls troops dressed as peasants. The rebels held out for three days.

be pursuing the thieves. The ruse failed. Even when captured, however, the colonel's nerve did not desert him. "It was a gallant attempt, however unsuccessful," he told his captors. "It was for a crown."

Whether Charles II was in some way implicated in this attempt to steal the Crown jewels is another of history's puzzles, but certainly the colonel was not only spared from the gallows, but also had his forfeited estates restored. Yet perhaps this was only a royal gesture in recognition of the superb arrogance of this remarkable exploit.

EXPLOITS OF THE CIVIL WAR

The Scottish regalia—the Honours of Scotland as they are called—which are now housed in the jewel room of Edinburgh Castle, were also once the cause of a noteworthy exploit. They were in Dunnottar Castle, which General Monk was besieging during the Civil War, and there are various accounts of how they were smuggled to safety. One story says that they were brought out of the castle hidden in a fishwife's creel; another, that they were hidden under bundles of flax; and yet another, that the wife of the minister of Kinneff Church rode out of the castle with the crown hidden in her lap and the sceptre disguised as a distaff. After being smuggled out of the castle, the Honours were buried behind the pulpit of Kinneff Church until the time of Restoration.

The Civil War, however, was more notable for military exploits with grim endings than for episodes so happy in their outcome as the saving of the Scottish regalia. When the Royalist cause was almost lost in Yorkshire, General Rainsborough was sent by the Parliamentarians to lay siege to Ponte-fract Castle, where a handful of reckless cavaliers were still holding out. Rains-borough's headquarters were at Don-caster, but that did not prevent the defenders of Pontefract Castle from trying to kidnap him. Twenty-two of them sallied forth from Pontefract on this reckless mission, and four actually succeeded in gaining an audience with the general by pretending to be bearers of a dispatch from Cromwell. The general came downstairs with them, but then, suddenly scenting that something was amiss, refused to mount his horse. So the cavaliers failed in their mission, but they left the general dead behind them as they galloped back over Don-caster bridge.

The Civil War was undoubtedly an affair of hard fighting and hard riding, but one of the most famous riding exploits in British military history was that of William Massey, who, after taking part in the rising of 1715, rode non-stop from Preston to his home, Puddington Old Hall in Cheshire. The horse dropped dead at the entrance to the hall and its reputed grave is still pointed out. But Massey's gallant ride in an attempt to establish an alibi proved in vain and after capture he died a prisoner in Chester Castle.

FAMOUS RIDES

Outstanding, too, among riding exploits is the story of Dick Turpin's ride to York—a ride, sad to relate, which never took place. But the ride to York which did take place was longer and more exhausting than the one which Harrison Ainsworth has credited to Turpin. It was accomplished by a highwayman named Nevison, who robbed a man on Gad's Hill, near Chatham, at four o'clock one morning, and then, with only half an hour's rest at Colchester and again at Huntingdon, rode a succession of horses all the way to York, a distance of two hundred and thirty miles, in fifteen hours. But the fact that Turpin never accomplished the famous ride did not prevent him visiting York, and the cell in which he was imprisoned before going to the gallows can be seen in the old gaol adjoining the barracks.

The Isle of Ely, in the days when it really was an island, was the setting for many of the exploits of Hereward the Wake. There it was that Hereward, in disguise, joined the Norman workmen who were constructing artificial mounds from which to attack his camp. Hereward worked side by side with his enemies—until the job was almost complete. Then he set fire to the woodwork of the mounds and made good his escape. The higher heathland near Brandon was the setting for another exploit. On this occasion Hereward, disguised as a potter, succeeded in penetrating into the very heart of the Norman camp, killing one soldier with his sword and knocking down another before escaping.

CHASTLETON HOUSE, OXFORDSHIRE

Chastleton House, Oxfordshire, was built in the early seventeenth century by one Walter Jones. It is associated with a remarkable exploit which is said to have taken place during the Civil War. After the Battle of Worcester, Captain Arthur Jones, a Royalist, escaped on horseback from the field to his home, Chastleton. Pursued by Parliamentary troops, the Captain hid himself in a secret chamber, and despite the fact that the Roundheads remained for some time on the premises he was not detected. Later he managed to get away safely from the house.

CHAPTER 5

SAILORS AND EXPLORERS

To the casual visitor Spilsby in Lincolnshire is a pleasant little market-town attractively set at the edge of the Wolds. It is an agricultural centre in an agricultural county, and for generations its fourteenth-century market-place has known talk of soil and crops, of good and bad yields, of cattle prices and other farming matters. But the fine bronze statue which stands in the square in memory of Spilsby's most famous son commemorates not a man of the land but of the sea; for he was Sir John Franklin, intrepid sailor, Polar explorer and discoverer of the North-west Passage.

Born at Spilsby in 1786, young Franklin was intended to be a parson, but a holiday visit to the seaside filled him with the desire for a sailor's life. To cure him of such romantic notions his father sent him on a short voyage thinking that this would sicken him of the sea. But the trip had the opposite effect on the boy, for on his return he promptly joined the Navy.

In the years of peace following the Napoleonic wars, in which as a youth he fought at the battles of Copenhagen and Trafalgar, Franklin spent much time in Arctic waters, exploring and surveying for the Navy. For his work he was eventually knighted, made a Fellow of the Royal Society, and later became Governor of Tasmania. In 1845 at the age of fifty-nine the lure of adventure was still strong, and he volunteered to take command of an Admiralty-sponsored expedition to discover the North-west Passage. In May, 1847, with H.M. ships *Erebus* and *Terror* he sailed for the far north: then he disappeared.

From 1848 onwards several relief expeditions searched for the missing vessels. At last in 1859 relics were found which told a grim tale of disaster. Franklin had indeed discovered the North-west Passage, but his ships had been caught in the ice and abandoned while their crews tried to reach safety overland. After suffering many privations the whole party had perished.

To the north of Spilsby, in the little village of Marton in Cleveland, tucked away in the North Riding of Yorkshire, a son was born to an agricultural labourer in the year 1728. When the lad grew old enough his father took him to the tiny seaport of Staithes and apprenticed him to the local grocer and draper. Eighteenth-century Staithes was an exciting place for an adventurous youth. Tucked away in a narrow inlet on the coast, sheltered on three sides by lofty hills, with its steep, winding little streets, picturesque cottages and fishing boats bobbing in the harbour, it is an enchanting corner of Britain. Young James Cook often lingered on his errands to listen to the yarns of the sailors as they mended their nets on the quay or worked about the decks of their craft, and, fired by their stories, he abandoned his shop counter and went off to Whitby and to sea. Nowadays the visitor to Staithes can no longer see the

CAPTAIN COOK'S HOUSE IN WHITBY

All the little seaward towns of the North Riding of Yorkshire have produced intrepid sailors. Nor is this surprising when it is remembered that many of the population are descended from Viking ancestors. Captain Cook was a Yorkshireman, but of an agricultural family. He moved to Whitby as a young man. He was the most famous navigator of the eighteenth century, exploring the coasts of Newfoundland and Australia as well as many parts of the South Seas and of the North Pacific.

little shop where the great navigator, Captain Cook, once served lengths of calico and slices of ham, for together with other buildings it was swallowed up by the eroding sea many years ago. But in romantically named Grape Lane in Whitby's historic Flowergate the old house still stands where Captain Cook lodged during his spells ashore from his seagoing apprenticeship.

EXPLORATIONS OF COOK

In 1755, on the approach of war with France, Cook joined the Navy, and service in North American waters showed him to be a first-class navigator. Chosen to command an expedition into the Pacific on behalf of the Royal Society, he twice afterwards voyaged into that, then little known, ocean, discovering, exploring, charting, and surveying with meticulous accuracy. But on his third voyage Cook met with a tragic and untimely end. Investigating the theft of one of his ship's boats in Karakakoa Bay, Hawaii, he was treacherously attacked by formerly docile natives and stabbed and bludgeoned to death.

In Whitby's museum is a model of Cook's famous ship, the *Resolution*, and on a cliff above the town itself, once so important a seaport that its piers were maintained at the personal charge of the King, stands a bronze memorial to this great Yorkshireman.

Over the border into the ancient Scottish "kingdom" of Fife, close by the famous golfing centre of St. Andrews, is the small fishing-town of Largo, whose inn bears a name well known in English literature. For the Crusoe Hotel is almost as much a memorial to Scotland's Alexander Selkirk as his statue which overlooks the harbour.

Selkirk was born at Largo in 1676, the seventh son of a shoemaker. Like

A LINCOLNSHIRE MAN

This statue of Sir John Franklin stands in the market place of Spilsby, a small market town in Lincolnshire. Franklin was born there in 1786. Much of his life was spent in Arctic exploration. In 1845 he sailed in command of an expedition formed for the purpose of discovering the North-west Passage and never returned.

Franklin he yearned to go to sea and eventually got his way. He was an impulsive young man, for while anchored off the uninhabited island of Juan Fernandez during a voyage to the Pacific in a vessel of Dampier's squadron he quarrelled with his captain and demanded to be put ashore. Here he had to stay until picked up by Captain Woodes Rogers in the ship *Duke* four years later. When this vessel returned to England, Rogers' stories of the young castaway on his lonely island attracted

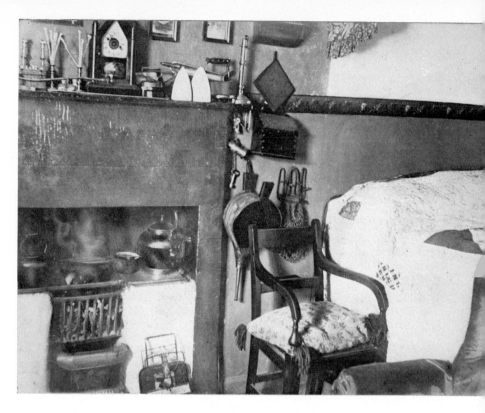

A LINK WITH DAVID LIVINGSTONE

This cottage at Blantyre, Lanarkshire, was the birthplace of David Livingstone in 1813. It was originally a single-room dwelling place of a poor type common enough in the Glasgow area a hundred and fifty years ago. Now it has been restored with great attention to detail and is the chief authentic link with the great man in what has become a museum of Livingstone's life and work. Livingstone was both explorer and missionary; he spent most of his working life in Africa and largely inspired the long agitation which ultimately resulted in the abolition of slavery. He died in 1873.

the attention of Daniel Defoe. The result was that classic yarn for young and old, *Robinson Crusoe*.

As for Selkirk, with the prize-money earned during his cruise with Woodes Rogers he retired to his father's house at Craigie Well, Largo, where, somewhat surprisingly, he lived in a cave in the garden. Then he suddenly eloped with a local girl to Bristol, and from there went to London, where he heartlessly deserted her and joined the Navy. Perhaps his long isolation at Juan

Fernandez had affected his health, for at the comparatively early age of forty-five he died on board H.M.S. *Weymouth* in 1721.

On the other side of Scotland, some ten miles from Glasgow, is the mining district of Blantyre. Today a small worker's cottage in Blantyre's Shuttle Row has become a national memorial as well as a constant reminder of one of Scotland's greatest sons. For here in 1813 young David Livingstone was born, and in a near-by cotton mill, still

BIRTHPLACE OF A GREAT ADMIRAL

Admiral Robert Blake was born in this ancient house of Bridgwater, Somerset, in August, 1599—in a street which has since been named, after him, Blake Street. Now known as the Blake Museum, No. 5 Blake Street has been reconstructed since the sixteenth century, but part of the interior remains as it was when Blake was born. Blake chiefly distinguished himself in naval engagements with the Dutch Navy.

MEMORIAL TO ANSON

The impressive triumphal archway of stone and marble in Shugborough Park, Staffordshire, is a memorial to Admiral Anson, who was born in the neighbouring mansion in 1697. Among Anson's most famous exploits were a successful voyage round the world, and in 1743 the capture of the richest Spanish galleon that ever fell a prize to an English commander.

preserved today, the rather awkward, stammering youth worked long hours as a piecer. But he was avid for learning and from his slender wages he bought himself books on Latin, botany, zoology and geology, which he studied while at his loom. In due course young Livingstone went to the University, qualified as a doctor, and then, as a missionary, went to Africa to become one of the greatest British explorers.

Going south into England, the West Country justly claims to have been the cradle of some of the most famous

British seamen. Bridgwater, in Somerset, preserves the memory of one of these. Sheltered by the Polden Hills, its ancient quays washed by the tidal waters of the River Parrett, Bridgwater is a town of many historical associations. Near-by were once the marshes where King Alfred wandered after his defeat by the Danes, and in a shepherd's cottage he burnt the cakes he was supposed to be watching. In Bridgwater Castle, of which only a solitary stone archway now remains, the ill-fated Duke of Monmouth crowned himself king. Then came his disastrous defeat on the field of Sedgemoor, when after the battle he was discovered cowering in a ditch.

REPUBLICAN ADMIRAL

But Bridgwater's most famous historical figure is her own son, Robert Blake, Cromwell's faithful admiral and "General-at-Sea," whose statue stands near his birthplace. Today Blake's four-hundred-year-old house is a museum, and upstairs the room in which he was born has been carefully preserved, even to some scrawls on its panels said to have been made by the admiral himself when a child.

Robert Blake, staunch supporter of Cromwell, was one of the greatest English seamen, yet had it not been for his ugliness and uncouth speech which offended the college authorities he might have ended his days peacefully as an Oxford don, for he tried hard to obtain a fellowship. As it was he became a merchant and eventually Member of Parliament for Bridgwater. When the Civil War broke out he sided against the King and earned fame by his military prowess during the conflict. But it is for his exploits afloat that Blake is most famous. In his battles with the Dutch he gained for Britain the mastery of the seas; in the Mediterranean he

A HOME OF SIR FRANCIS DRAKE

Buckland Abbey, near Yelverton, South Devon, was originally a Cistercian monastery founded in the thirteenth century. It had a comparatively uneventful but useful existence for over two hundred years, and was less affected by the increasing laxity of the monastic foundations than other larger houses. It did not, however, escape the fate of almost all the monasteries at the Dissolution at the beginning of the sixteenth century. For a time the buildings were allowed to decay. Then they were purchased by Sir Richard Grenville (of Revenge *fame), who made them into an up-to-date mansion which later became the home of Sir Francis Drake.*

exacted respect for the British flag at a time when our prestige had sunk low, and at Santa Cruz, in Teneriffe, he smashed Spanish aspirations in a terrific battle. But Santa Cruz was his last fight and he died, worn out, as his ship was entering Plymouth Sound.

Westwards into Devon lies Bideford, another town of ancient memories. Like Bridgwater, it stands beside a tidal river, enclosed by oak-clad hills that reach almost to the sea. In Bideford's ancient church of St. Mary is the

Grenville Chapel, tomb of one of the most famous families in the West Country. On the mellowed wall hangs a tablet engraved with the immortal last words of Sir Richard Grenville, whose heroic fight against overwhelming odds in the little ship *Revenge* is a glorious episode in English history.

Sir Richard, whose family was connected with other illustrious Elizabethans, such as the Raleighs, the Drakes, the Courtenays and the Gilberts, was born at Bideford in 1542 and soon

143

SOUTH WRAXALL MANOR

In this handsome Wiltshire manor-house is a farmers room in which the long-established tradition is that Sir Walter Raleigh (by birth a Devon man) and Sir Walter Long smoked the first two pipefuls of tobacco to be consumed in England. Raleigh had much to his credit apart from the debatable distinction of having introduced tobacco. He was the founder of the colony of Virginia and one of the architects of the defeat of the Spanish Armada. His star waned on the accession of James I and most of his later life was spent in prison. He was finally executed on a charge of treason.

proved himself a sailor and fighting man. Returning from his voyage with Raleigh's colonists to Virginia, he was attacked by a much larger Spanish ship, but outfought and captured her. When the Armada sailed against England Grenville commanded the defences of the West Country.

In 1591 he sailed as vice-admiral of an expedition under Lord Thomas Howard to attack the homeward-bound Spanish treasure fleet from America. But while the English ships lay in wait off the Azores a powerful Spanish squadron appeared and Howard hastily withdrew, leaving Grenville re-embarking his men from the shore. Surrounded by fifty-three great enemy galleons, Grenville and his crew fought for fifteen hours until the five-hundred-ton *Revenge* had been battered into a helpless wreck. Mortally wounded, Sir Richard died on board the Spanish flagship.

Devon and Cornwall are rich in historical associations with these great English seamen whose exploits added such lustre to the golden age of Queen

Elizabeth. Down a narrow lane just outside Tavistock stands Crowndale Farm, in a small cottage of which in 1542 was born Sir Francis Drake, perhaps the greatest of them all. Today the cottage has disappeared and there is only a stone tablet to show where it once stood. But the ancient cattle-troughs and the old well still remain, and the narrow, winding country lanes have changed but little during the centuries.

While he was still a child Drake's parents were forced to leave their home during a period of religious turmoil, and eventually the family found shelter in a hulk on the River Medway in Kent. When he was old enough young Francis was apprenticed to the owner of a small coasting vessel, upon whose death he inherited the ship. He made his first voyage to America before he was twenty, and during the second he and his famous relative, Sir John Hawkins, were treacherously attacked by a large Spanish squadron while sheltering in harbour. From then on he hated the Spaniards. In 1577 he sailed from Plymouth in his little ship *Pelican*, later named the *Golden Hind*, on a voyage to

PLYMOUTH—THE HOE

Plymouth's great distinction as a port is that it has remained in the forefront of the story of the sea since Britain's navy first established herself as a world force. In Elizabethan days, as now, it was one of the chief naval stations. It was here on the Hoe that tradition relates Sir Francis Drake was playing bowls when news was brought of the approach of the Spanish Armada. To the statue of Drake, one of the most conspicuous landmarks (not seen here), have been added part of a former Eddystone lighthouse (seen here on the right) and several memorials.

THE MAYFLOWER MEMORIAL, PLYMOUTH

The Mayflower Stone (set in the pavement) and the classical-style memorial recall the sailing of the Mayflower *with its complement of "Pilgrim Fathers" en route for the promised land of America in 1620. Originally two ships had been set aside for the expedition, the* Mayflower *and the* Speedwell, *which brought a contingent of settlers from the Low Countries. The latter was condemned as unseaworthy, however. So the* Mayflower, *carrying the passengers from both ships, set sail alone.*

explore the Pacific, but which took him round the world.

Three years later Drake dropped anchor in Plymouth Sound. Wild with excitement at the news of his return the whole population flocked to the quay to greet him, including the entire congregation of St. Andrew's Church who left their astonished parson preaching to empty pews. From this voyage Drake sent off to Queen Elizabeth five packhorses laden with gold and jewels. Soon afterwards he took the *Golden Hind* round to Deptford, where all London turned out to see the ship and the Queen knighted him on his own deck.

DRAKE IN DEVONSHIRE

After the annihilation of the Armada Drake enjoyed a peaceful period on shore during which he acquired the beautiful mansion of Buckland Abbey from the Grenvilles, became a squire of the manor, Member of Parliament and Mayor of Plymouth. In 1595 he commanded his last expedition to the New World, for in the following January he was stricken with illness and died at sea.

Five miles east of Exmouth is the charming little seaside resort of Budleigh Salterton, a century ago merely a smuggling cove. A short distance inland, behind the neighbouring village of East Budleigh, is the centuries-old farmhouse of Hayes Barton, lying in a dip of the hills. It is a beautiful thatch-roofed building set in flower gardens surrounded by a mellow wall. Here Sir Walter Raleigh was born in 1552. As a boy Raleigh often played on the shore at Budleigh Salterton, and it was here that Millais came to paint his famous picture of the youthful Raleigh curled up at the feet of a sailor listening eagerly to his yarn of adventure.

Soon after his arrival at court Queen Elizabeth began to load favours and honours upon this handsome courtier, who once spread his own cloak upon the mud before her so that she might walk dry-shod. In 1584 he was knighted, granted valuable wine licences, an estate of forty thousand acres at Cork, Waterford, and Tipperary, and made Vice-Admiral of Devon and Cornwall. An expedition fitted out by Raleigh discovered and took possession of the colony of Virginia.

After marrying one of the Queen's maids of honour, he settled down for a time on his beautiful estate of Sherborne in Dorset, presented to him by the Queen herself. But this was the golden age of discovery and Raleigh was fascinated by the talk of Eldorado, the fabulous city of the Spaniards in Mexico, and in 1595 he sailed in command of an expedition to the Orinoco. During subsequent voyages court enemies intrigued against him, and finally after the death of Elizabeth he was shut up in the Tower of London on a charge of treason. Released after being sentenced to death, he sailed once more to attack the Spanish treasure-fleet, but failed, and on his return he was arrested for making war and finally beheaded.

THE HOMES OF RALEIGH

Today the old church at East Budleigh, where Raleigh's father was once churchwarden, is redolent of memories of this great Elizabethan. Raleigh's arms are carved on one of the pew ends, and at the ancient font he was christened. Little remains today of Raleigh's old home at Sherborne, for it was battered almost to ruins by Cromwell's artillery during the Civil War.

Like many other Elizabethan adventurers, Raleigh sailed on his expeditions from Plymouth, premier seaport and naval base of the West. During the Second World War much of this ancient city was destroyed in air raids, but nothing can rob it of the memory of its past great men. From its venerable Barbican sailed the Pilgrim Fathers in their little *Mayflower* to found a new world of free men. Sir Humphrey Gilbert sailed from Plymouth to discover Newfoundland, Grenville took his colonists to Virginia, and Frobisher departed in search of the elusive North-west Passage. On the Hoe the statue of Drake still stands unscathed, and near-by the Armada Memorial.

HAWKINS AND PLYMOUTH

One of the most famous sons of Plymouth was Sir John Hawkins, born in the city in 1532, and a great merchant adventurer. When he became Treasurer of the Navy to Queen Elizabeth he introduced many improvements to Britain's ships of war, and instituted the "Chatham Chest," first system of pensions for disabled sailors. At the Armada action Hawkins was captain of the *Victory*, commanding the Inshore Squadron, and afterwards with his fellow captain, Frobisher, he was knighted for gallantry. Even when an ageing man he could not resist the call of the sea, and when Drake sailed on what was to be his last expedition to the Spanish Main, Hawkins went as his second in command. But off Puerto Rico in 1595 he was stricken with a mortal illness and was buried at sea.

Adjoining Plymouth is the naval town of Devonport, which was at one time known as Plymouth Dock. On the hills above the town towers a memorial to another West Country hero, Captain Robert Falcon Scott, Royal Navy, who was born there in 1868. His lovely old home, Oatlands, still stands, and here and at Stoke Damerel School the slightly built lad with blue eyes worked and played before entering the Navy in

1882. With a handful of companions Scott perished during an expedition to the South Pole in 1912.

A few miles from another great naval port is a tiny village composed of two rows of red-roofed cottages flanking an unusually wide street. This is Buckler's Hard, which stands near the head of the Beaulieu River in Hampshire. Less than one hundred and fifty years ago Buckler's Hard was a thriving shipyard, turning out such fine vessels as the sixty-four-gun *Agamemnon*, once commanded by Nelson himself, while no fewer than three of the "wooden walls" built at Buckler's Hard were present at Trafalgar. Today the old-time slipways are deep ruts in the fields and cattle graze where the shipwrights worked.

NELSON IN NORFOLK

Linked with Buckler's Hard through the immortal figure of Nelson is another country village, this time Burnham Thorpe in Norfolk, where, in 1758, the admiral was born. For forty-six years his father, the Reverend Edmund Nelson, was vicar of Burnham Thorpe, and today lies buried within the precincts of the little old flint church in which he so often preached. Above his tomb stands a marble bust of his famous son, and the church's cross and lectern have been fashioned from the timbers of H.M.S. *Victory*.

The rectory which once echoed to the childish voices of Nelson and his brothers and sisters was pulled down three years before Trafalgar, but many of Burnham Thorpe's cottages and farmhouses have been standing since the days when the young Nelsons were scampering about the village. When he was old enough Horatio became a pupil at Norwich Grammar School. Here in this ancient capital of East Anglia, once the second city of Britain, lived the

IN BURNHAM THORPE CHURCH, NORFOLK

A monument to Admiral Lord Nelson is seen on the right of this picture, taken inside the church of Burnham Thorpe. The famous admiral was born at the Rectory of Burnham. The house has been destroyed, but the church, in addition to the bust, contains several links with Nelson, including the lectern and cross which were made, it is said, from timber taken from the admiral's flagship, the Victory.

boy's uncle, Captain Maurice Suckling, under whose wing Nelson started his sea career. Suckling House, which dates back more than four hundred years, still stands in St. Andrew's Street, and in the Concert Hall near-by hangs the last portrait of Nelson for which the admiral sat, painted by Beechey.

But it is, perhaps, at Portsmouth that memories of England's greatest

admiral are more closely associated. For here in the naval yard, preserved in the oldest dry dock in the world, lies H.M.S. *Victory* herself, now a national memorial. Here also is the ancient Sally Port, where, after passing his last night in England at the old George Inn, the immortal Nelson stepped into his waiting barge, to be borne to Trafalgar and ultimately St. Paul's Cathedral.

THE SCOTT MEMORIAL AT DEVONPORT

Devonport, with its great dockyard, lies immediately to the west of Plymouth on the same side of Plymouth Sound. Its seafaring traditions are as deeply rooted in history as those of Plymouth; among its illustrious sons it counts Captain Robert Scott, the most fearless of Antarctic explorers, who was born here and spent much of his shore life in Devonport. The finely-sculptured memorial by A. H. Hodges is on Mount Wise, a high-level promenade. It shows Scott with his companions—Oates, Wilson, Bowers and Evans—on their last fatal expedition to the Antarctic.

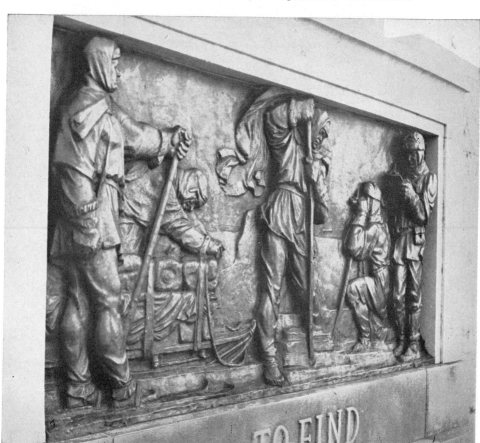

CHAPTER 6
FOLKLORE AND LEGEND

Our British countryside is full of ancient legends which have been handed down from father to son for generations. Queer and often lovely traditions, some purely mythical and some based on half-remembered facts, surround our pools, rivers, rocks and caves, our wells and moorlands, and our old houses and hamlets. Many such tales concern national heroes, like Arthur and Robin Hood. Others are legends of fairies and giants, or pagan nature-spirits who once haunted wild and remote places. Nearly all are very old and, while some are almost forgotten now, or have been altered beyond recognition by the passage of years, the majority are as familiar to us today as they were to our medieval forefathers.

Every nation has its traditional heroes whose deeds, real or imaginary, are celebrated in ballad and story. Of all the bright names that star our history, few are more cherished than that of the man we call King Arthur. Very little is actually known about him. Folklore has made him a king, but it is not at all certain that he really was one. His dates, lineage, birth and death are all alike obscure, and his very existence has been denied by some scholars who believe his entire story is a myth. Yet, through persistent folk-tradition, and through the works of countless poets and writers, he lives for us more vividly than many well-authenticated characters, and is the true type of chivalry, the embodiment of every knightly virtue.

All we know for certain is that in the sixth century, when the Britons, deserted by their Roman protectors, were fighting for their lives against successive waves of Saxon invaders, some great military leader seems to have arisen. This man rallied the scattered native forces, and by a series of brilliant victories checked the Saxon advance for a while. In his lifetime he was naturally the idol of the people, and when he died the loss was felt to be so overwhelming that his despairing followers refused to accept it. A belief sprang up, as it has about many other heroes, that he was not really dead but only absent for a time. He was sleeping in some secret place—in the mysterious Isle of Avalon, or in some hill or cave—and he would return in the hour of direst need to lead his people once more to victory.

Tintagel Castle is said to have been his birthplace. Cornwall thus claims him for her own, and all over that wild and lovely county innumerable rocks, pools, hills and barrows bear his name. But his legend is also found in many other parts of England, Wales and Scotland. At Cadbury Fort in Somerset he slept inside the hill, and rode out occasionally on moonlit nights. He hunted along an old track leading to Glastonbury which is known as King Arthur's Causeway, and watered his horses at King Arthur's Well. In this district there was no special tradition of his future return, but that he dwelt within the ancient British fort was

ROCKY TINTAGEL

Cornwall, the chief remaining stronghold of Celtic folklore and legend in England, has several sites associated also with legendary figures which are common to the more Anglo-Saxon parts of England. Here on the rocky promontory of Tintagel there are the ruins of a medieval castle which tradition has made one of the homes of King Arthur. The castle ruins are definitely later than the Norman occupation and so can have no connexion with King Arthur. Whether or not there was an earlier fortified residence on the site is not known. There are remains of an early monastery.

firmly believed by the local people until a few years ago. And when about 1890 a party of excavators came there, an old man asked anxiously if they had come "to take the King away."

A somewhat similar tradition existed at Alderley Edge in Cheshire. A farmer was once crossing the hill to sell a white horse at Macclesfield market when he was stopped by an aged man who wished to buy the animal. He refused, and was then told that he would not sell the horse that day. This proved to be the case. On his return he again encountered the stranger, who took him, with his horse, through some iron gates opening into the hillside and showed him a great circle of sleeping men in a chamber within. All were fully armed, and behind each stood a white horse, ready saddled. One was missing, and it was to replace it that the farmer's beast was needed. The old man told him that the sleepers were King Arthur and his men, who would remain there until they were needed to fight for Britain when "George, son of George, is king."

In this story the visitor fulfilled the task required of him, for he left the horse behind. At Richmond Castle in Yorkshire another man, Potter Thompson, failed through lack of courage. A chance-met stranger took him into an underground room where the King slept with his host and showed him a sheathed sword and a horn. He told Thompson that if he drew the one and blew the other he could deliver the sleepers from the spell that bound them. But when the sword was half-drawn they all stirred and seemed about to rise, whereupon Thompson in sudden terror let it fall back into the scabbard. The warriors sank down again to sleep, and a melancholy voice was heard reproaching him for his cowardice. Later on Thompson tried to return, but he was never able to find his way to the secret chamber again.

Arthur slept in the Eildon Hills in Scotland, and in several places in Wales. At Craig-y-Dinas he and his men guarded two heaps of treasure in a cave approached by a long passage, in which hung a great bell. Tradition said that if anyone struck the bell the heroes would

A FORTRESS TOWN OF YORKSHIRE

At Richmond town, in Yorkshire, pictured here on its hill, history and legend link hands. The walls and keep of one of the strongest medieval fortresses in the north can be seen on the left of the photograph, with the densely-packed little town clustered around them. The legend associated with the castle is that of Potter Thompson, who is said to have been shown, by a stranger he chanced to meet, King Arthur and his knights asleep in an underground room. A sheathed sword and horn were in the room, and Thompson was told if he drew the one and blew the other the sleepers would wake. Thompson had not the courage to do this and fled. Later he tried to discover the underground room for himself, but was quite unable to do so.

awake to lead the Welsh to victory. Once a Welshman went there seeking gold and accidentally touched it. The sleepers awoke and cried: "Is it day?" "Nay, sleep thou on," replied the man hastily, and they sank again to rest. This happened several times, until one day the robber forgot the right answer, whereupon the host fell upon him and beat him unmercifully.

Though Arthur's death is so strenuously denied in most legends there is one which says he was buried in Glastonbury Abbey. Many curious stories are associated with this ancient monastery. Here it was that St. Joseph of Arimathaea founded the first Christian church in Britain; and here he thrust his staff into the ground, where it took root and grew into the Glastonbury Thorn which blooms every year on Old Christmas night. In Henry I's reign the monks claimed to have discovered Arthur's grave through a dream, and in 1190 it was opened. A hollowed oaken log with an inscribed cross upon it was found. Within it were the bones of an immensely tall man on whose skull were the marks of ten wounds, all healed except one, of which presumably he died. Guinevere was also buried here, though according to another tale she lies in Meigle churchyard in Scotland. A lock of her golden

THE RUINS OF GLASTONBURY

The most venerable of all the monastic ruins in Britain, Glastonbury is the sole link in the south between the Christianity of the later Roman period and that of medieval England. There seems to have been a religious foundation on the site at least as early as the third century, while legend relates that St. Joseph of Arimathaea founded here the first Christian church in England. There is a thorn tree at Glastonbury which flowers about Christmas-time. This is attributed to St. Joseph. The legend tells that it sprang from his staff which he planted to mark the site of the church.

THE CASTLE OF THE PEAK

Sir Walter Scott immortalized the traditions surrounding Peveril of the Peak, who in legend was a bastard son of William of Normandy. To William Peveril his royal namesake granted a wide area of the barren uplands of Derbyshire. Peveril, it is said, founded the Castle of the High Peak, which is even today popularly known as Peveril Castle, a grim, fragmentary fortress standing on the summit of a high, rocky hill as pictured above. The castle is of Norman origin and largely substantiates the legend.

hair lay in the coffin, as bright and lovely as when she was alive; but when a monk lifted it in wondering admiration it crumbled into dust. The remains of the King and Queen—if indeed these were their remains—were translated to a tomb in the great Abbey church, but this, like many other ancient shrines, disappeared at the time of the Reformation.

Wild Edric haunted the lead-mines of Shropshire and rode out to warn the nation of any serious war. He was a rebel leader of the eleventh century who rose against William I in 1067, and fought for three years before he made peace with the Conqueror. Yet, though he was an undoubtedly historical character, curious legends were told about him from the first. He is said to have married a fairy wife, and lost her again because he reproached her with her alien origin. A fairy fish in Bomere Pool wore his sword at its side, holding

WARWICK CASTLE AND THE RIVER AVON

Warwick Castle is a fine blend of very ancient and more recent. Its façade dates from the fourteenth century, much of its interior from Elizabethan times. But it is known that there was a castle on the site for many centuries before the present building was begun. In this earlier castle in the thirteenth century there dwelt an Earl of Warwick whose daughter, so legend recalls, was wooed and won by an English commoner known as Guy of Warwick. This Guy of Warwick later became a hermit after a pilgrimage to the Holy Land. He was reconciled to his wife on his deathbed.

it in trust until one of his descendants should claim it. His ghost haunted Condover Hall, which was supposed, quite wrongly, to have belonged once to his family. His death-date and burial place are both unknown, and it is perhaps because of this that he was thought to be a sleeping hero. Tradition said that whenever war threatened he and Lady Godda, his wife, rode out with their followers, dressed all in green, in the direction of the enemy country. At other times they dwelt in the lead-mines, and the sound of their movements, like those of the Cornish Knockers, was the sign of a good lode.

Robin Hood was a hero of quite another type. No tales of military glory or patriotic self-sacrifice surround his name. The greater part of his life was spent as an outlaw and a robber. But he was beloved of the people because he successfully defied the hated Forest Laws imposed by the Norman conquerors, and managed to lead for years the sort of carefree, open-air life of which every young man dreams. With Maid Marian and a band of cheery followers he roamed Sherwood and Barnsdale forests, and retired to Robin Hood's Bay when things became too hot for him inland. From these fastnesses he robbed the rich and helped the poor, played innumerable tricks on the harassed authorities, and lived to the ripe old age of eighty-seven.

His exploits were the subject of countless ballads and stories repeated with chuckles in village ale-houses and wherever poor men met. Some at least of these tales make him the equal of giants and magicians. Robin Hood's Penistone, near Halifax, is an enormous boulder weighing several tons, but he is said to have kicked it to its present site quite without difficulty when he and his men were amusing themselves on Shackleborough. A rock in the Cheshire River Tame bears marks which are called his fingerprints. As an archer no

ROMANTIC RUINS OF BOLTON ABBEY

The ruins of Bolton Abbey are situated beside the River Wharfe in the West Riding of Yorkshire. They consist principally of the ruins of a church which was never the church of an abbey, as its name suggests, but of a priory of Augustinian Canons. Like almost all the monastic foundations of Britain, the priory was dissolved during the reign of Henry VIII. Among the legends associated with it is that of the Shepherd Lord who is said to have mastered the art of manufacturing gold at Bolton Priory— one of the many legends associating medieval religious foundations with alchemy.

DUNVEGAN CASTLE, SKYE

Dunvegan Castle, in the Isle of Skye, is said to be the oldest of Scottish castles still inhabited. It was probably founded earlier than the eleventh century. Formerly it was the home of the chieftains of the MacLeod clan. There is a legend that an early MacLeod chieftain took a fairy to wife; after twenty years this fairy grew weary of life on the earth and left her husband, bequeathing to him the Fairy Flag which was kept in the family for many centuries and regarded as the token of their success. The flag is said to have had the power of bringing victory and so was always carried in war.

THE FAIRY FLAG

Above are the Fairy Flag (see page 158), the Dunvegan Cup and Rory Mor's Drinking Horn in Dunvegan Castle. The flag is a square of cream-coloured silk embroidered in gold. The ancient chiefs of the MacLeods were not considered fit to rule until they drank, without a pause, the contents of the horn.

man could equal him except Little John. Once these two were competing on the tower of Whitby Abbey. Robin's arrow fell a mile and a half away, at Whitby Lathes, and Little John's fell a hundred yards farther on.

His reputed grave lies at Kirklees Priory in Yorkshire. The story goes that when he was eighty-seven years old he fell ill and came to this house to be nursed by his aunt, the Prioress. According to the custom of the time he was bled, but, whether through carelessness or evil intent, the operation was too drastic and he died from loss of blood. In his last moments he struggled to the window and shot an arrow through it, saying he must be buried

where it fell. Accordingly he was laid to rest in the Park, and there his grave is still shown, together with a window in Kirklees Priory Farm from which he is supposed to have shot his last bolt.

Many of our ancient legends concern the fairies, those curious beings, half mortal, half spirit, whom our ancestors both feared and admired. In medieval times no one doubted that they existed, or that they mingled freely with mankind, sometimes as friends and sometimes as dangerous and powerful enemies. Although they were supposed to live in splendour in a marvellous land where it was always summer, their ways were curiously human, and they often sought the aid of mortal midwives, or lent and borrowed household utensils, like cauldrons, kettles, and peels for bread-making. At Frensham a large cauldron in the church vestry is supposed to have belonged once to the fairies of Borough Hill, who frequently lent their goods to less fortunate housewives. For some reason or other the cauldron was not returned at the agreed time, and this gave such offence that all interchanges ceased, and the vessel itself was left in Frensham Church as a perpetual memorial of a broken promise.

FAIRY FLAG OF DUNVEGAN

The Fairy Flag of Dunvegan, a square of cream-coloured silk embroidered in gold, was given to the MacLeods long ago by a fairy. Tradition varies as to the manner of the gift. One story says that a MacLeod chieftain had a fairy wife who left him after twenty years and gave him the flag on parting. Another version is that a strange woman entered the castle and wrapped the banner round the infant heir, whilst singing the lullaby that has ever since been sung over any heir of the house who is born in the castle. But however they acquired it, the MacLeods have always regarded it as a sacred thing, which was carried into battle immediately behind the chief and was defended by him, if necessary, with his life.

It had the power to bring victory to the clansmen if it was unfurled in war, but only on three occasions. Consequently it was used only in dire need, once at the battle of Glendale in 1490, and again at the Battle of the Spoiled Dyke in 1580. On both occasions the MacLeods were victorious. In the sixteenth century a seer named Coinneach Odhar predicted that when it was unfurled for the third and last time the glory of the MacLeods would depart, much of their land would be sold and a

single coracle would be sufficient to hold all the gentlemen-tacksmen on the estate. In token that the time had come, Norman, the fourth of his name, would perish in an accident, and a vixen would have cubs in a turret of the castle.

The curious thing about this prophecy is that it was fulfilled almost to the letter. In 1799 Mr. Buchanan, the Chief's business manager, and an English smith then staying at Dunvegan, broke open the iron chest in which the flag was kept and unfurled the banner. This they did, apparently, from sheer idle curiosity, and without the knowledge of any member of the family. About the same time Norman MacLeod, the fourth of his name, was blown up in H.M.S. *Queen Charlotte*, and his tame vixen had cubs in the west turret. Thereafter the property gradually diminished, and with it the power of the clan. When the prophecy was made there were forty tacksmen on the estate; today none remains. Large portions of the land passed into other hands, and in 1915 the last male heir in the direct line was killed in France. The flag itself is now kept in the drawing-room of the castle, in a glass case on the wall.

FAIRY WIVES

Fairy wives often imposed difficult conditions on their husbands and left them instantly if those conditions were broken. The Lady of Llyn y Fan Fach consented to marry a farmer from Esgair Llanthony only if he promised never to give her "three causeless blows." She was a water-spirit of great beauty whom the farmer saw floating on the surface of the lake and enticed ashore with wheaten bread specially baked by his mother. She brought him a rich dowry of cattle, and for many years they lived happily together. But their story ended sadly, for in the course of time he did

ZENNOR, CORNWALL

The legend of Zennor is that of a mermaid who for some time attended the services at the village church disguised as an ordinary parishioner. One day a young man, the best singer in the church, fell in love with her and followed her out of the church. She thereupon took him by the hand and led him straight into the sea, and neither the man nor the mermaid was ever seen again. A bench-end carving in Zennor Church, seen in the centre of the picture, represents this mermaid of romance.

WAYLAND'S SMITHY

Wayland's Smithy, on the Berkshire Downs, near White Horse Hill, is the remains of a Stone Age burial-place or cist dating from about 2,000 B.C. In the Middle Ages any unexplained phenomenon such as a set of megaliths of this kind promoted legendary tales. The tradition most closely linked with Wayland's Smithy is that if a horseman came to the smithy, left a coin on one of the stones and turned away his head an invisible smith would shoe his horse for him. Another version of the legend was that a horse must be brought at sunset, tethered to one of the stones and could then be collected, magically re-shod, at sunrise next morning.

strike her three times without cause, though never with any intention of hurting her.

Once he tapped her playfully on the shoulder because she was slow in fulfilling a command. On another occasion they went together to a wedding, and the fairy wife, having second sight, wept because she knew the wedded pair would be unhappy. Her husband put his hand on her and asked her why she wept, and this, she said, was the second blow. The poor man did all he could for many years to avoid even the suspicion of violence, but it was all in vain. One

day, when their three sons were already grown men, she began to laugh at a funeral to the great scandal of all present. The farmer touched her and told her sharply to stop. She replied that the dead man was happy, for death had freed him from trouble, but that her husband's sorrows were just beginning, for this was the third blow. She then returned to the lake, taking all her cattle with her. The farmer never saw her again, but she used to visit her children secretly and instruct them in medical lore. Rhiwallon, the eldest son, became physician to Prince Rhys Gryg, and from his sons and nephews descended the famous Physicians of Myddrai whose book of remedies, compiled in the thirteenth century, still exists. It is said that skill in medicine persisted in this family right down to the nineteenth century, and that in every generation there was at least one man who had marked healing powers.

MERMEN AND MERMAIDS

Stories of mermen and mermaids abound along the coasts. In 1161 some fishermen off Orford caught a strange hairy creature in their nets which they said was a tailless merman. They took him to Orford Castle, where the Governor, Bartholomew Glanvill, tried in vain to question him, for he could not or would not speak. He was kept a prisoner for some time and fed on raw flesh and fish, the only food he would accept. Eventually he managed to escape and disappeared into the sea from whence he came. Who or what he really was no one ever knew, but he is still remembered in Suffolk as the Wild Man of Orford.

In Zennor Church a bench-end carving of a mermaid is supposed to represent a sea-woman who came there long ago. A beautiful but unknown lady, richly dressed, used to attend the services and sing so sweetly that she delighted all who heard her. No one suspected she was a mermaid, but obviously there was something unusual about her, for though she came to church for years she never seemed any older, nor did her beauty fade. Then one day a young man, the finest singer in the choir, fell in love with her and followed her out of the church. She took him by the hand and led him straight into the sea. Man and mermaid sank together to her submarine home, and there presumably he remained, for he was never

seen again on land, nor was his body washed ashore by any subsequent tide.

Mermaids sometimes appeared in inland waters also. At Rostherne in Cheshire one used to ring a sunken bell in the lake on Easter morning, and then rise to the surface and sing. This bell was one of a peal intended for Rostherne Church which broke its ropes when it was being hung and rolled into the water. This happened three times, and finally a workman lost his temper and cursed the bell roundly. It sank immediately to the bottom, and all later efforts to retrieve it failed. Another mermaid appeared in the lake at Hayfield in Derbyshire, also at dawn on Easter Day. Tradition said that those who heard her sing then would never die, but there is no record that anyone ever heard her.

WATER-SPIRITS

Many British rivers were once believed to harbour malignant spirits who demanded a tribute of human lives every so often. Probably in early times such lives were offered to them as a sacrifice; in later legends they took them for themselves. Peg o' Nell, who haunted the River Ribble, was undoubtedly a water-spirit once, but the story now told about her is that she was a servant at Waddow Hall. Her mistress bewitched her so that she was drowned whilst fetching water at Bungerley Stepping Stones. After her death she haunted the Stones and all the surrounding district. Every mishap to men or cattle was put down to her malice, as well as queer noises and disturbances at Waddow Hall itself. Not content with that, she claimed one life every seven years. It was firmly believed in the locality that someone would certainly be drowned on Peg o' Nell's night unless an offering of a bird or animal had previously been made to her.

The Rollright Stones in Oxfordshire are situated near the crest of the Cotswold Hills where they overlook the Warwickshire Plain. Until comparatively recent times it was believed that the whole body of Warwickshire witches met here frequently at dead of night. Associated with the witchcraft legend is the belief that the stones cannot be counted twice alike, and that at certain seasons they go down to a spring near-by to drink. Another legend states that a king, who was setting out with his troops to conquer England, once met a witch on the hill. The witch promised that he would be king of

On the Trent the strong spring tide which rushes up the stream and causes many fatalities is still known as the Aegir, after a Norse god who was at one time worshipped in that region. More bloodthirsty than Peg o' Nell, this tide is believed to demand three lives a year. It is easy to see how this superstition has persisted, for the bore is very dangerous and old memories of pagan sacrifice give it a personal and living character. The Tees had a malicious spirit called Peg Powler, and farther south, on the River Yore, a kelpie, or water-horse, used to rage along the banks at evening and take at least one life a year. On a stretch of the Swale known as Hoggett's Hole the ghost of Tom Hoggett dragged down swimmers. Hoggett was a highwayman who robbed travellers on the Great North Road in the eighteenth century. Captured at last, he was taken to the Salutation Inn to await the York coach, and from there

STONES, OXFORDSHIRE

England if he should reach in seven long strides the summit so as to see the village of Long Compton in the valley below. If he could not he would be turned into stone with his men. He was confident of success, but on reaching the hilltop in seven strides he was confronted by a long barrow which hid Long Compton from his sight. He was immediately turned into the King's Stone, now seen on the hilltop, his men becoming the King's Men, pictured above. Certain knights, who were plotting against him, were turned by the witch into the Whispering Knights, a group of stones some way off.

he managed to escape. He attempted to swim the river and was drowned, and from that time onwards every accident in the dangerous Hole was ascribed to his ghost.

Stones and rocks, especially those of odd shape, are the source of many legends, and so are single hills, patches of sterile ground, and barrows, cromlechs and stone circles. A long barrow in Berkshire called Wayland's Smithy was the home of Wayland, a famous Norse smith who was the son of a giant. He was captured and forced to work for King Nidruth of Sweden, who crippled him so that he might not escape. But he made himself a pair of wings and so flew away, presumably to Berkshire. There for many centuries it was believed that if any horseman came to the smithy, laid a coin on a near-by stone, and turned away his head, an invisible smith would come forth from the stones and shoe his horse for him.

WISHING STONE AT MATLOCK

The limestone hills which surround Matlock have a number of detached stone slabs lying on the surface. These are the remains of an older rock covering, most of which has been eroded away. In prehistoric times such isolated stones formed the megaliths from which Stone Age monuments were made. Through the ages many of them, like this wishing stone, have been credited with magical properties—a process of primitive thought which follows naturally from the mere fact that they are unusual.

The Devil was held responsible for many curious stone-formations, hills, dykes, circles and sterile patches. He is said to have built Stonehenge, bringing the stones from afar, and dropping one six miles off near the Devil's Ditch in Wiltshire. The Colwall Stone, a large boulder in Herefordshire, was thrown by him in a rage, and so were the three stones called the Devil's Quoits in Oxfordshire. On the Stiperstones in Shropshire a seat-like rock is named the Devil's Chair. Here he sat to preside over meetings of the local witches, and tradition says that if anyone sits in it now a storm springs up at once. At Kington in Herefordshire there is a barren patch called the Devil's Garden which he chose for his own use and on which consequently nothing will grow.

Sometimes pieces of ground remain sterile because of some crime committed there. In Montgomery churchyard lies the grave of John Davies (sometimes called Newton), who was falsely accused of robbery and executed in 1821. He declared that in proof of his innocence no grass would grow on

166

his grave for a generation, and in fact it did not, though several attempts were made to break the curse with new seed and fresh soil. The barren patch still exists, though it is smaller now than it was. A distinct cross of bare ground can be seen on the grave, and what makes it more remarkable is that the grass grows strongly all round it, yet never springs up on the cross itself.

All over Britain there are stories of farmers who took, or attempted to take, stones from ancient circles or cromlechs for some utilitarian purpose, and came to want and disaster in consequence. A Cornishman once broke up the Round-hags and sold them as building material for Penzance Dock. But, so goes the tale, he never prospered afterwards, and all the horses used to move them died within the year. A Leicestershire farmer in the early nineteenth century threw down the Hoston Stone near Humberstone to make his ploughing easier, and within six years he lost all his property and died in the workhouse. Several attempts have been made to take stones from the Rollright Stone Circle in Oxfordshire, or from the Whispering Knights near-by, and always disaster has followed and they have had to be replaced. In former times the Warwickshire witches met at Rollright, and fairies haunted the Whispering Knights. It is said that the Rollright Stones cannot be counted twice alike, and that at certain seasons they go down to a neighbouring spring to drink.

Some stones, like wells and springs, have healing or other magical powers.

THE DEVIL'S CHAIR, STIPERSTONES

Like prehistoric antiquities which were explained by fanciful tales when they could not be explained by known causes, any unusual feature of the countryside became the subject of legend during the Middle Ages. Many such natural formations, including these rocks, the Stiperstones, situated in Shropshire, were attributed to the Devil. Thus there are numerous examples of devil's jumps, devil's cauldrons, devil's punch-bowls and the like, all of them, of course, perfectly natural geological formations. The legend of Stiperstones is that the Devil sat on the rock which is shaped like a chair to preside over the meetings of the witches of the neighbourhood.

The Shargar Stone at Fyvie cured ailing children who were passed under it. The Long Stone at Minchinhampton cured young sufferers from measles or whooping-cough if they were passed through a perforation at the top. Near St. Ives, Cornwall, children with rickets used to be taken at midnight to the Nancledra Logan Stone and laid upon it. If it rocked they were healed, but it would only rock for the legitimate. The Wishing Stone at Matlock is still used by many who stand on it and wish, and at Overton in Cheshire there is a rock Wishing Chair which grants the desires of those who sit in it.

Some of the great chalk figures on our hills are so ancient and so mysterious in origin that it is scarcely surprising if curious tales are told about them. The White Horse of Uffington is supposed to commemorate one of Alfred's victories, though it is obviously much older than that great king. To stand and wish in the exact centre of its eye is lucky and ensures the granting of the wish. Just below the Horse is a knoll called Dragon Hill, where St. George is

COLUMBA'S PILLOW

This sacred stone enclosed in a brass cage is in the choir of Iona Cathedral and is a sacred relic from the monastery founded by St. Columba in the sixth century. St. Columba was the earliest of the saints from Ireland who made missionary expeditions to Scotland, and introduced Christianity there in the sixth century. Like many other important historical figures of early medieval times a large number of legends have collected around his name. These stories are largely derived from an early life by Adamnan.

MENANTOL, CORNWALL

This is another of the numerous megalithic remains in Cornwall. It consists of the usual group of megaliths (big stones), one of which is shown here with a circular hole bored through it. It is probably a ruined burial-chamber on the same lines as the quoits, one of which is illustrated on page 55. Like many other prehistoric remains the stones were popularly believed even in recent times to have magical qualities. The sick are said to have dragged themselves through the circular aperture in the hope of being cured.

locally said to have killed the Dragon. There is a small patch on it where no grass will grow, for the Dragon's blood gushed out and poisoned the ground.

The largest chalk figure in Britain is the Long Man of Wilmington, a huge, naked figure with a staff in each hand. No one knows for certain what he represents, but the local tradition is that he was one of two warring giants who lived in the district. They fought continually with rocks and boulders until finally the Wilmington giant was killed, and now lies for all to see on the north face of Windover Hill.

The savage-looking Cerne Abbas Giant is even more remarkable, and almost certainly represents some primitive fertility god. Legend says he once terrorized the whole countryside, devouring sheep and cattle and doing much other damage. One day after a hearty meal of stolen sheep he foolishly lay down to sleep on the hill. The people seized their chance, and, creeping up to him, they killed him as he slept. Afterwards they cut out the chalk figure as a memorial of the deed, and perhaps as a warning to other thieving giants.

Traditions of floods and sunken lands exist all round our coasts and in some inland places also. Most are founded on dim memories of actual inundations. In many coastal regions there are submerged forests, and even traces of buildings which show that the land once stretched much farther seawards and has since subsided. But if the floods

THE LONG MAN OF WILMINGTON

This is a well-known landmark on the South Downs between Lewes and Eastbourne. The figure is two hundred and thirty feet high and was for long thought to have been cut in the face of the chalk by the monks of Wilmington Priory. That theory has now largely been discarded, and the Long Man is believed to be a prehistoric symbol of fertility, mutilated in the Middle Ages by the monks. According to local tradition he was one of two warring giants, a good giant and an evil giant. The evil giant, who was threatening the valley homesteads, was finally killed by the good giant, and now lies for all to see on the slopes of Windover Hill, near Wilmington.

were a fact, we cannot always be so certain of the legends, usually concerned with sin and vengeance, which have sprung up in most districts to account for them.

Between Bangor and Great Orme's Head ran the land of Tyno Helig, where Helig ap Glannawg ruled over fertile fields and busy townships. His daughter loved a poor man, but she could not marry him because he lacked the indispensable symbol of gentility, a gold torque. With her connivance he murdered a nobleman and took his torque, and afterwards he buried the body in the sands. As he was doing so he heard a voice crying that vengeance would come "in the time of the children and the grandchildren and the great-grandchildren and the great-great-grandchildren." Overcome with terror, he would have fled, but the girl declared they need not fear, for they would both be dead before that time came. They were married and lived prosperously for many years. Both had forgotten the prophecy when, in their old age, they gave a banquet at which four generations of their descendants were present. Nevertheless the day of vengeance had come. A servant going to fetch wine found the cellar half full of water, with fish swimming about in it. She told the Bard and he, recognizing the signs, fled at once, taking the maid with him. As soon as they had gone the water rose and overwhelmed palace, field and township. The Bard and the servant were the only two who escaped, and since that day the sea has rolled over the land of Tyno Helig.

Lyonnesse and Lowland Hundred are both said to have sunk in the fifth or sixth century. The first stretched from Land's End to the Scilly Isles, and sank so suddenly that only one man

THE GIANT OF CERNE ABBAS

The similarity between the Giant of Cerne Abbas and the Long Man of Wilmington is obvious at first glance, and it is thought that the figure here, like the Sussex one, represents a primitive god of fertility. The Cerne Abbas Giant, the story goes, was terrorizing the whole countryside, devouring sheep and cattle and doing much other damage. One day after a huge meal of stolen sheep he lay down to sleep on the hill and was killed as he slept by the young men of the village, who later cut out the chalk figure as a warning of the fate that overtook all thieving giants.

IN CLARKE HALL, WAKEFIELD

Innumerable English and Scottish legends centre around the existence of secret hiding-places and underground passages linking houses with abbeys and with other houses. This picture substantiates the basis of many such legends, for it shows a primitive food hatch with sliding panel giving access to what is known as the priest's hole.

escaped to tell the dreadful tale. The second was a territory running between Bardsey Island and the River Teifi, in which were "sixteen noble cities" protected from the sea by a system of embankments and sluices. But one day Seithinnin, the keeper of the embankments, became drunk during a feast and forgot to close the sluices, with the result that the water rushed in and drowned the entire land. It is said that when the sea is very calm and the water clear the remains of buildings can be seen far below, and sometimes the faint sound of bells comes up from sunken churches in very quiet weather. The same strange ringing used to be heard off Blackpool from the submerged church of Kilgrimol, and also in the anchorage known as the Park, off Selsey Bill, where once stood St. Wilfrid's Cathedral, his palace and a park full of deer.

Many lakes are supposed to have come into being because of some sin committed by those who once dwelt on the site. Where Llynclys now lies near Oswestry, a towered palace stood. It was drowned because a Welsh king, its owner, wickedly refused to hearken to St. Garmon's preaching. Near Darlington, three deep pits called Hell's Kettles are said to have opened suddenly to engulf a farmer and his carts and horses. This man insisted on carrying hay on St. Barnabas' Day.

When he was reproved for working on a holy day, he replied: "a cartload of hay whether God will or nay," and was immediately swallowed up by the pits which opened beneath his feet.

Ellesmere in Shropshire was once fertile fields through which a causeway led to a well in the centre. Here the people came to draw water until a new owner bought the land and forbade them to do so. For this hard-heartedness he was quickly punished, for the well overflowed and turned the fields into a lovely but economically valueless lake. The causeway still runs into it and disappears beneath the water of the lake, but the well to which the causeway led has never been seen again.

ELLESMERE LAKE, SHROPSHIRE

The mere of Ellesmere is a shallow lake in Shropshire. During the last few hundred years it seems to have increased its depth, unlike the majority of lakes which are constantly filling up. The fact that a causeway appears to run into it at one point and continue beneath the water has suggested the legend that the mere was once a marsh with a causeway which led to a well in the centre. When a new owner bought the land he forbade the villagers to draw their water from the well and was punished by the well overflowing and inundating his estate to form a lake.

CHAPTER 7

GHOSTS AND PHANTOMS

Like every other long-inhabited country, Great Britain possesses a rich and varied ghost-lore. If an exact census could be taken of every house, field, pool or crossroads that is, or once was, reputed to be haunted, many large volumes would be needed to contain it; and even so it could never be complete, for new apparitions are still constantly reported, while old ones are forgotten or disproved. The belief that the dead can return to the scenes of their former life is as old as the human race itself. Primitive peoples dreaded even those they had loved best in this world, for death changed them into malicious spirits who were jealous of the living and harmed them whenever they could. Many funeral rites were intended not only to speed the dead man on his journey, but also to prevent his return. Christian teaching stressed the need for helping the departed, but it did not destroy the fear of ghosts, and even today, in spite of modern education and scientific progress, the old belief still persists and shows but little sign of dying out.

How far the belief is founded upon fact is still a matter for argument. Long tradition supports it, and so in some cases does the evidence of witnesses whose word it is impossible to doubt. Ghosts, like other old-established things, have lately been subjected to close investigation on scientific lines, and some at least seem to have stood up to the test. On the other hand, the very nature of the subject makes cut-and-dried proof difficult. Hauntings are seen and felt by some people and not by others. It is natural that those who do not see ghosts should ascribe them to the overheated imagination of those who do, and in some cases they are almost certainly right. Yet there seems to be no doubt that curious things do sometimes occur for which no rational explanation is forthcoming. It may be that in the future we shall be able to explain them, but in the present state of our knowledge the question is still unsettled and belief or disbelief remains a matter which everyone must decide for himself.

What is certain is that strong traditions of haunting are attached to many places. These traditional hauntings are of many kinds. Some legendary ghosts are clearly confused memories of old fairy traditions, or of nature spirits who were once worshipped by particular pools, trees or stones. Others are human souls who are earth-bound because of some sin or tragedy in their lives. Others again are merely temporary visitors who return to fulfil a special task and disappear when it is done, and some are spirits whose identity is unknown and for whom no explanatory story has ever been told.

Many families are said to be warned of death or disaster by the appearance of a ghost who is not seen at other times. At Newstead Abbey in Nottinghamshire a Black Friar walked whenever

NEWSTEAD ABBEY

Newstead Abbey is principally famous as the home of the poet, Lord Byron, although in fact he was seldom in residence and sold the property some time before his death. It was never an abbey in the strict sense, but the house was built from the remains of an Augustinian priory founded in the twelfth century and which continued as a religious foundation until the Dissolution. Like so many other residences which were originally priories or abbeys, Newstead is said to be haunted by ghosts, including the ghost of "The Monk of Newstead," who was seen by Byron on several occasions.

misfortune threatened the Byrons. This house was one of those ominous dwellings which are haunted by more than one ghost. Curious noises were frequently heard there. In one bedroom under the clock a startled visitor saw a White Lady glide out of the wall at night, cross the room without sound and disappear into the opposite wall. Sir John Byron the Little, to whom Henry VIII gave the Priory of Black Canons, appeared from time to time in the State apartments and was once seen in broad daylight, reading by the fire. These, however, were harmless spirits, unlike the Black Friar who was the evil genius of the family and came only before a death or some other misfortune. Lord Byron, the poet, declared that he saw him just before his unhappy marriage with Miss Milbanke, and on several other occasions, always followed by sorrow. He particularly haunted a room next to Lord Byron's bedroom, but he was also seen in the cloisters and other parts of the abbey, and at the bedsides of the dying. Who he had been in life was not known, but probably he was one of the many monks who, dispossessed at the Reformation, were supposed to haunt those who had acquired their old monastic homes.

ROSLYN CHAPEL, MIDLOTHIAN

This is one of the most elaborate fifteenth-century churches in Scotland, notable for its stone carving, here well seen. It stands near Roslyn Castle, but was built in 1446 by William St. Clair, Earl of Orkney. The legend connected with it is that before the death of any descendant of the founder the whole chapel appears to be on fire, an illusion to which, surprisingly, through the centuries many well-known people have borne testimony. The chapel is situated about seven miles south of Edinburgh.

At Cortachy Castle the sound of an invisible drum foretold a death in the Earl of Airlie's family. Tradition said that a former earl, driven by jealousy, had murdered a drummer by forcing him into his own drum and throwing him out of one of the tower windows. From that day onwards a mysterious drumming was heard before any death. In 1844 Miss Dalrymple heard it for two nights running whilst staying at the castle, and was so alarmed that she left on the third day. Six months later she learnt that her hostess, Lady Airlie, had died. Another visitor heard it in 1849, this time at a shooting-lodge called the Tulchan which also belonged to the family. Riding over the open moor towards the lodge he was astonished to hear sounds of distant music accompanied by a drum apparently coming from a low ridge of land near the house. No one was in sight, and there were no buildings anywhere that could have sheltered a musician. On arriving at the Tulchan he was told that the ninth earl was ill in London, and on the following day news came that he had died.

A FIERY PORTENT

An awe-inspiring manifestation foretold the deaths of the St. Clairs in Scotland. In 1446 William St. Clair built Roslyn Chapel, near Edinburgh, and there all the Barons of Roslyn were buried in their armour and without coffins. Before the death of any descendant of the founder the whole chapel appeared to be on fire. Those who saw it blazing in the night expected its utter destruction, yet it was always found quite undamaged next morning. William St. Clair's direct descendants died out in 1778, but the fiery portent persisted under another branch of the family.

Spectral birds or animals often appear as death-warnings. The Dun Cow of Warwick is seen in the grounds of Warwick Castle whenever death threatens the earl or any of his relations. This is that famous cow of gigantic size which Guy of Warwick killed in the remote and legendary past. But though it was enormous in life, its ghost is no bigger than other cattle, and this perhaps makes it even more terrifying. At first sight it seems only an ordinary beast, but there is a difference between it and other cows. Its trampling leaves no mark on grass or path and its hoofs make no sound, and at any moment it may vanish suddenly before the horrified eyes of the beholder.

SPECTRAL BIRDS

The Oxenhams of South Tawton were warned by a bird with a white breast which fluttered round the beds of those about to die. Two white owls perching on the house-top was a sign for the Wardours of Arundel. Perhaps the most curious of these bird-portents are the White Birds of Salisbury Plain, for here it is not a family that is concerned but an office. Before the death of the reigning Bishop of Salisbury two large birds of unknown breed are seen flying over the plain and the city. When Bishop Moberley lay dying in 1885 his daughter saw them rising from the palace garden and floating away towards the west. Twenty-six years later Miss Olivier saw them over Hurdcott meadows, and when she reached home she heard that the bishop had died suddenly that afternoon. On this occasion there was no preliminary illness, and the bishop's death was so little expected that most of his family were out at a flower-show when it occurred.

The Civil War left many ghostly traces, which is hardly surprising when we remember the hundreds of personal tragedies it caused. At Woodcroft Manor in Huntingdonshire, where Dr. Michael Hudson made his last stand for King Charles in 1648, sounds of fighting are heard, with cries of "Mercy!" and "Quarter!" Hudson was besieged there with only a few followers, and in the end he was the only man left alive. The Roundheads forced him over the parapet and cut off his fingers as he tried to hold on. He fell into the moat below, and as he struggled out of the water his enemies killed him.

At Ham House in Surrey Charles I stayed for a night on his last journey towards trial and execution. The gates through which he passed are now always kept locked, but few people would care to walk after sundown in the gloomy avenue beyond even if they were open. On certain nights a distracted cavalier rushes up and down, bemoaning his inability to save his master. Another cavalier is sometimes seen on Hook Common, near Old Basing House, which Oliver Cromwell destroyed in 1645 after the Marquis of Winchester had gallantly defended it for three years. Probably the cavalier

THE GREAT HALL OF HAM

Ham House was built in the first quarter of the seventeenth century. Charles I is said to have stayed here for a night on his last journey before trial and execution. The house is near the old main road between Richmond and Kingston. The gates through which he passed are normally locked at night, but until at least fifty years ago few local people would have cared to walk after sunset in the dark avenue, even if they were open, for the avenue is haunted, it is said, by a distracted cavalier who rushes up and down shrieking and groaning and declaring his inability to save his master.

FORDE HOUSE, DEVONSHIRE

Forde House, near Newton Abbot, was built about the same time as Ham House (opposite), and shows the typical grace and restraint of early Jacobean architecture. It is said that William of Orange stayed here after his landing at Brixham in 1689. Doubtless William suffered great anxiety of mind that night, not knowing whether his expedition would succeed or not. Even now in stormy weather, it is said, the footsteps of the king can be heard passing up and down the corridors of the house.

was one of the Marquis's soldiers. Not far from where he walks are some seventeenth-century houses, and it may be that death came to him from one of them in the form of a sniper's bullet.

Cromwell himself was formerly said to haunt a barn at Old Basing, though he has not been seen there of late. He appears also at long intervals in Red Lion Square, London, with two other cloaked figures who are thought to be Ireton and Bradshaw. There is a tradition that when the regicides' bodies were disinterred and hanged at the Restoration they were first taken to the Red Lion Inn, Holborn, though why this should have been done is not clear.

If it was done, however, it might account for a haunting that is otherwise inexplicable. President Bradshaw also walks in the Islip Rooms in Westminster Deanery. The reason for this is not far to seek, for it was here that he signed the warrant for the King's death. His restless footsteps are heard pacing up and down the rooms, the passages and the stairs that lead to them, as perhaps he really paced for many hours before coming to so terrible a decision.

Oddly enough, King Charles figures in very few ghost-tales. His headless phantom haunted Marple Hall in Cheshire, where Henry Bradshaw, the President's brother, lived, but it does

BURTON AGNES, YORKSHIRE

Burton Agnes, Yorkshire, another seventeenth-century mansion, is well known for its allegorical carvings in wood in the west screen of the great hall, shown here. Burton Agnes was built by three sisters called Griffith. The eldest of these, Anne, when dying persuaded her sisters to keep her skull in the house. Since then, it is said, every effort to bury or remove the skull has been the signal for an outbreak of extraordinary noises, and the skull is now bricked up in the house so it cannot be moved.

BLICKLING HALL

Blickling Hall in Norfolk was built between 1610 and 1630, probably by the same architect as Hatfield House. Its similarity to the style of Hatfield is clearly apparent. It was built on or near the site of an earlier mansion, the origin of which is unknown, but which became one of the estates of Sir Thomas Boleyn, father of the ill-fated Anne. There is a tradition that Anne spent some of her childhood here before going to Hever. On the anniversary of her death she returns in a coach drawn by four headless horses which proceeds up the avenue and vanishes at the entrance of the hall.

not appear at Whitehall, or Carisbrooke, or in other places intimately connected with his sad story. But if King Charles is absent, other kings and queens are not. The heavy-booted footsteps of William III can be heard in the corridors of Forde House, near Newton Abbot. Here he spent his first night in England in 1689, and here probably he endured great anxiety of mind, not knowing whether his perilous venture would succeed or not.

At least three of Henry VIII's unhappy wives were seen or heard long after one had died in childbirth and the other two on the scaffold. Jane Seymour walked in Marwell Hall, her childhood's home in Hampshire, where she is said to have been secretly married to Henry in May, 1536. She also appears at Hampton Court Palace, carrying a lighted taper from the Queen's Rooms, through the Silver Stick Gallery and down the stairs. Poor Katherine Howard's screams are still heard in the Haunted Gallery in the palace. When she was arrested in 1541 she escaped from her guards and rushed along the gallery to the chapel, where the King then was, intending to beg for mercy. But before she could reach it she was seized and hurried away, and her despairing shrieks still echo periodically through the palace.

Anne Boleyn is seen in several places. She haunts the Tower of London, where she was executed in 1536, as well as Hever Castle and Bollin Hall (now destroyed), in both of which she once lived. Part of her childhood was spent at Blickling Hall in Norfolk, and on the anniversary of her death she returns there in a coach drawn by four headless horses, which moves slowly up the avenue and vanishes at the hall door.

A gentle and beautiful ghost whose identity is quite unknown is the Radiant Boy of Corby Castle. He appears as a child dressed in white, glowing with mysterious light and having a mild and friendly expression. His coming foretells no evil and there is nothing terrifying about him except in so far as all

supernatural manifestations are in some degree disturbing. A very different appearance is that of Lady Hoby, who walks in Bisham Abbey, washing bloodstains from her hands in a ghostly basin. A persistent legend says she beat her little son, William, to death because he was slovenly and careless in his lessons. Years later some badly blotted copybooks, found behind a skirting-board, seemed to support the tradition. But the curious part of the story is that Lady Hoby never had a son named William,

DUNLUCE CASTLE, ANTRIM

Legends of the banshee are common in Ireland and in parts of the Highlands of Scotland as well. The banshee is a family fairy, the private property as it were of a family, her self-assigned duties being to protect the family and to give warning of the approaching death of a member of it. The wail of the banshee is the ear-splitting shriek with which she gives that warning. The idea of the banshee is so deeply rooted in Irish mythology that many country people still believe implicitly in banshees. Dunluce set on its abrupt cliff rising precipitously from the sea, as seen below, is appropriately haunted by a well-authenticated banshee.

GLAMIS CASTLE

Glamis figures in legend as the castle of Macbeth, though there is nothing to substantiate the tradition of a building here as early as the eleventh century, when the murder of Duncan took place. Modern Glamis is an early seventeenth-century mansion in the typical Scottish baronial style with a development of Gothic ornament never approached in England. Another legend attaches to this house, for long the home of the Earls of Strathmore; it is said that there is a secret room or sealed chamber which is haunted, and the entrance is known only to the Earl, his heir and his steward.

and her three known sons, Edward, Thomas and Francis, all grew up to healthy manhood.

In one or two houses the skulls of former inhabitants are carefully preserved because their removal is always followed by fearful shrieks and noises. Bettiscombe Manor in Dorset contains the skull of a negro servant whom Azariah Pinney brought from the West Indies in the seventeenth century. He died of consumption, and with his last breath begged to be buried in his own country. This was not done, and for some reason his skull was kept in the house. Thereafter appalling and continuous screams were heard whenever it was taken away, followed by cattle diseases and persistent bad luck on the farm. Only when it was brought back did these manifestations cease. Of late years it has been kept in a carefully closed niche; and though the tenants profess to disbelieve the old story, they are

183

careful to leave the skull undisturbed. The same violent upsets always followed any removal of Anne Griffith's skull from Burton Agnes Hall. This Yorkshire house was built by three sisters in 1628, and was so beloved by Anne that when she was dying she made her sisters promise to keep her skull at home. Since then every effort to bury or banish it has been the signal for an outburst of extraordinary noises, which cease only when it is replaced; and today the skull is safely bricked up in the house so it can never be moved.

Among the most eerie ghosts are those about whom very little is known. What, for instance, is it that haunts the sealed chamber at Glamis Castle? Many legends are told to account for the strange sounds heard. According to one story the truth is known only to the owner, his heir and his steward.

IN MORETON OLD HALL, CHESHIRE

Of all the magnificent homes in Cheshire and Lancashire which were built in the fifteenth, sixteenth and seventeenth centuries, Moreton Old Hall is probably the finest in the black-and-white half-timbered style of building which reached its fullest development in those areas. The date of its construction is about the middle of the sixteenth century, and the hall, which is pictured here, typifies the elaborate and graceful interior. Queen Elizabeth was a visitor more than once and probably danced in this hall. The house is said to be haunted by a ghost.

CHAPTER 8

PRISONS AND PRISONERS

FROM the sea-girt walls of Tantallon Castle, matching itself with the near-by Bass Rock, to the black battlements of Edinburgh, the grey towers of Alnwick, the sandstone bastion of Carlisle and the white pinnacles of the Tower of London itself, the early story of Britain's prisons and prisoners is largely the story of her fortresses.

It is only within the last two or three centuries that the idea of detaining a man in prison to punish or reform him has been accepted. Before then imprisonment was intended merely to keep him safe until he could be tried and sentenced. Up to feudal times justice was largely dispensed by the local overlord. It was rough and ready, and being carried out on the spot did not call for any prison other than the dungeon of his castle. In 1360, however, the title of justice of the peace came into being, and Tudor times saw the passing of many new laws, including an act of 1576 which set up bridewells—a name still to be encountered—where people judged wilfully idle were put to work. The bridewells did not long maintain their original character, however, and by 1720 justices could send minor offenders to them if they saw fit.

There were also common gaols, some two hundred of them, in which corruption and disease ran rife. Prisoners had to pay fees to the gaoler, and on the amount they gave depended their comfort. Even when acquitted the prisoner had to pay the gaoler release fees. One

of the horrors of these times was the "gaol fever," and judges carried bouquets, the fragrance of which was supposed to protect them from its dangers. The custom of handing the judges bouquets remains to this day. In Chislehurst Church in Kent there is a plaque to Sir Richard Adams, who died in 1774. "His death was occasioned by the gaol distemper which he caught at the Old Bayly in the Execution of his Office" runs the inscription. Through General James Oglethorpe, the founder of Georgia, a parliamentary inquiry was held in 1729, and this led to the first step in reforming the gaols.

Another reformer was John Howard, who was made High Sheriff of Bedfordshire in 1773. So wretched was the state of affairs he found in the county gaol, once the prison of John Bunyan, author of *Pilgrim's Progress*, that he gave up the rest of his life to prison reform. His name is remembered in the Howard League for Penal Reform which still works for prisoners. Later Elizabeth Fry was to make similar efforts on behalf of women in gaol.

British gaols, however, have seldom sheltered the most famous prisoners, since most of these were detained for some political reason rather than an actual crime. It is in the castles of England and not in the gaols that we find the romantic figures, sometimes living in comfort and even luxury, sometimes in the most pitiful circumstances. Up to the time of Queen Anne, indeed, most kings of England and Scotland knew imprisonment in one form or another, whether it was a guarded surveillance in their youth, or, as with Charles I and Mary, Queen of Scots, a careful watch because of suspected plotting, culminating in the block.

Typical of such castles is that of Pontefract, where the ruins today are a pleasant playground for children and the black walls that once ran with blood echo to schoolboys' shouts. Here in 1400 died Richard II. His murderers are said to have pursued him round his room while he sought desperately to escape the blows they dealt him with their battle-axes.

Pontefract Castle belonged to the De Lacy family for many years, and passed through marriage to the Earl of Lancaster in 1310. This was the man who broke Piers Gaveston, the favourite of Edward II, and had him executed. His own turn came when the barons under the Earl of Pembroke allied themselves with King Edward, and Lancaster was taken prisoner at Boroughbridge in 1322.

By a grim twist of fate he was taken to his own castle at Pontefract, and detained there until he could be tried

BOLTON CASTLE, WENSLEYDALE

Set on a gently rising hill above the fertile valley of Wensleydale in Yorkshire, Bolton Castle, even now that its battlements have been demolished and its ancient walls are a shell, seems a singularly appropriate place to have served as a royal prison. It is one of the largest of the later medieval castles in Yorkshire and was built in the last decades of the fourteenth century. For many years it was an effective bulwark against disorder in a part of the country which was always liable to be involved in the conflicts between England and Scotland. Mary, Queen of Scots, was held here in 1568-9.

CARLISLE CASTLE

This is another of the prison homes of Mary, Queen of Scots, though only for a time in 1568 before her incarceration at Bolton. The keep is a massive example of Norman workmanship and dates from the end of the eleventh century. During the 1745 rebellion Prince Charles Edward passed through here on his victorious march into England and here many of the Scottish rebels were imprisoned after the final defeat of the Young Pretender's army at the battle of Culloden Moor in 1746.

before the King and a party of peers. He was executed within sight of the castle walls. In its day Pontefract was an awe-inspiring building with seven towers and a deep moat. The dungeons were particularly unpleasant places. One of them was hewn out of the rock, twenty-five feet square, and entered only by a hole in the roof. The unhappy prisoner was thrown in, or if he was lucky lowered on a rope, and then left in darkness without hope of escape. The castle, after withstanding sieges in the Civil War, was demolished like so many others by Cromwell's orders.

Of all royal prisoners, however, Mary, Queen of Scots, is probably the most famous. She knew many prisons. One of the first was the castle of Dunbar, of which some ruins still remain, where Bothwell took her in 1567. Soon afterwards they were married. This was too much for the Scottish lords, who suspected them of murdering Mary's first husband, Lord Darnley. Rebellion broke out and Mary was imprisoned after the battle of Carberry Hill. Lochleven Castle was chosen as a prison, but less than a year later, in May, 1568, she escaped with the assistance of a

THE GATEHOUSE OF CARISBROOKE

A Norman castle occupying probably the site of Saxon fortifications, Carisbrooke has been the centre of the Isle of Wight's defences for nearly a thousand years. In the Middle Ages and for some time after castles were automatically prisons, and among the distinguished prisoners of Carisbrooke were Charles I and his children, Princess Elizabeth and Henry, Duke of Gloucester. Charles was a prisoner in the castle from the winter of 1647 until the end of the summer of 1648.

188

sixteen-year-old page, Willie Douglas, who brought the castle keys to her hidden in a napkin. Douglas rowed Mary across the loch in a little boat to her waiting friends. The episode, however, was in vain. Eleven days later the nobles defeated her at Langside, and she was forced to fly to England—and Elizabeth—for sanctuary.

Lochleven Castle, squat and black, still stands on its island, surrounded by the grey waters of the loch. When Mary crossed the Solway Firth she hoped to be well received in England and enlist Elizabeth's help in regaining the Scottish throne. That was not to be. Mary soon found herself instead in Carlisle Castle, which has not greatly changed since her day. Its sandstone walls look across to Scotland and over the town it guards. One sill is still shown with the stone worn away where prisoners rested their hands as they looked out hopelessly towards freedom. In the dark dungeons visitors can see a section of the wall that is always damp. The tongues of parched prisoners have licked grooves on the surface of the wall where a film of moisture appears.

ATTEMPTED ESCAPE

From Carlisle Mary was taken to Bolton Castle, in Wensleydale, North Yorkshire. She came over the lonely moors by way of Appleby with a retinue of forty persons, half of whom had to stay in the village that still clusters round the tall castle's handsome walls. The room in the south-west tower where she was detained is pointed out, and from the roof of the tower, on which Mary is said to have passed much of her time, a magnificent view of the rolling dales can be obtained. The Queen was not long in attempting a daring escape. She found that it was possible to climb through the narrow

west window of her room. An attendant lowered her carefully while others waited below. The party reached a place that is still known as Queen's Gap, in the hills at neighbouring Leyburn, before they were caught and brought back.

Mary's last prison was Fotheringhay Castle, near Oundle, Northamptonshire, but this was destroyed in 1627, and little remains. Pleasant Linlithgow, where she was born, still stands by the water's edge. It is now in ruins as a result of the sacking it underwent at the hands of English troops in 1746.

ROYAL PRISONERS OF ENGLAND

Another royal prisoner was Charles I. Carisbrooke Castle, though its grey walls are somewhat ruined, looks down on the Isle of Wight it was built to defend. Not only was it a prison for Charles, but also for his son and daughter, and the little princess actually died here nearly two years after her father's execution. Charles had gone secretly to Carisbrooke from Hampton Court, hoping for help from the Governor. Gradually, however, his movements were restricted, until one day, like King Lear in Shakespeare's play, he found all his attendants dismissed. This did not prevent the King plotting to escape. He wrote many letters making plans, and on one occasion everything was ready and promised well until the King, trying to leave by a window he had marked for the purpose, found it was too narrow for his shoulders.

The royal home of Windsor Castle has frequently been a prison for royalty. To protect the boy king, Edward VI, who succeeded Henry VIII in 1547, the Duke of Somerset sent him from Hampton Court to Windsor. Seeing its grey walls, and comparing them in his mind with the pleasant places of Hampton Court, the lad lamented: "Methinks I am in prison: here be no galleries nor gardens to walk in."

The Tower of London is one of the most famous prisons in history. It was built by William the Conqueror to guard London, but it has been in turn a palace, a home for the Royal Mint, a store for public records and the Royal Observatory. The buildings are grouped round the Keep, or White Tower, which now contains a splendid collection of armour. Some of its most famous prisoners were executed on Tower Green, close by the Keep, but many more met death on Tower Hill, in Trinity Square, which is outside the walls. As far back as 1388 Sir Simon Burley was beheaded on Tower Hill, and others who followed him, after languishing in the Tower itself, included the Earl of Essex, Sir Thomas More, the Earl of Strafford, Archbishop Laud and the Jacobite lords implicated in the Scottish risings of 1715 and 1745. The last to be executed here was Simon, Lord Lovat, as late as 1747.

IN THE TOWER OF LONDON

The Yeoman Gaoler's Lodging and the King's House are situated on the Green of the Tower of London. It was in the Yeoman Gaoler's Lodging that Lady Jane Grey was imprisoned before her execution in 1554. From the window of the lodging Lady Jane watched her husband, Lord Guildford Dudley, who had been held in the Tower, led out to Tower Hill for execution. After he was beheaded, it is recorded, she also saw his body being brought back into the Tower again.

TOWER OF LONDON, BYWARD TOWER

The Tower of London—fortress, royal residence and State prison—consists of a Norman fortress, known as the White Tower, and a number of towers at the angles of the outer walls. There are also a number of more modern buildings. The Byward Tower, pictured above, is one of the medieval wall turrets with later additions. It was in these detached "towers" that State prisoners were kept when awaiting trial or execution, most infamous of all being the Bloody Tower, in which the little Princes, the children of Edward IV, were probably murdered in 1483.

Queen Elizabeth, when a princess, was kept in the Tower in 1554, and her favourite walk along the walls is still called after her. It is near the Beauchamp and Bell Towers. The first of these towers takes its name from Thomas, third Earl of Warwick, one of the Beauchamp family, who was imprisoned in it by Richard II in 1397. This tower has held many prisoners and its ground-floor room has inscriptions which include the name of Robert Dudley, who as the Earl of Leicester rose to be a favourite of Elizabeth. He was luckier

A GRIM REMINDER OF HARSHER DAYS

In the Middle Ages life was not held so precious as it is today. Judicial execution, far more common than it is now, was carried out in a rough-and-ready manner. The Tower contains many links with this less sensitive past, including the axe and block on which the last political prisoner was executed at the Tower. Simon, Lord Lovat, paid the supreme penalty as late as 1747.

than his brother, Lord Guildford Dudley, who was executed on Tower Hill.

Married to Lady Jane Grey, Lord Guildford Dudley became involved in the plot to put her on the throne instead of Mary Tudor. Both were arrested, and from one of the windows of the gabled, red-tiled houses that stand between the Bell and Beauchamp Towers Lady Jane saw the headless body of her husband brought back from his execution on Tower Hill. A few days later she shared his fate, but her own sentence was carried out on Tower Green, near the royal chapel of St. Peter ad Vincula. Her head fell on the spot where those of Anne Boleyn and Katharine Howard, the second and fifth wives of Henry VIII, had rolled. Unlike the others, Anne was executed with a sword, the headsman being brought over from St. Omer, France.

ESCAPE OF NITHSDALE

The Beauchamp Tower contains also a Latin inscription carved by Philip, Earl of Arundel, in 1587. Kept a prisoner for ten years, he could have had his freedom had he been willing to give up his Roman Catholic religion. He refused and died in the Tower. Near the Beauchamp Tower stands the King's House, which saw one of the most daring escapes the Tower of London has known. Lord Nithsdale was imprisoned here after the failure of the 1715 Jacobite rising. He was rescued by the devotion and courage of his wife. With the help of two women friends she visited him on the eve of his execution. By sending the friends in and out of the Tower on errands she confused the guards over the number of visitors present in Nithsdale's room. This gave him the chance of leaving dressed in woman's clothing Lady

MARTEN'S TOWER AT CHEPSTOW

Chepstow Castle, on a bluff overlooking the Wye near its confluence with the Severn, was one of the chief Marcher fortresses, from which in the Middle Ages Norman barons made raids on the Welsh people and brought back as hostages leading men of the Welsh tribes. Later Chepstow became the prison home of Henry Marten, one of the judges who signed Charles I's death warrant. Marten was incarcerated here for twenty years until his death in 1680. He is buried in the parish church. In the time of the Commonwealth, Jeremy Taylor, who had been chaplain to Charles I, was for a period imprisoned in the castle. After the Restoration he was made a bishop.

RUINS OF MINSTER LOVELL

The ruined manor-house of Minster Lovell in Oxfordshire is famous for a grim tradition which may well represent authentic truth. Lord Lovell took part in the rising in 1487 in support of Lambert Simnel's claim to the throne, and fought at the Battle of Stoke. After the defeat of the rebels he escaped to his home, Minster Lovell, where he concealed himself in an underground secret chamber of which a faithful servant held the key. Then for some unknown reason the servant left the lord to starve to death in his hiding-place. Two hundred years later the secret chamber was discovered. At a table in the room the skeleton of Lord Lovell was found, still seated in a chair.

Nithsdale had brought with her, while she waited behind and pretended to keep up a conversation. When Lady Nithsdale left she asked the guards not to disturb her husband as he was praying. The friendly Venetian Ambassador allowed Nithsdale to travel to Dover, dressed in the livery of one of the servants, on the Ambassador's coach and he escaped by boat to Calais.

Although the Bloody Tower is the one best known to the public it has only a worse record than its neighbours in the sense that the little princes, Edward V and his brother, the Duke of York, are believed to have been murdered here in 1483 by order of their uncle, the Duke of Gloucester, later Richard III. In the Bloody Tower Sir Walter Raleigh and Archbishop Laud were also detained in Stuart times.

PRISON LIFE IN THE TOWER

Other famous prisoners in the Tower have included William Wallace, the fighter for Scotland's freedom; King John of France, who was made prisoner at the battle of Poitiers; Guy Fawkes; John Wilkes and, in 1820, the Cato Street conspirators. Most of the more distinguished prisoners arrived by Traitor's Gate, which gave on to the Thames. Since they came by water from trial at Westminster in a number of cases, it was a convenient entrance. Now dried out, the line where the water lapped the stone steps can still be seen. The prisoners lifted their eyes as they stepped ashore to see the forbidding bastions of the Bloody Tower and the Wakefield Tower confronting them. Taken over by the yeomen warders, who were practically confined to the Tower themselves, the prisoners were indeed in a world apart. They had to buy the furniture for their cells from the warders, who, having seen the execution

of their clients, and having perhaps assisted at it, cheerfully sold the tables and chairs again to the next batch of victims.

Dunure Castle still stands with its broken black walls frowning in majestic challenge at the sea south of Ayr. Its position is as commanding as any keep in Britain. The ancient home of the Kennedy family, it was the scene of a particularly grim torture devised for a man who had been foolish enough to defy the lord of the neighbourhood. A certain Allan Stewart was given an office which put him in charge of Crossraguel Abbey soon after the Reformation. The Earl of Cassillis considered that the post should have been his and promptly seized Stewart and took him to Dunure Castle. Here in a cellar known as "the black vault" he stripped the wretched man and fastened him round a spit. A roasting fire was lit and, while soldiers turned the spit slowly and Stewart was "cooked," others poured oil on him so that the meat might be basted. In fact, of course, it added to his tortures. Notwithstanding the terrible pain Stewart did not give in easily, but at last he agreed to sign a paper renouncing his claim. Once free he appealed to the authorities, but the Earl was merely bound over to keep the peace in the sum of £2,000.

COVENANTERS IN PRISON

Torture was not an unusual accompaniment of imprisonment, particularly if the offence was a religious one where a retraction was needed. The Galloway area of the south of Scotland was the scene of the ruthless persecution of the Covenanters. Originally these were men who in 1638 signed a covenant in Greyfriars churchyard, Edinburgh, against the attempt by Charles I to impose an English prayer book on

Scotland. Subsequent persecutions culminated in the battle of Bothwell Bridge in 1679, when, by a strange twist of fate, a thousand or more Covenanters who were taken prisoner found themselves gaoled in the very same Greyfriars churchyard.

Most of them were shipped to the plantations when they refused to recant. Wigtown, in Galloway, housed many Covenanters in its gaol in those times.

The most notable of religious prisoners is John Bunyan, who was gaoled in Bedford from 1660 to 1672 as a Dissenter. He was kept in the old county gaol which was pulled down in 1801, and later in the town gaol on Bedford Bridge, also long vanished. While imprisoned he wrote *Pilgrim's Progress*. George Fox, the Quaker, was another to suffer for his beliefs. He was held in Scarborough Castle, the white ruins of which stand out today on a great headland overlooking the North Sea and the town below.

Among tragic prisoners is Lord Lovell, who took part in the rising in support of Lambert Simnel's claim to the throne in the reign of Henry VII. The rebels were easily defeated at the

LEEDS CASTLE, KENT

Leeds Castle, a medieval stronghold with modern additions, is a still moated romantic-looking group of buildings (parts of which are built on islands in a lake), a little to the south of the main road from Maidstone to Ashford. At the end of the Civil War Leeds escaped the fate of "slighting" or dismantling which was the penalty meted out by the Parliamentarians to many castles which had stood for the Royalist cause, and many others as well. Instead Cromwell requisitioned it as a prison for Dutch and French prisoners of war. John Evelyn, the diarist, was governor of the prison for a time.

DUNURE CASTLE, AYRSHIRE

Situated on a still remote and wild part of the coast between Ayr and Girvan, Dunure Castle is a thirteenth-century ruin which was once the home of the Kennedy family and in the Middle Ages of the Earls of Cassillis. A grim tale is told of one of the earls (the legend is unsubstantiated). Soon after the Reformation, it is said, a certain Allan Stewart was given office under the Crown which gave him possession of nearby Crossraguel Abbey. Regarding the sinecure as being properly his, the Earl seized Stewart, threw him into a cellar of the castle, and proceeded slowly to roast him alive on a spit until Stewart agreed to sign a paper repudiating his claim in favour of the Earl.

battle of Stoke, near Newark. After the battle Lord Lovell escaped to the fine old mansion of Minster Lovell in Oxfordshire, which was his home. There he took refuge in a secret chamber built into the thick walls, and apparently ordered a servant to lock him in until his pursuers went away. That at any rate is the generally accepted explanation of his death. Two hundred years later, when the walls were being repaired, the room was discovered. At a table in the centre a skeleton was resting on a chair, the skull laid on the table. So Lovell had died waiting in vain for release. Either the servant had been murdered or had deserted his master.

Despite the cruelties practised, prison in the past did not necessarily entail the disgrace that it does today. Prisoners, especially when they were detained as a safeguard rather than for an offence, often enjoyed a certain amount of liberty. They could generally write as much as they wanted, and Raleigh, indeed, wrote his history of the world while in the Tower. The dungeons, which rightly appear to us inhuman and wretched places, were in keeping with the ideas of their day, when imprisonment rested largely on the whim of the monarch, and the man who was chained and in prison one week might be a court favourite the next.

CHAPTER 9

MURDERS AND MASSACRES

SOME of the fairest settings in Britain have been the scenes of the foulest crimes. They range from the imposing heights of Glencoe, brooding darkly over the valley where the Macdonalds were massacred, to the tall and stately towers of Canterbury Cathedral where Archbishop Thomas Becket was murdered eight hundred years ago. The story of these murders and massacres ranges through the centuries and finds links in every county of Scotland and England. It gives to many an old building or lonely moor an association of horror that the casual visitor, unacquainted with history, would never suspect.

War has invariably been accompanied by massacre. The Roman conquest of Britain, from which modern history really dates, was no exception. When the Emperor Claudius came to Britain in A.D. 43, ninety years after Julius Caesar, he was determined to complete the subjection of the country. He began by occupying Colchester, the bustling old town in Essex where the remains of Roman walls are still to be seen. One of his generals, Suetonius Paulinus, was sent to subdue Wales and marched to Anglesey, the pleasant island off the Welsh coast, to exterminate the Druids, the lawgivers and priests of the time whose influence on the people was feared by the Romans.

The Druids were believed to hold magic secrets. They advised the tribes and sacrificed human victims before battle. Under their orders the oak tree was held sacred for its mistletoe, which was cut off with golden sickles in complicated ceremonies. Anglesey was the site of a famous grove of oaks, all of which were cut down by Suetonius, who also exterminated the Druids in a frightful massacre. While he was still waging war in this part of England he was called back to Colchester, where the Iceni, a British tribe, had risen under Queen Boadicea. It was the Britons' turn to slaughter their enemies, and they killed all the Romans in Colchester and marched on London and St. Albans. Both places were burned to the ground, but Suetonius eventually defeated Boadicea, who poisoned herself rather than be taken prisoner.

With the departure of the Romans about A.D. 400 Britain became the prey of many invaders. The Hebrides, Iona and the Isle of Man were overrun by the Vikings and the inhabitants massacred. Anglesey suffered again and hundreds of the people living there were killed. On the other side of the country, Maldon, the quiet market-town on the Blackwater Estuary, was the scene of a desperate battle when ninety-three shiploads of Vikings arrived and beat the local tribesmen.

Treachery was rife on both sides. Ethelred the Unready came to the throne in 978 and bought peace with the Danes by paying them money, called Danegeld, and some of the Danes settled in Wessex. Six times he paid

THE ROMAN GATEWAY OF ANDERIDA

Anderida, or Pevensey Castle, as it is generally known, was one of the more important Roman stations along the south coast in the declining days of the Roman province of Britain. Fifteen hundred years later the Roman materials of this, the main gateway, still stand as eloquent testimony to the massive strength of the defences. Even so, the walls were not strong enough to withstand the attacks of Saxon pirate invaders, who in the fourth and fifth centuries made repeated forays on the Roman province and on the occasion of one particularly fierce attack put to the sword the entire garrison of Anderida. Later the Roman walls were utilized as the outer defences of a strong Norman castle, the fine ruins of which can still be seen today.

this bribe, amounting to £9,000,000 altogether.

Rumours of conspiracy among the Danes in Wessex caused Ethelred to order the massacre, which took place on St. Brice's Day in 1002. One of the victims, however, was the sister of Sweyn Forkbeard, the King of Denmark. It provided him with an excuse he had long sought. Vowing vengeance, he sailed up the River Humber and

along the Trent to establish a camp at Gainsborough. Soon he was King of England.

The victory of William the Conqueror at the battle of Hastings in 1066 was followed by one of the most ruthless crimes in British history. Rebellions broke out early in his reign and three of these centred on York. William decided to make an end of such happenings. His armies marched north and

RUINS OF JEDBURGH ABBEY

Jedburgh Abbey, founded by King David I in the twelfth century, was many times threatened in the wars between England and Scotland, though spared from deliberate depredation because of its religious fame. Then in the sixteenth century, during the English invasion of 1544, a battle developed for Jedburgh. The abbey was left in ruins.

laid waste all the land between York and Durham. Villages were burned to the ground and the terrified inhabitants forced to fly before the advancing soldiers. Those who collapsed in the path of the army were murdered in cold blood and even the cattle in the pastures were slaughtered. The only inhabitants to escape were those who succeeded in crossing the border into Scotland. From the Humber to the Tyne England became a barren country.

BORDER WARFARE

In the later wars between England and Scotland the border towns were often sacked and set on fire with cruel slaughter, but never again was the land devastated on such a scale. Life for the townsfolk, however, was never safe with the armies of the two countries constantly clashing. No town has suffered more terribly and over a longer time than Berwick-on-Tweed.

Walking today by the old walls which look down on the broad River Tweed and the fishing boats coming in from the sea it is hard to associate the place with the terrors of the past, but the tower on which hung the alarm bell still looks towards Scotland and the town was sacked by Saxons and Danes many a time. In 1296 Edward I of England arrived with a huge army reinforced by a great fleet. He captured Berwick and slew seven thousand of the garrison and inhabitants. In the wool market he set fire to a tower which thirty men were defending and burnt them alive. Said an old writer: "The mill wheels of the town could have been turned with rivers of blood."

On a far smaller scale, but better remembered because of its treachery, was the massacre of Glencoe. A rising by the Highlanders on behalf of James II of England, who fled when

William of Orange arrived in 1688, was settled when the clans agreed to take the oath of allegiance by 1 January, 1692. In the north of Argyllshire the chief of the Macdonalds of Glencoe was late in making his submission and Sir John Dalrymple determined to make an example. He secured an order against the clansmen from William without revealing that the chief had eventually taken the oath. Led by two Campbells, traditional enemies of the Macdonalds, a hundred and twenty soldiers arrived in Glencoe and were entertained for a fortnight. Then, at five o'clock one morning, they fell on the clansmen after shooting the chief and his wife. Although many escaped thirty-eight were killed, including two children and two women. The wretched deed was never forgotten and prevented an earlier reconciliation between the two countries.

MURDERS IN CHURCHES

Treachery is inevitably a part of many cold-blooded murders, and William was not the only monarch who was used as a tool by those anxious to rid themselves of an enemy. When Henry II came to the throne in 1154 he raised a young man named Thomas Becket to great power, first as his Chancellor and then as Archbishop of Canterbury. In this second office, however, Becket deemed it his duty to resist the King on certain matters in the interests of the Church. Both were imperious men, and it came about that Henry, in 1170, growled to his courtiers, more in exasperation than serious anger: "Are there none of the dastards eating my bread who will rid me of this turbulent priest?" Four were only too willing. They left Henry's court in France and reached Canterbury on the evening of 29 December while vespers were being sung in the great cathedral.

COURTYARD OF LINLITHGOW PALACE

The Palace of Linlithgow is on the site of a royal residence which is thought to date from the reign of David I. The present buildings are of various periods, but mainly of the sixteenth century, the fountain seen here in the forecourt being attributed to this rebuilding. In 1570 James Stuart, Earl of Moray and half-brother of Mary, Queen of Scots, appointed regent when Mary was imprisoned, was mortally wounded when riding through Linlithgow, was carried into the palace and died there.

THE GATEWAY OF BERKELEY CASTLE

Feudal castle and modern residence, Berkeley, in Gloucestershire, has the doubtful distinction of being the scene of Edward II's murder. The Norman castle was built by Robert FitzHarding, a merchant, in the twelfth century. Thereafter through the Middle Ages the castle was almost continuously held as a stronghold residence by the feudal barons of Gloucestershire. The fourteenth-century gateway is seen above. Edward II came to the throne in 1307 but soon incurred great unpopularity among the nobles because of his weak character and obvious subservience to ill-chosen favourites. In 1327 he was deposed, taken as prisoner to Berkeley Castle and there, without any semblance of a trial, he was cruelly put to death.

There was some parleying and the monks tried to hide Becket in the cloisters, but he refused to retreat. Finally the irritated knights struck out. Becket grappled with one of his assailants, while Grim, a German monk, put out his arm to stop another blow. The sword broke the monk's arm and wounded Becket in the head. Other strokes came at once, so fiercely that one murderer splintered his sword on the stone pavement. Becket's blood, says

tradition, was splashed across the altar. He died with a prayer on his lips.

Murders in churches are happily rare, but another such deed played an important part in Scottish history. Robert Bruce and Sir John Comyn were rival claimants to the Scottish throne.

On 10 February, 1306, they met in the church of the Grey Friars at Dumfries. Bruce accused Comyn of breaking a promise and in the quarrel that followed stabbed him with his dagger. As he came out shaken by what he had done, two friends asked him where Comyn was. Bruce replied that he feared he had killed him. "I mak siccar," said one of them, meaning that he would make sure. With his companion he rushed in and finished off the dying man. The present Greyfriars Church is named after the old one which stood near the Burns' monument.

MURDER OF SCOTTISH KING

But Scotland's history is dark with murder. Of the five kings who reigned from 1406 to 1542 only one died a natural death, and that was due to a broken heart following defeat in battle at Solway Moss. The murder of James I was a singularly dramatic episode in the nation's story. At Christmas-time in 1437 he travelled to Perth to stay at the Blackfriars monastery. On the way he met an old woman who held up his company and prophesied that if he crossed the Firth of Forth he would lose his life. James laughed at her words and rode on, unaware that one of his enemies, Sir Robert Graham, had planned his downfall with Sir Robert Stewart, the royal chamberlain. Stewart placed planks across the moat round the monastery and removed the bolts from the doors. One evening when James was joking with the ladies of the court before retiring the murderers burst in. One of the women, Catherine Douglas, thrust her arm through the clasps on the door. It was broken by the thrusts of the men outside. James had meanwhile pulled up a plank in the floor and hidden himself in the cellar, hoping to find a way out. Only a few days before, however, he had caused an exit to be closed because tennis balls were being lost there.

One after another the murderers jumped down after him. Despite a desperate struggle he was killed. Later his Queen enforced a terrible vengeance on the men responsible. Perth, beautifully situated on the banks of the River Tay with the Grampian mountains behind it, remembers the dead King with a plaque on a corner of Blackfriars Street where the monastery stood.

One of the coolest assassinations of history was carried out at Linlithgow, the town between Glasgow and Edinburgh where, in the now ruined castle, Mary, Queen of Scots, was born.

From a window looking on the street James Hamilton of Bothwellhaugh shot the Regent Moray as he rode by in 1570. The murder was planned very carefully. Hamilton put a feather mattress on the floor of the room so that his boots would not be heard below. He also darkened the walls with black curtains and hung up a white sheet to make the smoke from his gun less apparent. The door opening on the street was locked, while a horse waited ready saddled at the back. As soon as he had seen Moray fall Hamilton rushed away and escaped.

MURDER ON MAGUS MUIR

The late seventeenth century was a period of serious religious conflict between Catholics and Protestants, and religious murders were common at that time. From the castle, of which the ruins stand close to the famous golf club at St. Andrews, Cardinal Beaton looked out in March, 1546, to watch George Wishart burned as a heretic. Three months later Wishart's followers broke into the castle to take their revenge. Beaton was in bed and he tried to barricade himself in his room. The men battered down the door, however, and although he begged frantically for his life he was murdered and his body hanged from the castle walls in full view of the townspeople.

THE CAVE CHAPEL OF KNARESBOROUGH

*St. Robert's Chapel, at Knaresborough in Yorkshire, is hewn out of the solid rock.
It was originally a wayside chapel, founded in the beginning of the fifteenth century.
It won its unenviable place in the annals of notoriety when Eugene Aram hid in it the
body of his victim. Aram was convicted of murder and executed in 1759 many years
after his crime, which was given a romantic interest quite undeserved by a novel of
Bulwer Lytton. The figure is of a knight drawing his sword.*

THE APPIN MURDER

This unusual memorial marks the spot where James Stewart, known as "James of the Glen," was executed for the Appin Murder at Ballachulish, Scotland. The murder is generally considered one of the unsolved mysteries of Scottish crime. The victim was one Campbell of Glenure, who was passing through the district in 1752 in order to evict some Jacobites from their land. He was shot as he proceeded along a track beneath a wooded hill, and a man, whom some thought was James Stewart, was seen running away through the trees. The proceedings at the subsequent trial lend much support to the view that not James Stewart but another was the murderer.

A hundred or so years later another religious murder resulted from the harrying of the Covenanters by Archbishop Sharp under the instructions of Charles II. Sharp had a brutal servant and twelve men swore to kill him. On 3 May, 1679, they were waiting on the lonely Magus Muir, two miles from St. Andrews, expecting the servant to ride by. A carriage appeared in the distance and, as it came near, the watching men saw it contained the Archbishop and his daughter. Several shots were fired at him, but all missed. The carriage stopped, however, and Sharp and his daughter were dragged out, both pleading for their lives. There was no mercy for the Archbishop, who was stabbed to death in front of the girl.

MURDER OF EDWARD II

English history has been equally turbulent, though violence has often tended to be camouflaged by the trappings of justice. Murder was often cloaked by a court sentence. Cleverer, or luckier, than their Scottish counterparts, most English kings have died in bed. An exception was Edward II, who was murdered at Berkeley Castle in Gloucestershire in 1327. An old enemy, Lord Mortimer, had become the lover of the Queen, Isabella. They landed from France and Edward fled. He was captured and taken to Kenilworth Castle, where the dungeon that held him can still be seen. Under pressure he abdicated in favour of his son and was then moved to Berkeley Castle. Treated miserably by his captors, he was cruelly murdered, the traditional story being that a red-hot bar of metal was thrust into his body and that his screams were heard beyond the castle walls.

In more recent times no murder has been better known than the crime of Eugène Aram, the subject of a poem of Hood's and a novel by Lord Lytton. A Knaresborough shoemaker called Daniel Clark disappeared after swindling local tradesmen. After fourteen years, in 1758, a skeleton believed to be Clark's was found. An accomplice of Aram's turned King's Evidence and Aram was executed at York and his body hung in chains in Knaresborough Forest. The crime was commonplace enough, but the discovery of the remains and Aram's sentence so many years later gripped the public imagination. The cave where Aram hid the body is still shown a mile down the River Nidd.

Two years later, in 1760, the last peer hanged for murder died at Tyburn, where Marble Arch now stands. He was Earl Ferrers, who in a fit of temper shot his steward, Johnson, at Staunton Harold, near Ashby-de-la-Zouch. Johnson was responsible for an allowance paid to the Countess, who was separated from Ferrers. After accusing Johnson of trickery, Earl Ferrers forced him to his knees at pistol point and then shot him. While he lay dying the peer bullied and shouted at him. Ferrers was tried by the House of Lords and sentenced.

MURDER OF PERCEVAL

Assassination is a form of murder that is happily uncommon in Britain and few people remember that a Prime Minister was once killed in the House of Commons. He was Mr. Spencer Perceval and he was shot by John Bellingham, a man who had been imprisoned in Russia and had unsuccessfully demanded compensation. All his requests were ignored, although he wrote to the Prime Minister and the Prince Regent and time after time appealed to M.P.s for help. One afternoon in May, 1812, he put two loaded pistols in his coat pockets and left his rooms in King Street, St. James's. Crossing St. James's Park he arrived at the House of Commons, which then met in St. Stephen's Hall, where the public sit today while waiting for admission to the Strangers' Gallery.

Safeguards were laxer in those days and Bellingham found his way into the lobby, where he stood behind a statue. After a while Perceval entered and Bellingham calmly drew his pistol and fired. The Prime Minister groaned "Oh, God," and fell to the ground. His murderer did not try to escape and was arrested at once. At his trial he maintained that the insults he had endured justified his action. Asked if he felt no regret for his deed, he remarked: "I hope, sir, I feel as a man ought to do," and died calmly on the scaffold.

THE SAILOR'S GRAVE AT THURSLEY

This quaint memorial at Thursley is "in memory of a generous but unfortunate sailor who was barbarously murdered at Hindhead on September 24th 1786 by three villains after he had liberally treated them and promised them his further assistance on the road to Portsmouth." The carving represents the murder of the sailor.

CHAPTER 10

SOME FAMOUS WOMEN

BRITAIN did not begin the emancipation of her women until after she had emancipated her slaves. Until the nineteenth century was well on its way a woman could become famous only if the accident of birth ensured her a great destiny, if a romance or some freak of fortune sufficiently colourful to catch the popular fancy came into her life, or if an outstanding act of heroism aroused the enthusiasm of her contemporaries.

All over Britain there are memorials to women who reached distinction by one or other of these roads, and to others who, in a more recent age, have carved their own way to distinction. In the remote Western Isles, on the other side of Scotland, Kingsburgh House, in the beautiful island of Skye, is a memorial to a Scottish heroine who won great distinction by helping a prince of the House of Stuart to escape from his enemies.

In the original Kingsburgh House there lived in the year 1745, when the Stuart who was Bonnie Prince Charlie to his friends and the Young Pretender to his enemies brought war into Scotland, a "little woman of genteel appearance, and uncommonly mild and well-bred," whose name was Flora Macdonald. When the forlorn adventure ended at Culloden the prince was hard pressed by royal troops and his capture seemed certain. But when the hunt was keenest Flora arrived at Kingsburgh accompanied by a strapping maid named "Betty Burke." The new maid was greeted with the deference reserved for an honoured guest, although it was not until the danger was over that all Britain was aware that "she" was none other than the fugitive prince.

Of all places in Scotland made famous by feminine associations the Palace of Holyroodhouse at Edinburgh is, however, foremost in interest, for it is steeped in memories of the woman who, although born to the purple, found by bitter experience how often eminence and misfortune are allies. Even today, nearly four centuries after her death, the spirit of Mary, Queen of Scots, seems to brood over Holyroodhouse.

All over Scotland—and all over England, too—there are memories of the wanderings, voluntary or otherwise, of Mary Stuart. In the west wing of Linlithgow Palace is the spacious chamber in which she was born. A few days later she was queen, and the tragedy of her life fulfilled, in part at least, her father's gloomy prophecy concerning the fate of the Stuart dynasty when he was told of her birth. "It came," he said, "with a lass, and it will go with a lass."

Only the ruins remain of the castle of Loch Leven, in which Mary was imprisoned and in which she signed her enforced abdication. South of the Border, Maryport, in Cumberland, perpetuates her name on the map, and Queen Mary's Tower at Carlisle preserves the memory of one of her many places of imprisonment; while at Fotheringhay, in Northamptonshire, scarcely more than a grass-covered mound remains of the once splendid castle in which the final scene in her tragic life was enacted.

It was an odd coincidence that the last monarchs of England and Scotland as separate countries should be women, and that they should be at once so much alike and so different. Nature endowed Mary with the beauty denied to Elizabeth, but gave to Elizabeth and not to Mary the boon of a long and tranquil reign. The two Queens were sharply dissimilar in personality and temperament, yet each was shrewd and accomplished, and each has been alternately praised and vilified since her death. The memorials of English Elizabeth are even more numerous than those of Scottish Mary. In fact there is scarcely an old house or an historic inn that does not claim to have given "Good Queen Bess" lodging at some time or another, and scarcely a surviving sixteenth-century bed in which she did not sleep! Of all places associated with her memory, Hatfield House, in Hertfordshire, stands first in interest. In an upstairs room of the Old Palace she was virtually a prisoner in the precarious years when her half-sister reigned, and in the grounds is the "Great Oak" under which she was discovered reading when the news was brought to her that she was now Queen of England.

MONUMENT TO A QUEEN

In Hertfordshire also, at Waltham Cross, stands one of the three surviving monuments which a king erected in honour of his queen. Edward I was one of the fiercest of monarchs, but his savage qualities were redeemed by his tenderness for his wife, Eleanor of Castile. Never in history has there been a finer tribute to the qualities of a queen and a wife than the twelve crosses which marked the resting-places of Eleanor's funeral cortège on its way from the Midlands to Westminster. Only three of the twelve survived the intolerance of seventeenth-century Puritanism, Waltham's being one and the others those of Northampton and Geddington. All are spire-shaped columns, rising in three stories.

THE SHE-WOLF OF FRANCE

On a gentle eminence to the east of Castle Rising, in Norfolk, may be seen the walls and towers of the old castle which gave the village its name. Here is a sharp reminder of the contrast between the beloved Queen Eleanor and her detested daughter-in-law, Isabella the Fair—fair in face but not in fame, for the savage qualities which so belied her beauty earned for her the nickname, "The She-Wolf of France." For twenty-seven years Isabella expiated her many crimes in retirement at Castle Rising, and was at times visited by her son, Edward III, on which occasions his queen, the virtuous Philippa of Hainault, awaited him in her beloved city of Norwich.

Norwich owed much to Queen Philippa, who was largely responsible for the development of the thriving woollen industry of this "City of Churches." Norwich might also be described as the city of famous women, and there is one spot which, to a generation which knows Philippa only as a name, is more hallowed than any other. A plot of grass outside the cathedral is known as Life's Green, although the name is inappropriate since here a simple cross marks the grave of Nurse Edith Cavell. It is strange that her place of burial should be named Life's Green, whereas Tombland in the same city is

A FAMOUS ELEANOR CROSS

This well-restored cross at Geddington in Northamptonshire is one of the original Eleanor Crosses which Edward I caused to be erected at the places where his Queen's body had rested for the night on its final journey to her burial-place in Westminster Abbey. Queen Eleanor died at Harby in Nottinghamshire in 1290. At least twelve of these elaborate crosses were erected, including one at Charing Cross, but only three have survived—those at Geddington, Waltham Cross and near Northampton.

not a burial-ground at all, but a busy and spacious centre. Here a monument has been erected in memory of the heroic lady who, as all the world knows, was executed in the First World War for conniving at the escape of allied soldiers.

In Norwich, too, is a house in Gurney Court which, as memorial tablets record, was the birthplace of two notable Englishwomen who, although born in the same house, were not members of the same family. At one time this building was the headquarters of the famous Gurney banking-house, and just before the nineteenth century began a young girl of this old Quaker family started visiting the sick and relieving the destitute children of the city. She even persuaded her father to allow her to visit the local gaol, and thus began the work which, when continued at Newgate after her marriage to Joseph Fry, made the name of Elizabeth Fry famous for all time. So cynical a critic as Sydney Smith said that at the sight of Mrs. Fry at Newgate he wept like a child.

Harriet Martineau was born in Gurney Court two years after Elizabeth Fry's marriage. Harriet, who was a famous writer, shared Elizabeth's

IN LINLITHGOW PALACE

Linlithgow Palace, West Lothian (see page 202), is famous as the birthplace of Mary, Queen of Scots, in 1542. This unhappy and ill-fated Queen, daughter of Scotland's James V, was actually proclaimed Queen within a week of her birth at Linlithgow. When she was six years old she went to France, where she stayed to marry the Dauphin in 1558 and became Queen of France for a year (1560). It was not until her husband's death that she returned to Scotland to assume the government.

ENTRANCE TO THE KEEP, CASTLE RISING

Castle Rising, in Norfolk, was one of a number of strong fortresses, such as Norwich, Hedingham and Colchester Castles, erected by the Normans to protect the wealthy agricultural land of East Anglia and Essex. Rising retains much of its Norman architecture. Queen Isabella, mother of Prince Edward, later Edward III, and wife of the ill-fated Edward II, resided here for many years after the murder of her husband. She lived a life of seclusion in what was virtually a prison.

GURNEY COURT, NORWICH

Norwich was the birthplace of Mrs. Elizabeth Fry, the philanthropist and prison reformer. She was born a Miss Gurney and lived in Gurney Court. Harriet Martineau, the writer on political economy and social questions, also lived here for a number of years. Harriet Martineau died in 1876, Elizabeth Fry in 1845.

qualities, for it was said that "her existence was entirely and unselfishly devoted to the promotion of the happiness and wellbeing of mankind." In her girlhood she was sent to an aunt at Bristol, which was the metropolis of the west when Norwich was the metropolis of the east and rivals Norwich in its memorials of famous women.

Bristol Castle was the residence of the "Empress Maud"—the "queen" of England who never reigned—and was her headquarters during her long but futile struggle for the crown against King Stephen. But Bristol's most treasured memories are of two noble women who devoted their lives to the unfortunate among their own sex. In the north transept of the cathedral is a monument to Mary Carpenter, who founded at Bristol a reformatory for girls that was the model for all Britain; and Hannah More established in the neighbourhood of the city some of the earliest of the Sunday schools.

WOMEN DOCTORS

Bristol was, moreover, the girlhood home of Elizabeth Blackwell, who went to America to become the first woman doctor and died many years later at Hastings. Hastings, moreover, was the birthplace of Sophia Jex-Blake, who went to America to study under Elizabeth and returned to lead the long fight against the ban on women doctors, which ended in 1877 in victory.

From Hastings it is not a long journey to the old county town of Lewes, whose women, according to shrewd old William Cobbett, were "remarkably pretty, as indeed they are in most parts of Sussex." The old manor-house in the Southover High Street is, however, a reminder that at least one woman who lived at Lewes was by no means "remarkably pretty."

In fact, her unprepossessing features robbed her of a crown. Yet paradoxically it might be said that her plain face was after all her fortune, for she was Anne of Cleves, the fourth wife of Henry VIII; and although Henry discarded her because she was unattractive, had she been otherwise she might well have shared the fate of numbers two and five among Henry's six. As it was, the manor-house—known today as Anne of Cleves' House—was awarded her as a kind of consolation prize for the loss of her kingly husband, and perhaps she was content with the exchange.

FAMOUS QUEENS

It was at the Crown Inn in the High Street of Rochester, in the neighbouring county of Kent, that Henry obtained the famous "preview" of Anne which convinced him that she fell short of the Tudor beauty-standard; and ironically enough it was in the same county that he found much pleasure in the society of the other Anne—the first of his queens to lose her head. While his first wife was still queen Henry was in the habit of paying clandestine visits to Anne Boleyn at Hever Castle, Kent.

Surely no queen in history had a more magnificent memorial than Henry's first wife, Catherine of Aragon. She was buried in Peterborough Cathedral, and when it was suggested to Henry that "it would well become his greatness to rear a stately monument to her memory," he answered that he "would have to her memory one of the goodliest monuments in Christendom." Because it was her resting-place the abbey church of Peterborough was spared from the general destruction of the monasteries, and it is no exaggeration to say, therefore, that although only a marble slab in the north choir-aisle marks her grave, the cathedral itself is her monument.

AN ANCIENT HOUSE OF LEWES, SUSSEX

This ancient house, which is certainly in part of early Tudor date, is known as Anne of Cleves' House. It is situated in Southover, a suburb of Lewes. Anne of Cleves, a daughter of the Duke of Cleves, became one of the wives of Henry VIII, the King having fallen in love with her on the strength of a portrait by Holbein. Later he referred to her as a Flanders mare, and, totally disillusioned, quickly divorced her. Anne did, however, escape with her head, and lived for many years a life of quiet retirement in the small house which the King provided for her.

Only towers and a gable, with the chapel and fragments of the walls, remain of the once magnificent mansion of Bradgate, in Leicestershire, which is associated with two British queens. It was here that Lady Jane Grey, whose life was sacrificed for nine brief days of sovereignty, spent the only days of freedom and happiness she ever knew. Jane's high birth was her misfortune. It was because she was near enough to the throne to be used as a tool by those who

sought their own aggrandizement that she died by the headsman's axe.

In the previous century Bradgate had been the home of Lady Jane Grey's ancestress, Elizabeth Woodville, queen of Edward IV, although the house in which she lived was an earlier one than that which now lies in ruins. Elizabeth Woodville would never have met King Edward had it not been necessary for her to plead with him to restore Bradgate to her children by a former marriage. The King was hunting in the neighbourhood of the Northamptonshire home of Elizabeth's mother, and in order to present her petition she waylaid him, with a fatherless child in each hand, under a magnificent tree which still goes by the name of the "Queen's Oak." The mansion at Grafton Regis in which she was married to the King was, however, sacked and burnt during the Parliamentary wars, although part of it is incorporated in a new building on the site.

Crossing from Northamptonshire into Warwickshire we pass from the memory of queens to distinguished commoners.

South Farm at Arbury is a place of pilgrimage to the numerous admirers of "George Eliot" (Mary Ann Evans). Here she spent her youth, and the neighbourhood is vividly depicted in *The Mill on the Floss*.

Later she lived at Coventry, and it was there that her earliest work was written. Today a new Coventry is arising from the ruins of "the blitz," but memorials of the past are not being forgotten, and it will be remembered that not long since a statue was erected in Broadgate to the city's almost legendary heroine, Lady Godiva. There are many memorials of Lady Godiva's

THE ENTRANCE OF HEVER CASTLE

Hever Castle was the home of Sir Thomas Boleyn at the time when Henry VIII was courting his daughter, Anne. The King, accompanied by a small band of friends, frequently visited the Boleyns at their home, which lies on rather low ground near the valley of one of the Medway's tributaries. That is why on more than one occasion King Henry, riding on horseback, became hopelessly stuck in the mud and had to call for assistance from the castle to extricate him. Later the castle fell into complete disrepair, but was restored and enlarged in recent times.

PLAS NEWYDD, LLANGOLLEN

This was the home of the ladies of Llangollen to whom the poet Wordsworth dedicated his well-known sonnet. The "Ladies" were Sarah Ponsonby and Lady Eleanor Butler, who numbered among their friends Sir Walter Scott and the Duke of Wellington as well as Wordsworth. The two ladies lived here together from 1780 until the death of Lady Eleanor in 1829. Sarah Ponsonby died two years later. The fine house has been restored and enlarged since the death of the ladies, and is now used as the administrative headquarters of the Welsh National Theatre.

unconventional ride through the city's streets, and with the eye of faith we can see what Peeping Tom was not allowed to see with the physical eye, although the faith must be considerable, since Godiva's ride, like so many of the prized stories of history, changes from fact to legend when the remorseless light of research is brought to bear upon it.

In Warwickshire, too, are memorials to Shakespeare's wife and mother—the much-visited Anne Hathaway's Cottage at Shottery, and the less familiar Mary Arden's Cottage at Wilmcote, which has been restored to its sixteenth-century state and is now national property.

The industrial Midlands have their memorials to famous women not less striking than those of rural Warwickshire. At Walsall, for example, a marble statue surmounting the clock tower on the bridge commemorates Dorothy Pattison, who, as Sister Dora, became world famous in the 'seventies by her devoted nursing of the poor, and in particular of those afflicted with smallpox, thereby endearing herself to the miners and railwaymen of South Staffordshire.

The commercialism that has swallowed so much of Staffordshire has engulfed also vast areas of Yorkshire,

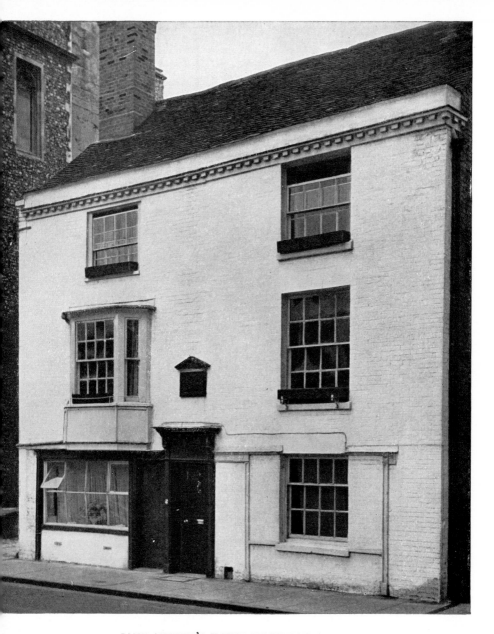

JANE AUSTEN'S HOUSE IN WINCHESTER

This house in Winchester was once briefly the home of Jane Austen. Jane Austen was the daughter of a country clergyman, and was born at Steventon where her father was rector. She remained at Steventon until early womanhood and later with her mother settled in a house at Chawton, near Alton. Chawton remained her home from 1809 onwards, but she was actually staying in this house in Winchester, in order to receive constant medical attention, in 1817 when she succumbed to her fatal illness.

THE TOMB OF BESS OF HARDWICK

This magnificently sculptured tomb is in the church of All Saints in Derby. It is in memory of "Bess of Hardwick," Elizabeth, Countess of Shrewsbury, 1518-1608. It was this Bess of Hardwick who rebuilt the houses of Chatsworth and Hardwick, the latter one of the most elaborate and advanced in style of Elizabethan mansions.

invading even the famous village of Haworth. But although industry has clutched Haworth in its tentacles it cannot entirely obliterate the bleak fascination of the moorland country of the West Riding, and it is still possible to recapture something of that wild spirit of the moors which Emily Brontë wove into the texture of *Wuthering Heights*.

Environment plays a notable part in moulding character, and the difference between the parsonages of Haworth in Yorkshire and Steventon in Hampshire is as apparent as the difference between the work of the famous women born in them. The sombre appeal of the moors permeates the Brontë novels, and similarly the smiling Hampshire countryside is reflected in the tranquillity which is a feature of the work of Jane Austen.

JANE AUSTEN AND HAMPSHIRE

The rectory in which Jane was born has disappeared, and only a pump and terrace taken from the garden of the former house remain. At Chawton, in the same county, a tablet indicates a house in which Jane lived for some years, and it was here that much of her best work was written. She died at a frequently visited house in College Street, Winchester, and a slab of black marble in the centre of the north aisle of the cathedral marks her grave.

Peaceful Hampshire became to another famous woman a battleground, although the battle she fought was not against people or policies but against disease and prejudice. Embley Park, in the parish of Wellow, has been considerably altered since the days when Florence Nightingale — who loved Hampshire as sincerely as Jane Austen did, and recuperated there when her labours had affected her health— became famous for all time as the "Lady with the Lamp" who ministered to Britain's sick and suffering soldiers in the Crimean War.

Passing into the centre of Hampshire to Alresford we find a memorial tablet in a house in Broad Street recording the birth of Mary Russell Mitford, but the Mitford Country is over the Berkshire border. Here is "Our Village" which Miss Mitford made famous, and at Swallowfield is her grave.

A GREAT BUILDER

At various places in the Midlands there are lavish memorials in brick which the famous "Bess of Hardwick," Countess of Shrewsbury, erected in honour of herself. The countess, who was four times a widow, and created two ducal dynasties, collected fortunes simultaneously with husbands, and surviving all her matrimonial entanglements was herself survived by the five stately homes of Britain she had built. In the park of Hardwick Hall in Derbyshire are the ruins of the older Hall which was her birthplace.

Another famous Derbyshire mansion is Haddon Hall, and everyone who visits Haddon is confronted with the romantic story of the elopement of Dorothy Vernon with Sir John Manners. Dorothy's bedroom may be seen, and the window through which she was courted in Romeo fashion by her lover, who heralded his approach by playing a lute in the wood. Dorothy Vernon's Steps, down which, says the story, she fled when she eloped, and Dorothy Vernon's Bridge are among the sights of Haddon Hall. But—alas for tradition! —the famous steps were not there in Dorothy's day, and there was no angry father and no elopement. The bridegroom was also the family's choice.

It is fitting to close with a reminder that not all Britain's famous women were ladies of high birth, and that some were of humble origin. Off the bleak and bare Northumbrian coast the seventeen rocky islets known as the Farne Islands thrust themselves into the North Sea, and among them the Longstone Lighthouse flashes its warnings to mariners. Here, more than a century ago, a keeper named Darling lived with his wife and daughter, Grace. On a stormy September night the steamer *Forfarshire* was wrecked, and in the morning it was seen by the Darlings from the lighthouse a mile away. To attempt to launch a boat in a raging sea seemed madness to Darling, but his daughter urged him to try, and herself accompanied him on the perilous journey. The survivors were saved, and England rang with Grace Darling's fame.

GRACE DARLING MEMORIAL, BAMBURGH

Appropriately set within sight of the North Sea and exposed to the full force of the north-easterly gales at Bamburgh, Northumberland, this memorial recalls the courage of Grace Darling, whose bravery has become almost a by-word among British people. Grace Darling was born in 1815, the daughter of the keeper of one of the Farne Island lighthouses. She won undying fame in September, 1838, by rescuing nine people with her father's help from the wreck of the steamer Forfarshire.

DOROTHY VERNON'S GATE AT HADDON HALL

A wealth of legend, some of it true, but much apocryphal, surrounds the name of Dorothy Vernon. What is certain is that Haddon Hall existed as early as Norman times and by the twelfth century was held by the Vernon family, who continued in possession until the sixteenth century, when Dorothy Vernon, the last of her line, married Sir John Manners. One legend recounts that a ball was in progress when Dorothy Vernon disappeared through this very gateway to keep tryst with her lover, Sir John Manners, who thereupon eloped with her. Nearby is Dorothy Vernon's Bridge.

CHAPTER 11

SOME MIGHTY MEN

IN every town and city of Britain, and in many of its villages, memorials of various kinds preserve the fame of men to whom the nation owes its greatness —Empire-builders and statesmen, pioneers of science and exploration, inventors and captains of industry, ecclesiastics and educationists, men of letters and of the arts, thinkers and philosophers, and men who made their mark in war.

Castles and ancient halls are treasure-houses rich in memories of the men who made them, but a no less striking feature of the towns and villages is the number of humble homes which gave illustrious sons to Britain. Often these modest memorials are dwarfed by the elaborate monuments which subsequent generations have raised in tribute, as, for example, at Stratford-upon-Avon, where the simple dwelling that was Shakespeare's birthplace is over-shadowed by the Memorial Theatre which a modern age has erected in his honour.

Nothing could be more fitting than to begin a search for Britain's mighty men in the home town of the greatest of them all; and it is appropriate that Shakespeare's birthplace is in the very heart of England. The stream of pilgrims pouring into Stratford shows how veneration for Britain's national poet increases as the years go by; and the fact that a considerable proportion of the annual invasion is from America is a striking recognition that Britain is still the hub of the English-speaking world.

Much of the charm of Stratford is that it has not changed appreciably since the days when Shakespeare lived there. About a century ago his birthplace in Henley Street was purchased so that it might be preserved for posterity, and a genuine attempt was made to restore this "small mean-looking dwelling of wood and plaster" to its condition in Shakespeare's own day. It is not difficult to cast one's mind back four centuries when one sees the living-room, with its bare walls and low ceiling; the kitchen, with its wide open-hearth; and above all the dim bleak bedroom, with its uneven floor, in which the poet was born. To assist the visitor in acquiring "atmosphere" the house is full of personal Shakespearean relics and of objects associated with the age in which he lived.

Although New Place, the house at the corner of Chapel Lane in which Shakespeare died, has long since been demolished, there is much of interest to see if the lane is followed to "the sweet-flowing Avon," on the banks of which stands Holy Trinity Church. Beautiful as is the church and its setting, the spot which most attracts the visitor is the chancel, for here is Shakespeare's grave, and above it the famous monumental bust which it seems really is an authentic likeness.

No visitor to Stratford will fail to walk or drive over to Shottery, a mile

SHAKESPEARE'S BIRTHPLACE

The date of birth of the Bard of Avon is 23 April, 1564. This house in Henley Street is the traditional scene of his birth. Most probably tradition is correct in this instance; as the house suggests, Shakespeare's father was a substantial citizen, an alderman of Stratford for more than twenty years and one of the leading citizens in the town. Among the other historic houses in Stratford and district associated with Shakespeare are New Place, where the poet went to live in middle age, and Anne Hathaway's cottage at near-by Shottery. The Henley Street house has been restored, but remains largely as it was when William Shakespeare was born there.

away, to see "Anne Hathaway's Cottage." This picturesque timbered farmhouse, with its low, thatched roof, was the scene of Shakespeare's swift and tempestuous courtship, and is the Shakespearean link whose authenticity is least questioned by the sceptical critic.

The ancient city of Lichfield tempts many of Stratford's tourists to extend their journey into the neighbouring county of Staffordshire, and again it is less the charm of the place than the

fame of its associations that attracts us. Although the delicate beauty of the "Lady of Cathedrals" and the slender grace of its three spires delights every visitor, a greater magnet is the three-storied house in the north-west corner of the market-square, for here Samuel Johnson was born nearly two and a half centuries ago; and if Shakespeare is the greatest Englishman, Johnson is surely the most typical—a rugged John Bull whose appeal to posterity is based more on his personality than on his actual achievement, and who by the freak of fortune owes his immortality to a lesser man, since it is the comparatively insignificant Boswell ("the Scotch cur at Johnson's heels") who, by preserving and recording the sayings and recapturing the spirit of the great Samuel, has made him a living figure to his countrymen.

It is a quaint old house that we see, with pillars supporting the overhanging upper stories, although the building has changed considerably since Johnson's day. Johnson's father was a bookseller, and the corner room was his shop. Above it is the room in which Samuel was born, and as in Shakespeare's case the house is now a museum of relics.

In the fine old county town of Stafford there is a reminder that some of Britain's greatest men have been those who paradoxically achieved nothing of any consequence. In St. Mary's Church there is a portrait-bust of Izaak Walton, the *Compleat Angler*, and houses in Greengate Street and Eastgate Street contend for the honour of being the birthplace of the man who is so revered by anglers.

ASSOCIATIONS WITH WASHINGTON

There is little similarity between the placid pilgrimage of Izaak Walton and the eventful career of George Washington. To Americans, Washington is the "Father of his Country," and when his compatriots visit England they flock, therefore, to Sulgrave Manor in Northamptonshire, where his antecedents are to be found. As recently as 1914 the house was purchased by public subscription and was suitably restored as a permanent memorial.

The old village of Lutterworth, in the adjoining county of Leicestershire, is memorable because in the fourteenth century the great John Wyclif was its rector. Although the rectory has vanished, there are many relics— genuine or otherwise—in the church. The east and south walls of the chancel remain from his day, and little more than half a century ago a memorial was belatedly erected in his honour.

RELIGIOUS REFORMER

It was from Lutterworth that Wyclif —reformer, idealist, and iconoclast— blazoned his way across medieval England as the "Morning Star of the Reformation," and it is not difficult to recapture in imagination the scene when his "poor priests" poured out over the English countryside, preaching a new doctrine that spread like wildfire among a poverty-stricken and illiterate people, who welcomed any ideology, whether social or spiritual, that promised alleviation of their miseries.

If we pass over the Leicestershire border into Lincolnshire we find, at Epworth, memorials of another of England's great religious leaders. Epworth is the Mecca of Methodists the world over, for in its rectory was born the great John Wesley, whose followers are numerous in both the Eastern and Western hemispheres, so that Epworth, like Stratford and Sulgrave, attracts transatlantic visitors.

The rectory they see is not the one in which Wesley was born. The old rectory was burned down when Wesley was six years old, and he had a remarkable escape from death when it happened. The church has changed little since his day, and in it is preserved the chalice from which, as a boy of eight, he first received communion.

Epworth is not, however, the only place of pilgrimage in Lincolnshire. At Woolsthorpe, on the Leicestershire border, Sir Isaac Newton—who became

DR. JOHNSON'S TOWN

Dr. Samuel Johnson has left links with many towns and villages in England, but Lichfield, Staffordshire, the town in which he was born, remained one of his favourite places throughout his life. In this picture is seen the three-storied house on the corner where he first saw the light of day in 1709. It is now a Johnsonian museum. The nineteenth-century statue of Johnson, seen above in the foreground, is embellished with several carvings depicting scenes from the great man's life.

SULGRAVE MANOR

This handsome manor-house of grey limestone was bought in 1539 by the Washington family. The family continued to live at Sulgrave until shortly before they emigrated to North America towards the middle of the seventeenth century. Sulgrave is thus the ancestral home of George Washington, first President of the United States. In 1914 it was presented by a British committee to the peoples of America and Britain. Its maintenance was subscribed for by various American societies.

TENNYSON'S BIRTHPLACE

Alfred, Lord Tennyson's father was rector of Somersby, Lincolnshire. The poet was born at the rectory (shown above) in 1809 and lived here for the greater part of his childhood. There is a memorial to him in the parish church. He went to school at Louth, a few miles away. There is no doubt that he was influenced by the quiet scenery and pleasant, rolling hill-country of the Lincolnshire wolds which he came to know so well as a child and schoolboy. But it is probably fanciful to identify, as some have done, any definite places in the neighbourhood with the poet's images.

President of the Royal Society in the year of Wesley's birth—was born in the local manor-house. It is a grey-stone building with mullioned windows, and has been preserved intact as a permanent memorial in honour of one of the greatest scientists and astronomers of any nation or of any age.

When a plague raged in Cambridge, Newton retired to Woolsthorpe to begin the researches that set the scientific world ablaze. A second bedroom in the house is shown as the study in which his investigations were made, but to the less erudite the principal attraction is the orchard, for here it was that, according to a tradition we are reluctant to discard, Newton saw the famous apple fall—and the fall of that apple has reverberated all over the globe and echoed down the ages, since it was the inspiration of the law of gravitation which was Newton's most striking contribution to science.

On the other side of Lincolnshire, between the Wolds and the North Sea, stands a house that was once the rectory of Somersby. In this attractive old residence, with its oriel window and pantiled roof, Tennyson was born.

Tennyson became Poet Laureate on the death of Wordsworth, and there is a gulf greater than that of mere geographical distance between the quiet streams and low hills of Tennyson Land and the rugged mountains and spacious lakes of the Wordsworth Country. Although the term "Lake Poets" is a literary misnomer, the "Poet of Nature" had as neighbours Southey, who lived at Greta Hall, and De Quincey. Thither, too, came Coleridge, while John Ruskin subsequently made his home at Brantwood, on the east side of Coniston Water.

LAKELAND POET

Transcending all these places in interest, however, is Dove Cottage at Grasmere, where Wordsworth lived in undisturbed tranquillity with his sister Dorothy in a house which is much the same now as it was then. Every year a numerous host of "Wordsworthians" gaze on the low-ceilinged sitting-room, the twisting staircase and the tiny bedrooms—and on such relics as Dorothy's work-box, and a wooden box made by the great man himself, for Dove Cottage, like so many of the habitations of Britain's famous men, is now a museum.

From this small cottage it is not a very long journey across the Scottish border to a quiet little churchyard—or rather kirkyard, since we are now in Scotland—where Thomas Carlyle is buried. His birthplace, like his burial-place, is in the village of Ecclefechan, in Annandale, and this is no roomy rectory or spacious manor-house, for Carlyle's father was a stonemason, and the famous "Arch House" is, in consequence, merely an arched entry into what was formerly the mason's yard.

At the time that Carlyle was entering the world at Ecclefechan, Robert Burns was lying ill at Dumfries in the same county, and he died seven months later, in a house in what is now Burns Street. The chair in which he sat in state at the local Globe Inn is preserved, and there is a Burns' statue in the High Street, while in the churchyard of St. Michael's his grave is embellished by a mausoleum.

It is in the neighbouring county of Ayrshire, however, that the more youthful associations with Burns are to be found. Streams of visitors pour into the town of Ayr to see the "auld clay biggin" at Alloway, on its southern outskirts, where the poet was born.

Everywhere in the town of Ayr ("wham ne'er a town surpasses, for honest men and bonnie lasses") there is something to remind us of the immortal Robbie. In the High Street stands the Tam o' Shanter Inn, where Tam's famous ride began, and we see farther on the Auld Brig o'Doon, which was his salvation, since the witches who pursued him could not cross running water. Alloway's "auld haunted kirk" and many another familiar landmark perpetuate the poet's memory, and towering over the "banks and braes o' bonnie Doon" is a colossal monument in the base of which such memorials as a snuff-box, Jean Armour's wedding-ring and the Bible Burns gave to Highland Mary are preserved.

SCOTT COUNTRY

The Burns Country is the Western Lowlands, but the Eastern Lowlands is the Scott Country, the point of contact being Edinburgh, in which city the plebeian Robbie and the patrician Sir Walter met on an historic occasion. Edinburgh's streets, and even the handsome Waverley railway station, remind us of Scott, but he who seeks more personal memories will turn south from the "Modern Athens" to the Tweed, and in particular to Abbotsford, that

WORDSWORTH'S HOME AT GRASMERE

Wordsworth, the greatest of the nineteenth-century poets of nature, who was born at Cockermouth, on the fringe of England's Lake District, and educated at the Grammar School at Hawkshead, stayed at Dove Cottage in Grasmere before and after his marriage to Mary Hutchinson for about nine years from 1799. Later he lived at other houses, but did not move out of the district for any length of time before his death in 1850. Much of the inspiration of his poetry was derived from the scenes and sights of the Lake District countryside. Wordsworth is buried in the churchyard of Grasmere.

magnificent mansion which contrasts so strikingly with the humble home of Burns, though each is a treasure-house of personal associations.

Abbotsford has been altered since Scott's day, but the original rooms remain as they were, and his study is almost as he left it. The treasures preserved include not only relics of Scott himself, but some "heirlooms of history" that he collected, including the sword of Montrose, Rob Roy's gun, a drinking-glass belonging to Burns, and the keys which Mary, Queen of Scots, threw into Loch Leven when she escaped from the castle.

In Edinburgh itself Scott's birthplace no longer stands, but one may see in North Castle Street the house in which he lived, and one of the dominating features of the city is the magnificent Scott monument which is the capital's tribute to the "Wizard of the North."

At Stirling the castle stands like a sentinel over the field of Bannockburn, on which the standard of Scotland still

BIRTHPLACE OF THOMAS CARLYLE

This small two-storied cottage at Ecclefechan, Dumfriesshire, is the birthplace of the great historian and philosopher, Thomas Carlyle. Carlyle was born on 4 December, 1795, the son of a stone-mason who later became a farmer. He was educated at the local school, entering Edinburgh University at the early age of fourteen. Most of the rest of his youth was spent in Edinburgh. The Ecclefechan house is now the property of the National Trust of Scotland. Carlyle's burial-place is also at Ecclefechan.

proudly floats to mark the scene of the crowning victory of Robert Bruce, and from the same vantage-point a prominent object in the landscape is the imposing Wallace Monument, which commemorates Scotland's other great national hero, Sir William Wallace, a brave but less fortunate man.

The story of Stirling reminds us that Scotland produced warriors as well as poets, but she has been even more prolific in her output of engineers, and of Empire heroes, such as David Livingstone, whose house still stands at Blantyre, a subscription having been raised to save it as recently as 1928. Blantyre lies by the banks of the Clyde, on the estuary of which is the port of Greenock, where a monument in Union Street reminds us that this is the birthplace of James Watt. Everyone who knows the pleasing legend—if legend it

LITERARY SHRINE IN THE VALLEY OF THE TWEED

Abbotsford, near Melrose, in the valley of the Tweed, was the home of Sir Walter Scott for the greater part of his life after 1812. Its magnificent pseudo-Gothic architecture reflects the material as well as the literary success of the novelist. Scott was born in 1771, but the period of great novel-writing which brought him fame did not begin until 1814, by which time he had completed the building of Abbotsford. He was living at Abbotsford when he wrote Waverley *in 1814, followed by* Guy Mannering, Rob Roy *and most of the other Scott favourites. In 1819 he was seriously ill, but recovered to write a further large number of novels, including* Ivanhoe *and* Kenilworth.

is—of Watt's boyhood days remembers that whereas Newton derived inspiration from a falling apple, Watt found his in the rising lid of a kettle, for his attention, says the old story, was directed thereby to the power of steam, and the result was the evolution of the steam-engine.

It was the Tyne and not the Clyde, however, which produced the man who consolidated the work that Watt began. Watt's invention may be said to have been the basis of Britain's manufacturing supremacy, but it was George Stephenson who, as the "Father of Railways," created the transport system that transformed Britain in the later stages of the Industrial Revolution.

Newcastle's striking monument to George Stephenson is overshadowed by the lofty High Level Bridge which was the creation of his equally famous son, Robert. The Newcastle home of the Stephensons was at 17 Eldon Place, and although it is down on Tees-side (at Darlington's Bank Top Station) that *Locomotive No. 1* is preserved, all their earlier memories are on Tyneside, and George's birthplace was at Wylam, a few miles up the river from Newcastle.

ANGLO-SAXON HISTORIAN

If, crossing Robert Stephenson's famous bridge, we leave Northumberland and enter the county palatine of Durham, we find, on the southern bank of the estuary of the Tyne, the town of Jarrow, which has been so widely associated with a depressing phase of modern industrialism that its ancient history is often forgotten. More than a millennium ago the Venerable Bede spent nearly the whole of his useful and active life in Jarrow's ancient monastery, and so vividly has his fame spanned the centuries that people visit the town today to see such relics as Bede's Chair, which is preserved in the chancel of the

parish church. Bede's tomb is in the twelfth-century Galilee Chapel in Durham's stately cathedral, which stands on a rocky cliff above a deep gorge made by the River Wear.

There are, of course, many famous memorials in Yorkshire. An old house in Hull's High Street, for example, is preserved as the birthplace of William Wilberforce, the man who freed the Empire's slaves, and the figure of the liberator triumphantly surmounts a lofty column standing in the heart of the city's dockland. And in rural Yorkshire, at Coxwold, near Thirsk, stands Shandy Hall, where Laurence Sterne lived when he was presented to the curacy of Coxwold. Here he wrote *Tristram Shandy* and *Sentimental Journey*.

LANCASHIRE INVENTOR

The county of the White Rose leads us across the Pennines to the county of the Red Rose, and we are reminded that the royal dynasties of York and Lancaster each ended in violence. But Lancashire is more famous for its industrial history than for its royal associations. Bolton, for example, was the cradle of the cotton industry, and here in the eighteenth century Sir Richard Arkwright—the man who boasted in his old age that he could pay off the National Debt if he wished—began his career as a "subterranean barber" shaving his customers for a penny, until fierce competition forced him to cut his prices by half. But Bolton's "halfpenny barber" became Britain's "cotton king," finding the invention of the spinning-frame so much more profitable than shaving the chins of his fellow-Boltonians that it was said he became the richest commoner in England.

Lancashire has produced a number of remarkable statesmen, and the famous

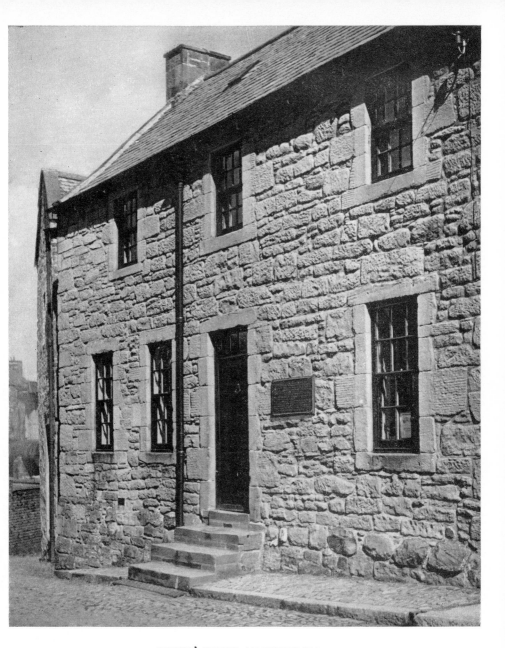

BURNS' HOUSE AT DUMFRIES

Robert Burns, the national poet of Scotland, was born in Ayrshire to a peasant family. He himself twice undertook a farm career and twice failed. Already famous for his poetry, and at the same time in failing health, he came to Dumfries as exciseman in 1791, first taking lodgings and then settling in this house two years later. He died here in 1796 at the age of thirty-seven and was buried in the graveyard of St. Michael's Church. A statue of Burns is in the High Street of Dumfries.

235

GEORGE STEPHENSON'S BIRTHPLACE

This cottage at Wylam on the Tyne was the birthplace on 9 June, 1781, of George Stephenson, father of the British railways. Stephenson's youth was one of poverty and hard work as an agricultural labourer and later as a colliery fireman. It was not until 1815 that he gained an award for a miner's safety-lamp. By then he had mastered the application of steam to machinery and had invented in 1814 the first locomotive for use on a colliery road. After that progress was rapid and he became consulting engineer for most of the railways constructed between 1820 and his death in 1848.

boast that "what Manchester thinks today London thinks tomorrow" is not by any means an empty one. Besides the famous Victorian politicians of the Manchester School, three of Britain's greatest Prime Ministers were born in Lancashire—Peel at Bury, Gladstone at Liverpool, and Lloyd George at Manchester — though each, oddly enough, is more closely associated with another county.

The "county of Prime Ministers" is, however, Buckinghamshire. Disraeli once said that five Buckinghamshire squires (of whom he was one) were Prime Ministers. Appropriately enough, Chequers, the official country residence of the Prime Minister, is in Bucks, its estate including the highest point in the Chiltern Hills. A few miles to the south is Hughenden Manor, where Disraeli lived and died.

How packed with seventeenth-century history is this picturesque "Chiltern corner" of Buckinghamshire! Between Chequers and Hughenden is Hampden House, which was the home of one of the greatest of Britain's bygone

THE TOMB OF ST. BEDE THE VENERABLE

St. Bede the Venerable, the first great historian of England, was a monk, residing first in the abbey of Wearmouth and after that in the abbey of Jarrow. His chief work was the Ecclesiastical History of the English People. *He died in A.D. 735. His remains lay in the Galilee Chapel of Durham Cathedral until dispersed in 1541.*

A FAMOUS CHURCH IN BUCKINGHAMSHIRE

The parish church of Great Hampden, set high on a hill in the midst of attractive and thinly peopled countryside, is famous as the burial-place of John Hampden (1594-1643). The church also contains a monument in memory of Hampden erected in 1755. Hampden was a cousin of the Protector, Oliver Cromwell, and from 1621 onwards, when he was elected to Parliament, played a conspicuous part in opposition to the King's party. It was indeed the unsuccessful attempt of the King to have Hampden and some others arrested which precipitated the Civil War. Hampden himself was fatally wounded at the battle of Chalgrove Field.

heroes. Part of the mansion—the "brick parlour," for example—is as it was in the days when all England was ablaze with enthusiasm at the news of the courageous stand of John Hampden against Stuart tyranny. Various relics of the statesman are preserved here, including the silver chalice from which he drank sacramental wine as he lay dying after being mortally wounded at Chalgrove Field. The site of the battlefield is indicated by an obelisk that is a

landmark for miles around, and in the church of Great Hampden, where he was buried, is another Hampden memorial.

Across the Chiltern range, a few miles from Great Hampden, is the only surviving house of several in which Hampden's great contemporary and colleague, John Milton, lived. Milton's Cottage at Chalfont St. Giles is a picturesque half-timbered house packed with Miltonian relics, and it was here that the poet finished *Paradise Lost* and began *Paradise Regained*.

In Buckinghamshire, too, is Stoke Poges, where the poet Gray is buried near the east wall of the church he immortalized in his famous *Elegy*; and in an adjoining meadow there is an obelisk to his memory, although a more enduring monument is the churchyard itself, for here are the "ivy-mantled tower," the "rugged elms," and other features familiar to readers of the *Elegy*.

Buckinghamshire's memories of Puritan England are continued in the adjoining county of Bedfordshire. Here is the country of John Bunyan, and Bunyan House (considerably restored and of doubtful authenticity) still stands in Elstow's village street, on the right-hand side of the road from Bedford, although the original birthplace has been pulled down. Hard by is the village green on which Bunyan played tip-cat on Sundays in his unregenerate youth, and in Elstow Church, where he rang the bells in the detached campanile (although he subsequently regarded this as sinful), are two memorial windows.

HUGHENDEN MANOR, BUCKINGHAMSHIRE

Here is a corner of the famous library at Hughenden Manor, Buckinghamshire, showing over the fireplace a portrait of Benjamin Disraeli by Sir Francis Grant. This portrait, painted in 1852, is an excellent picture of the statesman at the period when he was coming to a position of pre-eminence in Britain's politics. Hughenden was the home of Disraeli from 1848 until his death in 1881. His father had settled at Bradenham House, Buckinghamshire, many years before, so that his connexion with the county was continuous (his father died at Bradenham in 1848).

THE JOHN BUNYAN COUNTRY

The ancient half-timbered Moot Hall of Elstow, in Bedfordshire, apart from its own intrinsic interest, recalls John Bunyan's story of how he came to "see the light" while playing on the green opposite the Moot Hall on a Sunday afternoon early in his life. Bunyan was born at Elstow in 1628, and spent some twelve years of his life in prison at near-by Bedford as a penalty for his adherence to a sect which upheld a reformed type of religious instruction. The first part of Pilgrim's Progress *was actually written in the gaol at Bedford and many of his subsequent works at Elstow.*

We have only to pass into Huntingdonshire to find memories of the greatest of all Puritan leaders—Oliver Cromwell, who was Milton's "Chief of Men," and is the only Englishman who has stood in the place of a king. The registers of All Saints' Church at Huntingdon contain Cromwell's baptismal entry, although the words added by an irreverent hand—"England's plague for five years"—have been erased. It was in a house at the foot of the High Street that the Protector was born, but only a brick wall remains, although the building now occupying the site is known as Cromwell House. Cromwell's real memorial is the Grammar School, at which he and Samuel Pepys were pupils.

Cambridge, too, has associations with Cromwell, and Cambridge, like its sister 'varsity, is rich in memorials of the famous men who have studied there. The beauty of the town is in its "Backs"—which means that its colleges are seen to best advantage where the lawns behind them slope to the placid Cam. Macaulay, in a famous passage, pointed out that "Cambridge had the honour of educating those celebrated

THE OLD GRAMMAR SCHOOL, HUNTINGDON

The moulded Romanesque arches which are a feature of the High Street in Huntingdon form part of the façade of the old grammar school, which has had at least two very famous pupils. One was Oliver Cromwell, who was born in Huntingdon in 1599. An inscription on the wall reads: "Oliver Cromwell, Lord Protector of the Commonwealth, attended this school about 1610." The other was Samuel Pepys, who was a pupil at the same school about thirty years after Cromwell.

FLATFORD MILL, SUFFOLK

This beautiful group of mill house and cottages, together with the adjacent Willy Lott's cottage, has been immortalized in the paintings of John Constable, greatest of English landscape painters. Constable's father owned Flatford Mill, though the artist was born in a house which has since been demolished at near-by East Bergholt. The whole of this group, including the old mill and mill house, was purchased out of the proceeds of a public subscription, and restored in 1927 as a school and guest-house for artists in memory of Constable. Two of the most famous pictures in which Willy Lott's cottage appears are the "Hay Wain" and the "Valley Farm."

Protestant bishops whom Oxford had the honour of burning; and at Cambridge were formed the minds of all those statesmen to whom chiefly is to be attributed the secure establishment of the reformed religion in the north of Europe."

The burning to which Macaulay refers is, of course, the tragedy commemorated by the famous Martyrs' Memorial opposite the west front of Balliol College at Oxford. An iron cross in Broad Street marks the spot where, it is believed, Ridley, Latimer and Cranmer suffered martyrdom at the stake.

It is not far from Cambridge into that part of West Norfolk where Sir Robert Walpole built Houghton Hall during the long years of his Premiership, and there is one rather odd point of resemblance between Cromwell and Walpole. Cromwell was a farmer, and but for the Civil War he would probably have remained a farmer until the end of his days. Farming, too, should have been Walpole's vocation, for it was his father's ambition that Robert should be "the first grazier in the country." Instead he became Britain's first Prime Minister, and by holding that office for a generation accomplished something none of his successors has achieved up to the present time.

In the rectory of Burnham Thorpe, near the North Norfolk coast, Nelson was born two centuries ago. The rectory has been demolished, and today the Nelson relics consist of a bust in the church and a lectern made from the timbers of the *Victory*. At Norwich, capital of the county, a statue outside St. Peter Mancroft commemorates the fact that Sir Thomas Browne, the great prose stylist, is buried at the church.

Norwich had its own school of landscape painting, its founder being John ("Old") Crome, who is buried in St. George's Church. An even more famous landscape painter came from the neighbouring county of Suffolk. Flatford Mill and the adjacent oft-painted Willy Lott's Cottage are in the heart of the Constable Country, and have been restored as a school and guest-house for artists in memory of John Constable, whose father owned the mill.

Another artist's home that has been preserved for all time is Blake's Cottage

IN HOLKHAM HALL

Below is seen the state bedroom of Holkham Hall, near Wells, Norfolk, one of the finest houses built in the first half of the eighteenth century, with the restrained exuberance of interior decoration which marks the finest of Georgian work. The architect of the house was William Kent. He worked under the direction of the first Earl of Leicester, better known as "Coke of Norfolk" because of his unremitting and successful efforts to transform the barren sandy wastes of the Holkham estate into a productive and fertile countryside. Coke's success in Norfolk paved the way for the later eighteenth-century resurgence of Britain's agriculture.

at Felpham, in Sussex, where the poet, painter and mystic spent "three years' slumber on the banks of the ocean."

There are notable literary birthplaces in the neighbouring county of Hampshire. At Portsmouth the house in Commercial Road in which Charles Dickens was born is now the Dickens Museum; and George Meredith was born in a house in the High Street. Hampshire's most interesting literary memorial is, however, Selborne, the village made famous by Gilbert White, author of *The Natural History of Selborne*. White's house — known as The Wakes — is

shown, although it has been altered since his day, and his grave in the churchyard of St. Mary's is distinguished only by a plain headstone bearing initials and dates.

The jealous way in which Britain safeguards the memorials of her famous sons is seen also in the Hardy Country in Dorset. At Higher Bockhampton (Upper Mellstock in his novels) the thatched cottage which was the birthplace of Thomas Hardy is preserved in memory of the man who did so much for his beloved Dorset. Outside the cottage stands a granite column which

HAYES BARTON, DEVONSHIRE

Hayes Barton is another house which has a twofold interest. First it is a well-preserved example of traditional Elizabethan architecture, showing little sign of the Renaissance trends and perpetuating the irregular façade which had characterized English building from Gothic days onwards. Secondly it has a world-wide fame as the birthplace of Sir Walter Raleigh in 1552. The house is in the parish of East Budleigh and about two miles from the seaside resort of Budleigh Salterton. It was the seat of the Raleighs, an ancient and prosperous Devon family, for many generations.

A LINK WITH SIR HENRY IRVING

In this grey-stone house in the village of Keinton Mandeville, on the main road between Castle Cary and Somerton, John Henry Brodribb, better known as Henry Irving, was born on 6 February, 1838. Brodribb went to London early in life as a clerk, but in 1856 at the age of eighteen he was appearing on the provincial stage. By 1874, as Henry Irving, he was well established as a successful tragic actor and remained a leader in his profession until near the end of his life in 1905.

was erected by American admirers after the First World War, and rather more than two miles away is Max Gate, the house which Hardy built, and in which he lived during the latter part of his life.

Wessex was the creation, or rather resuscitation, of Thomas Hardy, and adjoining it are the rugged hills, bold cliffs and verdant valleys of Devonshire. In such a setting a naval arsenal might seem out of place were it not that Devon's greatest glory has been her

bold Elizabethan navigators. Some came from the north of the county, but the richest maritime memories are at Plymouth. On the famous Hoe stands Smeaton's Eddystone Lighthouse—and a statue of Sir Francis Drake, the greatest of all the Devonian seamen.

At Hayes Barton, an old seat, now a farmhouse, in that part of eastern Devon which lies between the Exe and Dorsetshire, Sir Walter Raleigh was born four centuries ago; but it was over the Dorset border at Sherborne, it seems, that Sir Walter enjoyed the first pipe of tobacco ever smoked in England—although, according to the old story, he was not allowed to enjoy it for long, since a startled servant, displaying more zeal than judgment, appeared to think his master was on fire, and threw a pail of water at his head.

Tobacco was one of the first benefits the New World bestowed upon the Old World, and it is as well to remember that although Columbus discovered (or re-discovered) America, Britain had some share in the credit. The Cabot Tower which stands on Brandon Hill at Bristol bears the inscription: "Commenced in the fourth centenary of the discovery of America by John Cabot and Sons, Lewis, Sebastian & Sanctus."

The discoveries of the Bristolian Cabots were in the North American continent—and on the village green of Westerham, in Kent, is a memorial to the man who gave Britain her principal possession in that continent. A handsome bronze statue commemorates

IN PENSHURST PLACE

Penshurst Place is one of the most interesting of the genuine medieval manor-houses of southern England. The buildings which compose the historic pile span the finest era of English architecture, from the fourteenth to the eighteenth century. The gallery shown here belongs to the later part of the house. Its walls are lined with portraits of the Sidney family, who have held Penshurst since the sixteenth century. Sir Philip Sidney, most famous of the line, was born here in 1554. The present lord of Penshurst Place is also a Sidney, Lord De L'Isle and Dudley, V.C.

DOWNE HOUSE, IN KENT

This pleasant Georgian-style house in the village of Downe, Kent, was the home of Charles Darwin, most eminent of English naturalists and biologists. Darwin was born at Shrewsbury in 1809. As a young man he sailed round the world in the Beagle *between 1831 and 1836. In 1842 he settled at Downe to write his definitive treatise,* The Origin of Species by Means of Natural Selection. *Darwin continued at Downe, until his death in 1882, writing a number of further scientific works which were mainly supplementary to* The Origin of Species. *These works revolutionized profoundly the scientific approach to the theory of evolution.*

General Wolfe, who was born in the local vicarage, and spent his boyhood in a red-brick Elizabethan mansion, now known as Quebec House in honour of the capture of Quebec which led to the English conquest of Canada.

Not far from Westerham is Hayes Place, which was built by the Earl of Chatham (better known as the Elder Pitt or the Great Commoner), who, in the days when he was entrusted with the destinies of the nation, made the decision which sent Wolfe to Quebec.

Famous residents of Kent have included scientists as well as soldiers and statesmen, and at Downe House— which has been given to the nation— Charles Darwin lived for forty years. The study in which he worked may be seen much the same as in his own day, and here also is the chair in which he sat when writing *The Origin of Species*.

THE MARTYRS' MEMORIAL, OXFORD

A well-known landmark in the university city of Oxford, the Martyrs' Memorial, an elaborate nineteenth-century pseudo-Gothic monument by Sir Gilbert Scott, is in honour of the Protestant martyrs, Archbishop Cranmer and Bishops Latimer and Ridley, Bishops of Worcester and London respectively. Latimer and Ridley were burnt at Oxford in 1555, Archbishop Cranmer one year later.

CHAPTER 12

FAMOUS MARTYRS

WE may find it difficult to associate Great Britain with the passion and brutality which led to a martyr's death, but martyrdom has nevertheless played a significant part in Britain's stirring history. Every martyrdom stresses the inescapable challenge which men of principle have had to face at moments of great crisis. Throughout history loyalty to ideas higher than those which the State may accept has driven men to prefer death to sub-servience to a creed which they believe to be wrong. Every martyr does not believe in free speech or religious toleration—the opposite is sometimes true—but he stands for loyalty to the highest as he knows it. He is not merely courageous. He is prepared to go to the last extreme to safeguard what he believes for the sake of future genera-tions. No martyr has suffered death in Britain for well over two hundred years, but in many parts of the world the Christian may find himself faced with the same alternative as that which con-fronted the English martyrs long ago. The same spirit that led men to give their lives for Christ's sake may make a poor peasant or an ignorant priest reject the demands of a totalitarian State, backed by all the armed might of modern militarism. And here and there as we wander through the length and breadth of Britain we may find a solitary memorial, the dedication of a church, the very name of the town itself, recalling the courageous stand which

some man or woman made against tyranny that we, in our turn, might be free to profess our faith.

And it is appropriate that we should begin our journey where the first recorded martyrdoms took place, at the Roman garrison towns of Verulamium and Caerleon. The town of St. Albans, built near Roman Verulamium, stands placid and undisturbed upon the edge of an upland plateau in Hertfordshire. On the crest the magnificent abbey church with its massive central tower dominates the situation, recalling the first of the English martyrs by its name and by its faith. We know very little of Alban himself. He was, the English chronicler Gildas tells us, a Roman soldier who sheltered a Christian priest and through conversation with the refugee was himself converted to Christianity. In doing this he defied the orders of the Roman emperor, Diocletian, who had ordered a general persecution of the Christian Church throughout the Roman Empire; he realized that no pagan ruler could long endure the continued existence of a society that placed its loyalty to God before its loyalty to the emperor. And so persecution spread from the con-tinental churches to the poor and uninfluential British Church and num-bered Alban among its victims. A church was built on the supposed site of the martyrdom, which the Mercian king, Offa, improved and possibly rebuilt towards the end of the eighth

THE NAVE OF ST. ALBANS ABBEY

The nave of St. Albans Abbey is one of the most massive works of Norman architects still extant. A feature of the pillars of the nave is the series of paintings recently uncovered and seen in the photograph on the two pillars nearest to the camera. The present abbey church was built early in the twelfth century on the site of a much earlier foundation, and was composed in part of materials taken from the ruined city of Verulamium, a quarter of a mile to the south. It takes its name from Albanus, a citizen of Verulamium, who was martyred late in the period of Roman occupation.

century, enclosing the miracle-working relics of the saint in a new shrine. Offa's abbey was in turn replaced by the existing building, which largely owes its birth to the Norman abbot, Paul of Caen.

In the four hundred years which followed the Romans' evacuation of Britain, all that the Romans had built, their towns, their roads, their bridges, fell into disuse and decay. One set of invaders, the Vikings, were pagans from Scandinavia, as rich in courage as in their desire for plunder. They sailed up the rivers in their longboats and found that the undefended churches and monasteries were often full of treasure. There must have been many victims, clergy and laity alike, of their pagan pride and brutality. The name of the pleasant town of Bury St. Edmunds, situated amidst a rich and fertile district, commemorates the best known of their victims. It recalls the East Anglian king, Edmund, who had his chief town here and who was shot to death by the Danes with arrows at the quiet village of Hoxne near-by, on

THE MARTYRDOM OF ST. ALBAN

This is the carving on the shrine of St. Alban in the cathedral. According to the legend, Albanus was executed by order of a judge of Verulamium because he confessed the Christian faith. The place of martyrdom was on a hill situated outside the precincts of the Roman city. When Christianity was generally accepted hundreds of years later under the Saxon kings the abbey was founded on the site.

HOXNE, THE SCENE OF ST. EDMUND'S MARTYRDOM

Hoxne, in the county of Suffolk, by the River Waveney, is associated with the martyr-dom of St. Edmund. A tablet on Goldbrook Bridge (above) records that this was where the saint was taken prisoner in 870 by the Danes. Edmund was a Christian king of East Anglia, born about 840. He was prominent in organizing resistance against the bands of pagan Norsemen who had been harrying the eastern marches of England for many years. There are two legends of his death, one that he was killed in battle, the other that he was martyred for his profession of Christianity.

20 November, 870. Nothing, except some ruins in picturesque gardens, remains of the abbey which was erected to house his bones, brought here in 903; but two noble churches, St. Mary's and St. James's—now the cathedral—bear witness to the town's former importance as a religious centre. Farther south in Essex the parish church of Greenwich recalls in its dedication another and later victim of Danish savagery, no less a person than Archbishop Aelphage of Canterbury. The Danish soldiers put him to death in April, 1012, with par-ticular cruelty in defiance of the protests of their own leader, Thorkell, because he had refused to pay the ransom they demanded.

From Greenwich we may now pass into Kent, to Aelphage's own city, Canterbury. Canterbury, important as the ancient capital of Kent, as the seat of the primate of all England, as the site of two of the richest and most important monasteries in medieval England, Christ Church (now the cathedral) and St. Augustine's (now a theological college), and as the first major town visited by all travellers from Dover to London, has had a long and fascinating history. The bare spaces around its cathedral, which today witness to the acrid smoke of burning buildings fired by Hitler's airmen, have themselves helped to prove Canterbury's antiquity, for they have revealed something of Canterbury's medieval and Roman past. Looking through the apple-blossom in spring-time towards the Bell Harry Tower of the cathedral, or walking through this city of many inns, the mind is instinctively watchful of the past, of cavalcades making their way to or from London, or of the pilgrims, immortalized by Geoffrey Chaucer, whiling away the time in story-telling as they made their way towards Harbledown and the great shrine in the apsed ambulatory of the cathedral. There is no longer a shrine behind the altar—though you may see the Black Prince's armour—but there once was and to it flocked pilgrims from all over England as well as from the Continent. This shrine, once rich with jewels, commemorated the most memorable of all the incidents in the city's history, the martyrdom of Thomas Becket, Archbishop of Canterbury.

MARTYRDOM AT CANTERBURY

"One martyr"—he meant Aelphage—"they had already," Archbishop Becket told his intently listening congregation at Christmastide, 1170, and he added that "it was possible they would have another very soon." The place of the martyrdom, then by the altar of St. Benedict in the north transept, can still be seen in the cathedral. The archbishop was an unusual personality, a histrionic, forceful, clever and religious man. He had served the king, Henry II, as an efficient chancellor. In securing his appointment as Archbishop of Canterbury the King thought that he had

rewarded a friend but found that he made an enemy. The King represented the traditional rights of the monarchy, the customs of the realm, which the Church represented by Becket sought to overthrow by the introduction of the newly-formed church or canon law and by exerting the superiority of the spiritual over the secular power. Four knights, hearing a violent outbreak on the part of the high-tempered King against his imperious archbishop, hastened to Canterbury to rid the realm of so "turbulent a priest." After a stormy interview with the archbishop at the monastery the knights made for the cathedral, where Thomas had gone to attend Vespers. Rushing the doors which he had ordered to be unbarred, the knights, after a short altercation with Becket, murdered him as he stood before the altar of St. Benedict.

SMITHFIELD MARTYRS

Although cathedral towns like Canterbury and small villages have had their toll of martyrs, there is one place which for nearly two hundred years was inseparably linked with the martyr's fate, Smithfield in London, now better known for another form of butchery. It was on what was then an open space north-west of the city walls, often made cheerful by games and joustings, that many a devoted man and woman were burned at the stake. It was here in March, 1401, that the first Lollard martyr, William Sawtre, paid the penalty of heresy. He was a follower of the priest and writer, John Wyclif, who demanded that the English should be allowed to read the Bible in their own mother-tongue and in other ways broke away from Rome. He had died in his own bed, but many of his followers were sentenced to burn for their ideas. Although Lollardy never completely

MARTYRDOM OF ST. THOMAS OF CANTERBURY

Thomas Becket, Archbishop of Canterbury, was murdered in the north-west transept of the cathedral by a group of four knights in 1170. A rich shrine was constructed and dedicated in 1220 in the presence of King Henry III. The rebuilt Trinity Chapel was thereupon named the Chapel of St. Thomas and the shrine was visited by hundreds of thousands of pilgrims every year until Tudor times. King Henry VIII, when the monasteries were dissolved, stripped the shrine of its treasures, and all that can now be seen is the place in the cathedral where it once stood.

died out, its fires began to burn sporadically and low. Yet Sawtre's death at Smithfield formed as it were the prologue to a long, frightful but courageous story. Nor was it for one thing only that men and women were burned here. Roman Catholics were burned for refusing to accept Protestantism. Protestants were sentenced for denouncing the Pope.

It was in the reign of "Bloody" Mary (1553–8) that Smithfield witnessed the greatest number of burnings, mainly because Protestantism was strong in the capital and Smithfield formed a convenient open space on which the sentences could be carried out. The list of martyrs is too long to be detailed, but as we gaze at modern Smithfield's busy crowds we may recall how the first of Mary's victims, John Rogers, who arranged and printed a Bible in English, walked to Smithfield on a February morning,

THE CHOIR OF CANTERBURY, LOOKING EAST

This view of Canterbury Cathedral shows the east end of the cathedral. The cathedral was founded by St. Augustine when he came to Kent at the invitation of Ethelbert, King of Kent, in 597. The present cathedral was started in the eleventh century and was added to at intervals from then until the fifteenth century. After the martyrdom of St. Thomas (see page 254) the cathedral became a popular centre of pilgrimage.

ENTRANCE TO THE OLDEST CHURCH IN THE CITY OF LONDON

Here is the half-timbered gatehouse of the church of St. Bartholomew the Great, Smithfield. The entrance is Elizabethan, but the priory of St. Bartholomew, with its church and hospital, was founded by Rahere in 1123. Within a few yards of the gatehouse is the site where some hundreds of martyrs were burnt at the stake for their religion, most of them during the Marian persecutions. Remains of burnt human bones and parts of the charred stakes were found during modern excavations.

BISHOP HOOPER'S LODGINGS

The old house in Westgate Street, Gloucester, is remembered as that in which Bishop Hooper spent his last night before being burnt at the stake. The Bishop had been trained for the Catholic priesthood, but was converted to the Reformed Faith and fled the country. On the accession of Edward VI he returned and was installed Bishop of Gloucester. Then when Mary came to the throne and sought to extirpate every trace of the Reformed Church he was seized and committed to prison, later being brought to trial and condemned as a heretic. He died at the stake in 1555.

accompanied by his sorrowing wife and eleven children, "ten able to walk and one sucking at her breast," a sight which aroused much sympathy.

If Smithfield was the scene of the majority of martyrdoms in the mid-sixteenth-century England, it had its counterparts in other parts of London and Great Britain. The execution-block on Tower Hill, of sombre memory, replaced the stake, by permission of Henry VIII, as the method by which

the death of two men, who refused to admit that the King was the head of the Church of England, was compassed. This open space outside the sternest and most fascinating of all royal palaces, sometime royal fortress, once royal zoo, and now a handsome watchdog of the destinies of a great city, has been the scene of many violent actions. Justice has not always been tempered with mercy; innocence has not vanquished reason of state. The Tower is today the finest museum in London, but even if it is on the "retired" list its every room remains redolent of past trouble. John Fisher, Bishop of Rochester, executed on Tower Hill on 22 June, 1535, was a learned scholar and a generous and saintly priest. Sir Thomas More, who had been Henry's Lord Chancellor, was an intelligent and cultured man whose gracious good-humour lasted to the end (6 July, 1535). "I pray thee," he told the lieutenant as he reached the steps of the scaffold, "see me safely up, and for my coming down let me shift for myself."

EXECUTION OF CHARLES I

One other place in London is worth visiting for the memories that throng it, memories equally harrowing as those associated with the Tower. As we may today walk down Whitehall, our imagination seldom carries us back three hundred years when a vast crowd thronged Whitehall from end to end to watch an event unique in British history, the execution of a king before the Banqueting Hall of the old royal palace of Whitehall. Crowds are indeed an inevitable link with martyrdom; they are drawn by mere sensation, by the sordid majesty of the spectacle, even by the courage of a lonely man. They had watched the Christian martyrs in the Colosseum at Rome and their successors suffering, be it at Oxford or Tyburn, Canterbury or Tower Hill, and now they crowded Whitehall. Was Charles really a martyr? Historians do not agree over the answer; but the King's obstinacy, duplicity and weakness tend to obscure the injustice of the sentence passed on him as well as his prolonged and sincere attachment to the principles of the Church of England; for a time his name appeared in the prayer-book, and more than one church has been named in his honour (e.g., King Charles the Martyr Church, Plymouth). "For the people," he told those within hearing from the scaffold, "I desire their liberty and freedom as much as anybody whomsoever; but I must tell you that their liberty and freedom consists in having of Government those laws by which their life and goods may be most their own. . . . If I would have given way to an arbitrary way for to have all laws changed according to the power of the sword, I needed not to have come here; and therefore I tell you (and I pray God it be not laid to your charge) that I am the Martyr of the People." However disliked and distrusted King Charles may have been, Parliament's action in executing him was undoubtedly unpopular; when the executioner held up the King's head, a long groan arose from the crowd.

But the martyrs' story cannot be confined to London. In Mary's reign the fires glimmered all over England. High-principled Bishop Hooper was burned in his own cathedral city of Gloucester. Carmarthen in Wales was the scene of the death of the Welsh-speaking Bishop Ferrar of St. David's.

OXFORD MARTYRS

But the most important victims in Mary's reign were reserved for one of the loveliest of English cities, the university town of Oxford. That busy place, full of gleaming spires, populous with students, has always been the centre of dispute and discussion, as becomes a community concerned with the pursuit of truth. The tourist who passes hurriedly through Oxford's crowded High Street, or even saunters for a moment in Magdalen's lush park, is barely able to catch a glimpse of the past, but he who stands silently in one of the more deserted of Oxford's

A FAMOUS WINDOW IN WHITEHALL

This window is in the façade of the Banqueting Hall of the unfinished Palace of Whitehall, masterpiece of the architect, Inigo Jones. A plaque in the wall commemorates the tradition that Charles I stepped through the window on to the scaffold which had been erected in Whitehall for his execution. There is some evidence, however, that Charles stepped out on to the scaffold not from the window, but through a specially constructed door. The execution of the King took place on 30 January, 1649.

IN STIRLING CEMETERY

This monument was erected in the cemetery of the parish church of Holy Rood in Stirling to the memory of the Wigtown martyrs. The martyrs, two ladies of Wigtown, were among the last to be put to death in the persecution of the Covenanters. They were tied to a stake far out in the Solway Firth at low tide and left to drown as the tide came in. Both were members of the band of Covenanters called the Cameronians.

quadrangles, or listens to the sounds of many bells, or visits Merton Library or Christ Church Hall, can hardly fail to catch something of the atmosphere of past Oxford, to perceive, however inadequately, how the intellectual vitality and principle of toleration which dignify a modern university slowly evolved. It was here, as the much-maligned Martyrs Memorial outside St. John's College commemorates, that Bishops Latimer, Ridley and Archbishop Cranmer paid the penalty for the acceptance of Protestantism. Hugh Latimer, a pithy preacher, now bowed down with years, was of indomitable faith. His companion, Nicholas Ridley, was a younger man and had been Bishop of London until the accession of the Catholic queen, Mary. The answers that he gave his accusers were rapier-like, but the issue had been pre-judged. On the evening before his death Ridley had supper with his keeper's family. "Tomorrow," he told them, "I must be married." Next day Ridley "in a furred black gown, such as he was wont to wear as a bishop, and a tippet of velvet, furred likewise about his neck, a velvet nightcap upon his head, and a corner-cap over it," and Latimer, "in a poor Bristol frieze frock, all worn, with a buttoned cap, and a handkerchief, a new long shroud hanging over his head, and a corner-cap over it," went to the place of execution "on the

THE MARTYRS' GRAVE AT WIGTOWN

Below is seen the Wigtown martyrs' grave (see page 260). The two martyrs, Margaret McLachlan and Margaret Wilson, were citizens of the town, the former over sixty years old, the latter under twenty. The vertical tombstone on the right is that of Margaret McLachlan, the large tombstone lying before it that of Margaret Wilson.

north side of the town, in the ditch against Balliol College." As the fire was kindled the old man told his younger colleague in words so often repeated: "Be of good comfort, brother Ridley, and play the man; we shall this day light such a candle by God's grace in England as I trust shall never be put out." Latimer was the first to die; after crying vehemently: "O Father of Heaven, receive my soul," he received "the flame as if embracing it." After he had stroked his face with his hands, and as it were bathed them a little in the fire, he soon died. "Ridley lingered much longer, for the wood was wet; in his terrible agony he called: 'Lord, have mercy upon me, let the fire come to me, I cannot burn.'"

DEATH OF CRANMER

Oxford's other major victim was a Cambridge man, Thomas Cranmer, the archbishop, now approaching seventy years of age. He was not the subservient office-seeker and coward that he has sometimes been called. He was a gifted writer of English prose and a learned and religious man. His guiding principle was his belief that the sovereign was appointed by God to be the head of the Church in England. If in other matters he hedged and sometimes changed his mind, to this principle he remained true. As soon as Mary became queen he was committed to the Tower of London and after prolonged discussion he was condemned as a heretic. He then retracted his opinions, but learning that such recantation was in any case vain he repudiated what he had said. In this struggle for his soul we must remember his old age, the constant pressure which his enemies brought to bear upon him and his own hesitant mind. He realized that his recantation had been a mistake, even a sin. "Ah, my masters," he said,

"always since I lived hitherto, I have been a hater of falsehood, and a lover of simplicity, and never before the time of my recantation have I dissembled." In bare feet, clothed in a long shirt, with long and tangled beard, he was taken to the place of execution. "And when the wood was kindled, and the fire began to burn near him, stretching out his arm, he put his right hand into the flames . . . oftentime he repeated 'This unworthy right hand!' And so long as his voice would serve him, and using often the words of Stephen, 'Lord Jesus, receive my spirit,' in the greatness of the flame he gave up the ghost."

Scotland had fewer martyrs than England, but the vigorous northern air, bracing mentally as well as physically, stimulated the spirit of controversy in the sixteenth and seventeenth centuries when the Scots turned away from the religion of Rome to the presbyterianism of John Knox and his colleagues. It was inevitable that men should die in the process of trying to defend or find what they held to be the truth.

SCOTTISH MARTYR

St. Andrews, doyen of Scottish universities, a town by the sea on the east coast, most frequented now for study and for golf, was once the scene of more violent conflict; for here on 2 March, 1546, the best known of the Scottish Protestant martyrs, George Wishart, was arrested, tried and burned. Wishart's death proved a stimulus to further action. It formed a motive for the brutal murder of the Catholic leader, Cardinal David Beaton, "a bloody butcher of the saints of God," as his enemies termed him, which took place a few months later.

If many parts of Scotland henceforth experienced comparative religious peace, the Lowlands were repeatedly disturbed by religious strife. And the

TOLPUDDLE CHURCH

This is the parish church of the quiet Dorset village of Tolpuddle, famous for a "martyrdom" which was very different in character from the religious martyrdoms recalled on previous pages. The Tolpuddle martyrs were six agricultural labourers who attempted to form a branch of the Grand National Trades Union in 1834 in defiance of the Government of the time and the employers, who were opposed to any form of organized labour. The six men of Tolpuddle were arrested, tried on charges of administering "oaths" and were sentenced to seven years' transportation. Popular indignation at this sentence did a great deal to further the cause of labour.

suffering to which this gave rise is summarized by what took place near Wigtown, whence the little Bladenoch river flows through the sands into the Cree river and so into the wider waters of Solway Firth. For it was the waters of Bladenoch which tested the faith of two Scottish presbyterians, members of a fanatical band of Covenanters known as the Cameronians who defied King Charles II. As an example to other disloyal subjects, two women, both Cameronians, an elderly widow named Margaret McLachlan and a young girl of eighteen, Margaret Wilson, were sentenced to be tied to stakes within the flood-mark of the water of Bladenoch. At low tide the women were attached to the stakes and then the salt water from Solway Firth slowly rose; as she died Margaret McLachlan's voice came over the rising waters:

> My sins and faults of youth
> Do Thou, O Lord, forget;
> After Thy mercies think on me,
> And for Thy goodness great.

A MONUMENT TO COVENANTERS

During the sixteenth and seventeenth centuries Scotland was repeatedly distracted by religious conflicts. In the reign of Charles II this gave rise to a severe persecution of the Covenanters, and there were many martyrs. Below is seen a gravestone on Magus Muir, St. Andrews, in memory of Covenanters who died for the cause.

CHAPTER 13

SMUGGLERS AND PIRATES

At the lowest extremity of the island of Barra, southernmost of the Hebrides, the little town of Castlebay stands dour and neat about its landlocked harbour. Today it is the centre of the western Scottish fishing industry, and behind its seventeen piers are concrete gutting tables, and curing and storing huts. At the height of the season the harbour is a hive of activity and the streets and jetties echo to the clump of fishermen's boots. Brooding over this busy scene from a small rocky islet in a corner of the bay stands a silent crumbling monument to Castlebay's romantic past: it is the ruin of Kismull Castle.

Four hundred years ago when Castlebay was merely a collection of rude huts this was a powerful fortress at which every day a strange scene was enacted. On to the stout ramparts strode a rough, bearded figure whose bellowing voice rang round the quiet waters, startling the roosting sea-birds into protesting flight. "The MacNeill of Barra has dined," declaimed this lusty herald, "the other lords and peoples of the earth may now dine."

Anchored beneath the frowning walls of Kismull Castle, stronghold of the proud and arrogant MacNeills of Barra, chieftains of the isles, lay their war fleet of *birlinns*, the finest ships in the whole of Scotland. These vessels, manned by fierce and piratical clansmen, ranged far and wide, preying on passing ships and holding crews to ransom, levying toll on all who entered those northern seas.

But one day the pirate fleet of the MacNeills seized an English ship. A complaint that could not be ignored was lodged by Queen Elizabeth's ambassador to the Court of King James of Scotland, whose problem was how to arrest his erring but powerful noble. Then a rival lord, the Mackenzie of Kintail, vowed to his worried master that he would bring the MacNeill to justice. By a piece of trickery he took the island chieftain prisoner and conveyed him to Edinburgh. Subsequently the Lord of Barra was released and pardoned, but his power began to wane, until today the only relic of this fierce sea-rover, whose proud boast was that his family had their own boat at the Flood, is the ruin of Kismull Castle.

Over on the mainland of Scotland the Solway Firth was for years a highway of pirates and smugglers, and today the bold and rocky Galloway coast holds many a romantic memory of those bad old days. One of the most famous spots along this stretch of coastline is Dirk Hatteraick's Cave, which has achieved the dignity of a name on the map.

This smuggler's cavern, which is to be found on the shore of Wigtown Bay, some six miles from Gatehouse of Fleet, was once the hiding-place of a notorious eighteenth-century Dutch smuggler named Dirk Yawkins, immortalized as Dirk Hatteraick in Sir Walter Scott's novel, *Guy Mannering*. Yawkins ran his cargoes of tea, tobacco and spirits over from the Isle of Man and landed them in a cove near Kirkcud-bright.

Once when Yawkins was landing a cargo at Manxman's Lake in the Dee estuary, two Revenue boats suddenly appeared and bore down on him, cutting off his escape. The bold Dutch-man is said to have weighed anchor and steered straight between the King's ships, tossing his hat contemptuously on to the deck of one and his wig on the deck of the other. Then he defiantly hoisted a keg of spirits to his masthead and outsailed the Revenue men.

Centuries ago Cheshire was an important maritime county, for her forty-mile coastline includes the tidal estuaries of the Mersey and the Dee. In early medieval times the beautiful old city of Chester was a considerable port. But as early as the reign of Richard II the port had already begun to decay by reason of "the abundance of sands which had cloaked the creek." By the time that Queen Elizabeth came to the throne the "shifting sands o' Dee" had so far done their fell work that a new harbour was urgently needed. In 1560 a collection was ordered to be made throughout the churches of the kingdom for a "New Haven," and soon after-wards Parkgate, several miles to the

CASTLEBAY, BARRA

The island of Barra is the most southerly of the larger islands in the Outer Hebrides. On an island in Castlebay stand the ruins of the stronghold of Kismull, a castle of the MacNeills of Barra, for many centuries chieftains of the Isles. The castle was built in the sixteenth century and continued to be a fortress until early in the nine-teenth century. Barra is associated in tradition with an era of piracy in northern waters when vessels manned by clansmen preyed on passing ships, held their crews to ransom and levied toll on those who sailed in what were then almost uncharted seas.

ON LUNDY ISLAND

There are tales of smugglers in every part of the country, but particularly where caves protected by rocky and precipitous coasts made detection more difficult. The island of Lundy, in the Bristol Channel, was ideal as a place of temporary concealment. Here tales of smugglers in later days are paralleled by even more bloodthirsty tales of pirates in the Dark Ages. This landlocked bay is known as the Landing Cove and may well have been used by sailors bringing contraband goods into the country. With the island as their headquarters they could distribute the contraband along the English coast.

west, came into being as the landing-place for the Irish packets.

Today Parkgate is locally known as "the village all on one side," for its quays and esplanade now face stretches of empty sand from which the errant tide has receded. But in its heyday Parkgate's narrow, winding streets saw much gaiety and social life, when the Irish trade was booming and Cheshire's brine baths were the fashionable mode.

But Parkgate saw other traffic, equally fashionable, albeit conducted under the cover of darkness to outwit the Revenue

men, and its dark, twisting warren of lanes and alleys between the quiet houses with their secret rooms and hiding-places knew the swift passage of smugglers with their illicit burdens. Contraband was both inward and outward bound at Parkgate, Chester, Hoylake, and sinister little Hilbre Island in the Dee estuary. For from Roman days the ancient Cheshire towns of Northwich, Nantwich and Middlewich have produced salt.

From ancient times salt was taxed in Britain, and as recently as the eighteenth century the salt dues from Northwich alone amounted to £85,000 annually. Smuggling of salt went on inland as well as by sea, and at Rudheath on the old "salt trail" leading out of the county the number of funerals at one time suddenly became startlingly numerous. At last a suspicious Revenue man ordered one of the coffins to be opened, and there, instead of a corpse, lay bags of salt!

Like deserted, grass-grown Hilbre Island, once the lair of smugglers and pirates, puffin-haunted Lundy Island, in the Bristol Channel, was for years the stronghold of nefarious sea-rovers.

Today Lundy is a privately owned domain whose tiny population under the beneficent rule of their "king" is thoroughly law-abiding. This three-mile-long granite crag, whose five-hundred-foot cliffs rise sheer from the sea, is the breeding place of many rare sea birds, and the abode of seals, ponies, deer and goats, while its inhabitants rear their flocks of sheep and cattle in quiet content. But in Lundy's roisterous past Algerian pirates roamed its mountainous paths, and Dutch and French privateersmen launched their raids from its rocky fastnesses. One sinister owner, M.P. for Barnstaple in 1748,

PRUSSIA COVE, NEAR PENZANCE

This is one of the many small natural harbours on the Cornish coast which were certainly the resort of smugglers in the eighteenth and nineteenth centuries. Smugglers preferred to style themselves free traders; they carried on for many generations a successful running fight against the coastguards. The most famous of all the eighteenth-century free traders was John Carter, who out of admiration for Frederick the Great styled himself the King of Prussia. Today Prussia Cove, his former "stronghold," is a well-known beauty spot. Nothing remains of Carter's old home.

BODINNICK, THE ROAD TO THE FERRY

The Bodinnick ferry crosses the River Fowey and links the port of Fowey with Bodinnick itself. Like every other coastal village in Cornwall, Bodinnick treasures many tales of intrepid smugglers in the eighteenth century and later. Cornish sailors never took kindly to regulations imposed by the central government. A tradition of independent action was firmly established, and the Act of 1779 which made the importing or exporting of dutiable goods without paying the duties imposed by law a felony provoked especial resentment in the south-west peninsula. Even in the nineteenth century a great deal of smuggling was carried on between Cornwall and Brittany.

bamboozled the Government into allowing him to ship convicted criminals to "colonize Virginia." It was some time before the authorities discovered that the gaolbirds got no farther than Lundy, where they were enlisted into Mr. Benson's private army of smugglers.

Of all haunts of smugglers and sea-rovers around Britain, the long indented coastline of Devon and Cornwall with its rocky coves and convenient creeks backed by wild and lonely moorland has for long held pride of place in history. Smuggling in Britain during the eighteenth and early nineteenth centuries was an important factor in the economic life of all classes. In 1787, for instance, no fewer than fifteen hundred articles of merchandise were dutiable, from silk to playing cards, while tea, salt, clothing and liquor were the most highly taxed of all.

The shipwrights of Mevagissey were famous for their speedy fishing-craft, and these were much in demand all round the coast, for they could easily outsail the few King's ships that could be spared from the wars to watch for smugglers. From Mousehole and Sennen, from Looe, Cawsand and

THE STAR INN AT ALFRISTON

This half-timbered Tudor inn is at Alfriston, on the River Cuckmere, about three miles inland from Cuckmere Haven. The haven was frequently used by the small vessels of early smugglers, who transferred their contraband to rowing boats and took them up the Cuckmere on moonless nights. Alfriston was said to have been the headquarters of a murderous gang of smugglers led by Stanton Collins. The regular rendezvous of the gang was the black-timbered Market Cross Inn at Alfriston.

Polperro, from Padstow, St. Just and Fowey, and from almost every town and hamlet fringing the sea, the "free traders" made regular trips to France, bringing over in one run as many as six thousand gallons of brandy and ten to twelve tons of tea.

The most famous eighteenth-century "free trader" in the whole of the West Country was John Carter, who so admired Frederick the Great that he styled himself the "King of Prussia." Today Prussia Cove, his former stronghold, which lies to the eastward of Mounts Bay, near Penzance, is a noted beauty-spot, but there is no trace of Carter's old home. A narrow ledge of rock divides this natural inlet into two havens, one of which is called "Bessie's Cove," after a Miss Bessie Burrows who in Carter's time owned a "kiddley-wink," or smugglers' inn, which stood at the head of the cove. On the opposite crag Carter and his eight brothers lived in a house impregnably built under the overhanging cliff, and into the bay below they regularly ran their cargoes.

A DARING RAID

But although the Carters were daring lawbreakers the Revenue men had a sneaking regard for the "king" and his gang who forswore violence and bore no grudges. Once the Excise men captured one of Carter's cargoes and stowed it along with other seized contraband in the Customs warehouse at Penzance. But the "king" had promised this cargo to a special client, and he determined to deliver the goods. Next day the Revenue men discovered that their warehouse had been broken into. But the only goods missing were those impounded from the Carters. Although the culprits were thus known the authorities respected their "honesty" and took no further action in the matter.

Not all smugglers, however, were of the calibre of the "King of Prussia," for around the Sussex coast where "owling" was equally rife the gangsmen did not balk at killings. The delightful old-world village of Alfriston, four miles from the coast at Seaford on the banks of the River Cuckmere, was once the haunt of a murderous gang led by an individual named Stanton Collins.

SUSSEX "OWLERS"

Alfriston's black-timbered Market Cross Inn with its secret hiding-places was once the regular rendezvous of this gang, the last survivor of whom died in 1895 in Eastbourne Workhouse. Here the "owlers" planned their coups, and along the winding waters of the Cuckmere they ran their luggers from Cuckmere Haven between Birling Gap and Seaford Head.

Collins and his men had a short way with any Preventive Officer who ventured to interfere. One Excise man began to patrol the cliffs near their beaching area at night, using whitened stones to guide his route. The smugglers discovered these and arranged them so that they led directly to the cliff edge. Unaware of his peril, the unfortunate man followed his usual trail and went over the cliff, but hung on by his hands. Then Collins and his henchmen appeared and stamped on the officer's fingers until he let go and crashed to his death on the rocks.

Across the border into Kent the ancient and picturesque villages of Goudhurst and Hawkhurst are the centre of a famous district of hop gardens. Goudhurst's church, which stands between giant elms, is so old that at the foot of its tower can still be seen the marks where the early villagers sharpened their arrow-heads. Guns for the Armada ships were forged in the

A COBBLED STREET IN RYE

The cobbled streets and old houses of Rye remain much as they were nearly a hundred and fifty years ago when the town was the headquarters of several bands of smugglers. The activities of these contraband runners were very different from those of the early free traders. What started as an adventurous calling had become a desperate career of crime. Smuggling gained added impetus after the close of the Napoleonic wars, when there were many desperate characters discharged from the forces and ready to turn a dishonest penny in any way open to them. Because of this the Coastguard Service was organized and a constant watch was kept along the coast. In a short time the smuggling racket on an organized scale was effectively checked by the coastguards.

near-by manor of Bedgebury, and here some of the first Flemish weavers came to teach their craft to Kentish workers. Damaged by land-mines and flying-bombs in the great air battles of the Second World War, Goudhurst still preserves memories of another battle which took place in the eighteenth century when a notorious smuggling gang which was terrorizing the district threatened to massacre the whole village.

The headquarters of this gang was at the neighbouring village of Hawkhurst, from which the smugglers took their name, their leader a scoundrel named Hugh Kingsmill. Today Hawkhurst is a charming place delightfully set in rural surroundings, whose picturesque old houses are romantically honeycombed with secret passages and mysterious hiding-places. The ancient inns are noted for the excellence of their food and the shopkeepers for their dignified old-world courtesy. But in the days of the "Hawkhurst Gang" honest men stayed indoors at nights when they heard the rumble of the smugglers' dog-carts laden with liquor and bales of silk and lace as the two-hundred-strong gang passed through from assignations as far apart as Shoreham, Lydd and Hastings. Because of the opposition of the good citizens of Goudhurst, Kingsmill prepared to carry out his murderous threat. The defence was organized by an ex-soldier named Sturt, and after a prolonged battle between the opposing forces troops arrived, the smugglers were defeated and Kingsmill hanged.

While the Alfriston and Hawkhurst gangs were running their illicit cargoes up from the Sussex coast, the lonely stretches of the Romney Marshes were also dotted by night with dim, hurrying figures. For here, too, smugglers had long been active. Led by a ruffianly farm labourer named Cephas Quested, one gang, called the "Blues" from the dim blue lights they carried, were ready to do battle with any Excise men bold enough to challenge them.

Soon after the opening of the nineteenth century the East Coast smugglers found themselves up against a doughty opponent in the person of Captain M'Culloch of the Royal Navy, whose preventive work eventually led to the establishment of the Coastguard Service. Two famous characters who gave M'Culloch and his colleagues plenty of

THE HARBOUR OF STAITHES

The little harbours of the North Riding of Yorkshire were as well adapted to serve as smugglers' haunts as the coves of Cornwall and South Devon. Staithes, pictured here, a perfect natural harbour (quite apart from the breakwater), is protected on every side but one by steep hills, with no easy access from the landward side until about a hundred years ago, when the track formerly leading into Staithes was built up into a road. Staithes was often a refuge of those seeking to escape the authorities.

trouble were "Smoker" Browning and "Stoney" Fagg, both of whom hailed from Robin Hood's Bay on the Yorkshire coast.

Robin Hood's Bay, or more properly Fylingdales, is a quaint little fishing-harbour, superbly set in a break of the cliffs which sweep from Scarborough to Whitby. The picturesque huddle of old fishermen's houses looks out over the curving bay, and its narrow, twisting streets wind steeply upwards to merge into the green background of Fylingdales Moor.

Before the advent of steel ships killed its trade Robin Hood's Bay, which once had a slender connexion with that romantic outlaw, was a port of some consequence, and its ships and men were widely known on the Seven Seas. It was the centre, too, of much smuggling, and in its rocky coves the old-time "stowholds" which could conceal the whole of a lugger's illicit cargo may still be explored. The bold "Stoney" Fagg, whose ferocity daunted many of the Revenue men, was eventually killed in a fight with four of the King's ships, and his companion in crime, "Smoker" Browning, shifted his activities to Kent, where he was finally captured.

SUFFOLK SMUGGLERS

Farther south, in ancient and historic Ipswich, where Chaucer's father once owned property and the great Cardinal Wolsey's parent plied his trade of butcher, a more romantic smuggling memory is preserved. For many years the creeks and havens of the Orwell estuary, from Felixstowe to the port of Ipswich itself, were the haunts of "free traders." But none perhaps was so bold and daring as the gang run by the self-styled "Captain" Bargood, a respectable merchant of Felixstowe, who for fifteen years outwitted the law.

One member of his gang, handsome boatman Will Laud, fell in love with pretty Margaret Catchpole, servant to a Mr. John Cobbold of Ipswich. Margaret was born near the village of Trimley in 1773, and entered domestic service at an early age. She was brave as well as pretty, for when only thirteen, her mistress having suddenly been taken ill, she galloped off for help on the back of an unharnessed Suffolk punch. She wanted her lover to give up smuggling, and several times he renounced the gang, only to rejoin.

ESCAPE FROM PRISON

After trying to trick her into marrying him, Laud finally wrote to her from London swearing that he had given up his evil ways and begging her to meet him in the metropolis. Disguised as a sailor the infatuated girl took one of her employer's horses without permission and galloped the seventy miles to London in just over eight hours. But there she was arrested for horse stealing, tried and sentenced to death. Through her employer's intervention her sentence was commuted to life imprisonment.

Then one day in prison the lovers came face to face, and together they plotted their escape. But ill luck still dogged them, for although the daring midnight dash over the spiked walls of Norwich Gaol was safely accomplished the couple were pursued and Will Laud was shot dead. Poor Margaret was put on trial for her gaol break and again sentenced to death. But again she was reprieved and this time sentenced to be transported. Only then did she find happiness, for in Australia she married a settler, had three children and died in 1841 at the age of sixty-eight. In Ipswich Museum is the skin of a lyre bird sent home as a curio by Margaret Catchpole.

IN OLD SCARBOROUGH

Since the Middle Ages there has been a seafaring community in the huddle of old houses under the castle hill at Scarborough, and many of this community, like those of Staithes and Robin Hood's Bay and Whitby, were of Viking descent and brought up to have scant respect for English lawgivers. Smuggling was rife along the coast, Scarborough and the ports near-by witnessing many daring deeds by the free traders.

IN OLD NORWICH

Tombland Abbey today looks through its medieval arch to the cathedral entrance. In the Middle Ages the piece of land known as Tombland was a constant cause of trouble between the citizens and the monks of Norwich Abbey. There were many riots against the increasing wealth of the monasteries at this time. An annual fair was held at Tombland, and fair day seldom passed without a riot. On one Sunday in 1272 there was a riot in which several lay brethren of the abbey were killed by the citizens.

CHAPTER 14

RIOTS, RISINGS AND REBELLIONS

THE whole constitution of Britain, as we know it today, is one forged in the white-heat of riot and rebellion. The very relationship between the Crown, Parliament and the people has been hammered out with sword and shield; the law itself has been more than once cast into the twin melting-pots of rising and riot to emerge tempered and moulded anew; even our religious freedom has been won only through bloodshed and burning. The things we now take for granted—freedom of speech, freedom of thought—had their beginnings in turbulence and violence.

There were risings against the Romans, against the Normans, against the throne for century after century; there were riots against unjust laws, against the introduction of new machinery, against the oppression of the monasteries. . . . It was from somewhere in Norfolk, which in those far-off days was almost completely cut off from the rest of Britain by the marshes of the Fens and the great stretch of sea which swept inland from where Great Yarmouth now stands, that the warlike Iceni, led by their gaunt warrior-queen, Boadicea, whose memory is commemorated by the chariot memorial near Westminster Bridge, London, swooped down on the newly-established Roman colonies at Camulodunum (Colchester), Verulamium (near St. Albans) and Londinium (London). All three places were virtually razed to the ground, and some seventy thousand of their inhabitants slaughtered, before the revolt was finally put down.

The flat lands of East Anglia's fenland, which in Norman times was a vast, steaming swamp, were the scene of Hereward's rising against the Norman conquerors. Ely, where the splendid pile of the cathedral now stands, was then an island entirely surrounded by reeds and mud and stagnant water, and it was from there that Hereward carried on his sporadic campaign of rebellion. For almost a whole year he and his little band defied the might of the Norman army, and even William the Conqueror recognized Hereward for the gallant warrior he was. The Conqueror rewarded the monks of Ely with the sum of £150 for their treacherous betrayal of Hereward, but soon after he marked his contempt for their action by finding a pretext to fine them something like £20,000.

Scotland has had its rebel heroes, too —Wallace and Bruce—though few will argue that these great patriots were rebels in the worst sense of the word. Certainly Wallace never acknowledged Edward I as his king, even though he was finally convicted of rebellion and high treason. But rebel or patriot, he was a man of courage and resource, a genius at military tactics, and a man of herculean proportions and great strength. He deserved a much better fate than that which finally overtook him. There is a memorial to him at Dryburgh and another at Stirling, where one can also see the sword which was by his side when he was finally betrayed. The Stirling memorial marks the spot where he gained his brilliant victory over the English on a hill near the Abbey of Cambuskenneth, while at Robroyston another monument marks the site of the house where he was sleeping at the time of his ultimate betrayal.

The days when Robert Bruce was waging his war of independence against the English constitute perhaps the most glorious period in Scottish history. Scotland possesses numerous associations with Bruce, but the best known of his adventures—the encounter with the spider—took place on the Isle of Rathlin, off the coast of Northern Ireland, and there may be seen the ruins of the castle in which he took refuge. Most famous of the Scottish associations is the field of Bannockburn, where Bruce won his great victory over the English, though there is little enough that is romantic in the cultivated fields which now cover the site of the battlefield. More romantic is Loch Trool, at the north end of which an enormous boulder balanced on a plinth marks the spot where Bruce scored his first victory over the English, by hurling down rocks on them from the heights of Mulldonach, and opened his campaign of independence.

Wales, too, had its heroic rebels waging campaigns of independence against the English. Greatest of these

IN GLEN TROOL

This boulder placed on a plinth on the heights of Mulldonach, near Loch Trool, Scotland, marks the spot where Bruce gained his first victory against the English in the Scottish wars of independence. In the course of the battle the Scottish troops hurled boulders down the side of the hill into the English below.

RUINS OF ELGIN CATHEDRAL

The Wolf of Badenoch, brother of King Robert III of Scotland, is a notorious example of the lawless behaviour of many nobles in medieval times. From his head-quarters in the district of Badenoch, Inverness-shire, the Wolf and his followers brought fire and destruction into the surrounding countryside on many occasions, once devastating Elgin Cathedral, which had been begun at the beginning of the thirteenth century and was then one of the finest churches in the whole of Scotland.

279

THE MEDIEVAL CATHEDRAL OF ELY

The draining of the Fens has only been carried out on a systematic scale during the last two hundred years. Before that Ely, with the surrounding district, was an island raised above the general level of morass and swamp. There was an abbey at Ely in Saxon times; later in the Middle Ages the Bishops held important civil as well as ecclesiastical rights, making the Isle of Ely in many ways a self-governing entity. It was here that Hereward the Wake organized a temporarily successful rebellion against Norman rule in 1070–1. Hereward and his men made themselves masters of the Isle, retreating into the marshes whenever danger threatened.

THE CATHEDRAL OF ST. ASAPH, NORTH WALES

This is another famous church which was destroyed during a medieval uprising.
There is a tradition that the see was founded in the sixth century by St. Kentigern.
The cathedral was certainly rebuilt in the fourteenth century in a modified style of
Decorated Gothic. Then during one of several rebellions led by the Welsh chieftain
and hero, Owen Glendower, whose struggle was not only against the English but against
Welsh people who favoured the English, it was fired and all its interior fittings destroyed.
That is presumably why the oldest woodwork is of a later date than the outer fabric.

was the heroic Owen Glendower, during whose rebellion the palace and cathedral of St. Asaph and the cathedral at Bangor were destroyed. Three times an English army was sent to subdue Glendower and three times it was forced to withdraw with its task unfulfilled. Even when his allies in England were defeated at Shrewsbury, and he himself defeated in an engagement which followed, Glendower was far from subdued. He went into hiding until the French, with whom he had concluded an alliance, landed twelve thousand men at Milford Haven. With ten thousand troops of his own Glen-

dower joined the French and the two armies advanced as far as Worcester, where they were confronted with the whole strength of the English army. For three days and nights the two armies were drawn up facing each other, neither anxious to attack. The Welsh and French with their provisions running short were the first to retreat —and the rebellion was over.

Shakespeare, who was never above adapting history if it made for good drama, is responsible for the confusion between Wat Tyler's rebellion of 1381 and Jack Cade's rebellion of 1450. In 1381 it was the unpopular

NORWICH CASTLE

The upstanding Norman fortress, now painstakingly restored and serving as a museum, was the centre of some of the bloody events of Kett's rebellion in 1549. Robert Kett was lord of the manor of Wymondham. He rallied the local peasants to revolt against the social abuses of the time, and in particular the increasing enclosure of common lands. Unable to obtain redress by a mere display of force, he seized Norwich at the head of sixteen thousand men and was only driven out after a royal army had been specially raised and sent to relieve the city. There is a tradition that the body of Robert Kett was hanged from the walls of Norwich Castle after his execution.

poll-tax which brought about local revolts in Kent and Essex, these in turn being the signal for a widespread insurrection to break out in twenty-eight counties. According to tradition, it was the insulting of Wat Tyler's daughter by a tax collector which fanned the spark of discontent into the flame of revolt. Tyler struck down the collector. Peasants gathered to support him and almost in an instant the whole of Kent was up in arms. Abbeys and manor-houses were attacked, charters and manor rolls were destroyed. Then came the attack on London. The Essex insurgents had already pitched camp to the north of the city, and when the men of Kent arrived on the scene the capital was in such a state of panic that the gates were flung open to admit them. Fleet Prison and Newgate Prison were burnt, John o' Gaunt's Palace was

THE ABBEY GATEWAY, BURY ST. EDMUNDS

In the fourteenth century the power of the monastic orders was still increasing; the abbots of many of the great monasteries were also landlords and empowered to impose what was in effect heavy taxation on the people, the proceeds of which went to elaborate the abbey buildings and provide the means of extravagant living for the officers of the monasteries. The unrest produced by this situation was one of the many causes of the Peasants' Revolt of 1381. During the revolt the peasant armies attacked many of the monasteries, including Bury St. Edmunds, one of the wealthiest houses.

ST. ALBANS ABBEY, THE GATEHOUSE

The abbey of St. Albans was another of the monastic establishments which was attacked by local people during the Peasants' Revolt of 1381. The strength of popular animosity against the Church at the time is illustrated by the fact that Simon of Sudbury, Archbishop of Canterbury, was not spared during one of the murderous attacks of Wat Tyler's insurgents. Although the revolt collapsed after the death of Wat Tyler at the hands of the Lord Mayor of London, it showed clearly the shape of things to come and began a train of events which led to the dissolution of the monasteries.

wrecked, Archbishop Sudbury was killed and his head placed over London Bridge. The Tower of London surrendered to the insurgents. The young king, Richard, met the rebels at Mile End and, later, at Smithfield. It was at Smithfield that Tyler put his hand to his dagger as he spoke with the King. In an instant, Walworth, the Mayor of London, who was at the King's side, had cut Tyler down with his sword. The insurgents began to reach for their weapons and it seemed certain that the King's little company would be slaughtered. But the King himself really saved the day. Riding towards the rebels he cried: "I will be your leader. Follow me." The rebels, to everyone's surprise, quietly followed him as he led the way towards open fields to the north. Walworth seized the opportunity to gallop back to the city and rally the citizens, arriving back on the scene with a powerful force while the King was still parleying with the rebels. With the odds no longer in their favour and their leader dead, the rebels dispersed and the rising was over.

Jack Cade's rebellion of 1450 was against the sins of the Suffolk-Somerset

CARFAX TOWER, OXFORD

Carfax Tower is the sole remaining part of St. Martin's Church, Oxford. The bell, housed in this tower, was used in the late Middle Ages to summon the townsfolk to arms whenever rioting broke out. Almost from the foundation of Oxford University there were differences between town and gown, aggravated by the fact that each part of the community had its own government. The town and gown riots were often serious and for long a curfew was imposed on the undergraduates. The bell of St. Mary's, which is the university church, was used to summon the scholars to arms.

THE LIBRARY AT KEN WOOD

This Georgian mansion was the home of Lord Mansfield at the time of the Gordon Riots in 1780. Lord George Gordon was the chairman of the Protestant Association which instigated the "No Popery" riots. Lord Mansfield, Lord Chief Justice at the time, had expressed himself forcibly in condemnation of the Protestant Association. During the disturbance the rioters destroyed Lord Mansfield's town house and then marched on Ken Wood. They were headed off by troops before reaching the house.

administration. Like Tyler before him, Cade, an adventurer of some education and military experience, led his men to London, where they were admitted to the city. But the rioting which followed turned the citizens against them and the rebels were forced to retire, and the revolt collapsed. Cade himself was caught and killed.

Robert Kett's rebellion of 1549 was directed against the illegal enclosures. On Mousehold Heath, overlooking Norwich, where the rebels encamped, they slaughtered some twenty thousand sheep as a protest against those landlords who kept their sheep on common land. After repeated assaults the rebels forced an entry to the city at Bishops Bridge, and among the many buildings which they sacked was the beautiful church of St. Helen, now part of a system of almshouses.

The rebels were finally driven from the city by an army of foreign mercenaries and the final battle took place on Mousehold Heath. Over two thousand of the rebels were killed, and Kett, who was captured in a barn at Swannington, was eventually hanged.

RIOTS IN NORWICH

Throughout the Middle Ages there were frequent risings and riots against the growing opulence of the monasteries. At Norwich the piece of land still known as Tombland, on which an annual fair was held, was a constant cause of trouble between the citizens and the monks. Seldom did fair-day pass without a riot. And on a Sunday in 1272 the citizens stormed the monastery, setting fire to it and killing a number of clerks and laymen. At Bury St. Edmunds there were grave riots in 1305 and 1327. On the second occasion twenty thousand of the townsfolk besieged the abbey with swords, spears and billhooks. The abbey gate was destroyed and the monastery pillaged. The gateway which stands today was built twenty years later and it is significant that it has grooves for a portcullis and apertures from which arrows could be fired against any attackers. There was more rioting in 1381. This was quelled, but only after much fighting had taken place.

GORDON RIOTS

London's worst riots were in 1780, when Lord George Gordon led some twenty thousand people in a protest march against the activities of the Roman Catholic Church. The march itself, from St. George's Fields to the Houses of Parliament, was orderly enough, but it attracted the worst element among the Londoners as it progressed, and that night they and the more fanatical among Gordon's followers started ransacking Catholic property. For four days the rioting went on, becoming steadily worse. Then came the burning of Newgate Prison, from where the mob, now reinforced by the released prisoners, went on to burn the house of Lord Mansfield, the chief justice, in Bloomsbury Square, and were only just prevented from burning his mansion at Ken Wood by the timely arrival of the military. The Bank of England and the Temple were both attacked, nearly every prison in the city was destroyed, and private houses were burnt and pillaged. The final riot lasted for thirty-six hours, and only when the military were given instructions to open fire was some sort of order restored.

The Luddite and reform riots of the nineteenth century resulted in the burning of Nottingham Castle and the tragedy known as Peterloo—an ironic twist on the name of the battle said to have been won on the playing-fields of Eton School. This was a period of low wages, unemployment and virtual starvation in Britain's industrial north, and when riots broke out things were made very much worse by the heavy-handed manner in which the authorities handled the situation. Peterloo was the outcome of an open-air protest meeting attended by sixty thousand people at St. Peter's Field, Manchester. The cavalry was called out, and in the fighting eleven people were killed and many injured.

At Nottingham there was rioting which resulted in broken machinery and the firing of factories. The worst outbreak was during the Goose Fair of 1831, when a great deal of property was damaged and the castle was burnt.

It was at Lyme Regis that the Duke of Monmouth, son of one of the mistresses of Charles II, landed with barely a hundred followers in an attempt to assert his legitimacy and proclaim himself James II. At Taunton he put up his standard and was proclaimed king.

Later, on the marshy area of Sedgemoor, Monmouth's brave little army of Devon and Somerset countrymen was routed. From the tall octagonal spire of Bridgewater Church Monmouth watched the royal army take up its position near Weston Zoyland. The village church at Weston Zoyland still has marks on its stones where the pikemen of the royal army sharpened their weapons in readiness for the fray.

Monmouth planned a surprise attack by night. The accidental discharge of a pistol as his men moved into position

THE LAST BATTLE ON ENGLISH SOIL

This roughly-hewn block of Cornish granite is in a meadow on King's Sedgemoor, Somerset. Known as the "Stone of Memory," it is a monument to the last battle on English soil which took place on 5 July, 1685, when the Duke of Monmouth made his ill-fated bid for the Crown. Monmouth's troops attempted a night attack on the royal army on the plain of Sedgemoor. The attack failed, and many rebels were killed.

GLENFINNAN

The Fort William area of Inverness-shire has numerous links with Bonnie Prince Charlie—Prince Charles Edward, the Young Pretender, grandson of James II, who in 1745 landed in Scotland and gained much support among Scottish people. Marching into England at the head of a well-disciplined force, he won several victories over the royal forces, but was finally defeated at the battle of Culloden. This memorial in Glenfinnan is set up at the traditional place at which the standard of revolt was raised before a gathering of clansmen in 1745 soon after Prince Charles had landed.

robbed the attack of its element of surprise, however, and took away the only real hope he had of victory. His ill-equipped army was completely routed.

Probably the most colourful of all risings in British history was that led by Bonnie Prince Charlie. It was as dramatic, as daring, as hopeful as the rising led by his father thirty years before had been colourless, negative and hopeless. The rising of 1715 was without organization, enthusiasm or support. It was at Braemar, where some Highland chiefs gathered on pretence of

attending a hunting expedition, that the Earl of Mar first flew the blue banner of the rising of 1715, and it was at Kelso, a Scottish town which looks curiously French, that James VIII was proclaimed, and the Scottish rebels united with the Jacobites who had risen in the north of England. But the English would not march north and the Highlanders would not go south. So came the skirmish at Preston, where the English rebels were bluffed into surrendering, and the indecisive battle of Sheriffmuir. From Montrose James was rowed out to a waiting boat—and the rebellion was over.

The rising of 1745 started in Inverness-shire when Charles landed near Moidart, on the coast of the county, with a handful of trusted officers, some borrowed money and arms for fifteen hundred men. The Highland chiefs, at first doubtful, flocked to his banner after Cameron of Lochiel had given them the lead. At Glenfinnan, eight miles from Fort William, a statue of Charles in Highland dress stands on the exact spot where he stood that day when the royal standard was unfurled. At Spean Bridge the first blood of the rebellion was shed, two companies of the Royal Scots being captured by the Highlanders. Edinburgh welcomed Charles with open arms, except for the garrison of the castle, who saluted him with hostile grapeshot. For five weeks after his victory at Prestonpans he held court at Holyrood. Then came the dash south—Carlisle, Manchester, Derby. Charles would have pressed on, but more cautious counsels prevailed. Small though his chance of success might have been had he gone on, it was smaller still once he started to retreat. Then came Culloden Moor, a grim game of hide-and-seek in the Highlands with £30,000 on his head, and eventually escape by ship to France.

THE HARBOUR OF PORTREE

Portree is a fishing village in the Isle of Skye, a modest place today which still recalls with pride its association with Flora Macdonald and Bonnie Prince Charlie. Flora Macdonald was one of the most devoted to the Jacobite cause, and she assisted actively when the Prince launched his ill-fated attempt to secure the throne. She was directly the cause of saving his life after his defeat at Culloden. Prince Charles had fled to the Isles. At Benbecula in the Hebrides his pursuers nearly caught him. Flora Macdonald concealed him and escorted him to Portree, whence he took ship to France.

CHAPTER 15

SIEGES OF HISTORY

IN MANY parts of Britain may still be seen reminders of those turbulent times when sieges were commonplace. The crumbling ruins of what were once wellnigh impregnable fortresses, and the defensive walls of such places as Colchester, Chester, York and Southampton, remain to remind us of the days when a determined garrison could close the gates or raise the bridges and retire behind the defences, as the citizens of Hull did when refusing admission to Charles I—an action which was followed by the Civil War during which Hull was twice besieged.

But because the Royalists never gained control of the Humber, and supplies and reinforcements could be obtained by water, the sieges of Hull lacked the ferocity and grimness that characterized many other Civil War sieges. How different was the siege of Chester by the Parliamentarians. At a time when an enemy force was entrenched in the suburbs, and the defences were already badly battered by two years of attack and siege, the citizens of Chester, with a gallantry that has seldom been equalled, responded nobly to an appeal by the King to hold out for him for eight days longer. Hurriedly the walls were repaired; additional fortifications were thrown up, the women working beside the men even after the enemy bombardment had begun.

Chester held out for those eight days, but the expected relief force did not materialize. Days became weeks and weeks became months, with the enemy bombardment continuing almost without respite. Every building outside the town walls was reduced to ruins. Within the walls everything made of metal that the defenders could lay their hands on was melted down to provide ammunition. Food supplies were cut off and the citizens were forced to live first on horseflesh and, later, on cats and dogs. And not until the last cat and dog had been eaten did that weary, starving, unwashed, but very gallant garrison agree to surrender.

At Colchester, where the garrison surrendered after a siege of ten weeks, the Parliamentarians were in no lenient mood. Two of the garrison commanders, Sir Charles Lucas and Sir George Lisle, were shot under the walls of the castle they had helped to defend. An obelisk marks the spot where their execution took place, and in St. Giles' Church a monumental slab is inscribed in their honour. The picturesque old Siege House at Colchester derives its name from the fact that its timbers are pitted with bullets fired during the course of the siege.

The siege of Gloucester, which probably marked the turning point of Parliamentary fortunes, was perhaps the most important siege in the whole Civil War. The Royalists, having taken Bristol, dared not march on London while Gloucester remained hostile in their rear. So they laid siege to it. But the citizens, after first destroying those parts of the city outside the defensive walls, defended the remainder valiantly until relief forces arrived from London.

Because of the positions they occupied in what was at one time a no-man's-land between England and Scotland, Carlisle and Berwick-on-Tweed endured many a siege. Berwick, at the mouth of the Tweed, changed hands no less than thirteen times before it was declared a neutral town in 1551, and to this day for certain legal purposes it is neither in England or Scotland. Considerable remains of the early defences still exist.

Carlisle was besieged for ten days by Robert Bruce, who had sworn to eat no flesh until he had avenged himself on the garrison of the castle. But the citizens of the town defended themselves so valiantly—they hurled great stones on the heads of the besiegers whenever an attempt was made to storm the walls—that Bruce was eventually forced to raise the siege. Sixty-five years later the town was again besieged by the Scots, and on that occasion many of its buildings were burnt by the flaming arrows which were fired into the roof-tops. Then, in 1644, came the great siege of the Civil War. Carlisle was garrisoned by seven hundred Royalists. Leslie, with four

THE WALLS OF SOUTHAMPTON

Southampton has been an important port and garrison town since the early Middle Ages. The walls, of which a nearly intact length is illustrated, date from the fourteenth century at a time when the wars between England and France were at their height. The town was often subjected to French attack; that of 1338, in the reign of Edward III, resulting in the town being plundered and burnt after its capture. Southampton has been one of the chief ports from which British armies have embarked for foreign service from the time of the twelfth-century crusades to the Second World War.

THE SIEGE HOUSE, COLCHESTER

This picture shows bullet holes in the timber front of the Siege House at Colchester.
The holes derive from the siege of Colchester in 1648, one of the fiercest of the Civil
War, when the Royalists held off the Parliamentarians for seventy-six days. The
Parliamentarians were in no lenient mood after the surrender, and two of the comman-
ders of the garrison, Sir Charles Lucas and Sir George Lisle, were shot.

thousand men, destroyed the bridges, burnt the suburbs and laid siege to the town. That was in October. By February the defenders were living on horseflesh. By June even that was a luxury. Dogs and rats were the staple items of diet and the garrison were so feeble that they could scarcely walk many yards at a time. Yet when discussing surrender terms they were still audacious enough to make the envoys drunk on the town's only remaining barrel of ale, themselves drinking water, so that the envoys might go away again with the idea that the garrison were well supplied. The trick appears to have succeeded, for surrender followed on honourable terms and the garrison marched out with colours flying.

On the south bank of the Tweed, where it divides England from Scotland, is Wark Castle—besieged many times by virtue of its position. On one occasion the besieged garrison was headed by the

NORHAM CASTLE, NORTHUMBERLAND

In the foothills of the Cheviot range a large number of small castles or fortified houses were built between the twelfth and fourteenth centuries. In view of the continued hostilities between the English and Scots such fortified manors were essential if agriculture was to be carried on without interruption. Invading armies generally by-passed a castle where they would have sacked an unfortified house. Norham was one of the most important fortresses in the border country; from the twelfth century, when it was built, until the close of the wars between England and Scotland, it suffered numerous sieges, mainly unsuccessful ones. For a time it was held by the Bishops of Durham, who had special civic as well as religious privileges.

Countess of Salisbury, whom Edward III thanked personally after the Scottish besiegers had withdrawn. The tale that the Order of the Garter was founded at Wark Castle, when Edward smilingly returned a garter the countess had dropped, is now discredited by historians. Norham Castle, too, withstood many a siege in those days because of its position close to the ford by which English and Scottish armies invaded each other's territory on many occasions.

During the Civil War the Parliamentary forces demolished many a castle after taking it by siege. Beeston Castle in Cheshire was demolished in this way after it had surrendered. Today a few crumbling ruins perched precariously on top of what appears to be a sheer, unclimbable wall of sandstone still give an excellent idea of how strong this fortress must have been before artillery came into general use. History records, however, that the castle surrendered to

Edward when it was garrisoned by Simon de Montfort's men, and later, without striking a blow in defence, to the Duke of Lancaster—this after Richard II had thought it so impregnable that he stored his gold and jewels there. In the Civil War the castle was twice besieged. During the second siege temporary relief was provided by a whirlwind sortie on the part of Prince Rupert, but when he and his men left again there was to be no further relief. Food and ammunition dwindled steadily. Then came the Royalist defeat at Rowton Moor—and the position of the garrison became hopeless. The siege had lasted nearly a year when they finally surrendered on honourable terms, and provisions had run so short that they were living on cats' flesh.

Raglan Castle, a picturesque stronghold in Monmouthshire, was also partly demolished after its capture by the Parliamentary forces. The great tower, which had sustained hardly any damage during the siege itself, though twenty-pound shots were pumped into it at the rate of sixty a day, was undermined and made to collapse. It was at Raglan that Charles took refuge after the battle of

ON THE ROCKY COAST OF NORTHUMBERLAND

Bamburgh Castle is built on a cliff overlooking the North Sea and commanding the coastal lowlands of Northumberland. A small village today nestles under its walls, but for the most part it remains in appearance much as it was when it was built in Norman times, though only the keep of that first castle has survived, while the outer walls and the other buildings are new or heavily restored. The castle rock was fortified long before the Norman occupation, its first traditional siege being during the war between Northumbria and Mercia, when it was attacked and almost captured by Penda, the powerful and warlike King of the Mercians, in 642.

CHEPSTOW, MONMOUTHSHIRE

The castle of Chepstow (see page 193) suffered a long siege by Parliamentary troops during the Civil War. The Constable of the castle was Sir Nicholas Kemys. With a small garrison he held out against the Cromwellian army until all the provisions of the castle had been exhausted. Even then he refused to surrender, hoping to evacuate by boat across the River Wye, but one of the besiegers swam the river armed with a knife and cut the boat adrift. The garrison wasted away from starvation and the castle was eventually taken by assault, nearly half the defenders being killed in the fight.

Naseby. He left again in September, 1645, and the siege began the following June. The Marquis of Worcester, who commanded the garrison, although nearly seventy years of age, replied defiantly to a summons to surrender, saying that he had "made choice (if it soe pleased God) rather to dye nobly than to live with infamy." After ten weeks, however, he accepted honourable terms of surrender. The brave old Marquis died a few months after the end of the siege.

Cromwell himself marched to subdue Chepstow Castle, the crumbling ruins of which rise from a rock overhanging the Wye. In the days when it was first built the landward side of this stronghold was defended by massive walls, lofty towers and a moat. A drawbridge and three portcullises guarded the entrance. Sir Nicholas Kemys and a garrison of a hundred held out against Cromwell's much larger besieging force until their provisions had run out. Even then they refused to surrender, hoping to escape by boat. But one of the besiegers swam the river with a knife in his teeth to cut the tow-rope of the boat. With the garrison growing steadily weaker and weaker for want of food, the castle was eventually taken by

RAGLAN CASTLE

Raglan was one of the last of the medieval castles intended for military use. The present ruins date from the period 1450–1650. The keep is of a hexagonal design and the moat is still well filled. During the Civil War it was garrisoned in the Royalist cause. The Constable, the Marquis of Worcester, held the castle intact for long after the defeat in the field of the Royalist armies. After a siege of six weeks in 1646 the Marquis accepted honourable terms of surrender from the Parliamentarians.

ANCIENT CASTLE, MODERN MANSION

Arundel Castle today is the seat of the Dukes of Norfolk, the main range of its buildings being a comparatively modern imitation of the Gothic style. From the time of the Civil War until the nineteenth century the old castle lay in ruins. Before that it had been three times besieged since the building of a Norman fortress at the end of the eleventh century. In 1102 it withstood a long siege, when it was held by the rebel baron, Robert de Bellême. Thirty-seven years later it was besieged by King Stephen in his war with the barons; once more it fell to a besieging force at the time when it was being defended for the Royalist cause during the great Civil War.

assault, Sir Nicholas and forty of his hundred dying in the last skirmish.

Donnington Castle, the remains of which dominate a wooded rise overlooking the Kennet, about a mile from Newbury, suffered badly during a siege by the Parliamentary forces. And what a siege it was!—lasting, on and off, for two years. The castle, commanding the road from Oxford to Newbury, was a place of some importance, and after their first attack had been beaten back the Parliamentary forces brought up an artillery battery which bombarded the castle incessantly for twelve days, reducing it wellnigh to ruins. Three of the towers and part of the outer wall were demolished by the guns. But still the defenders refused to surrender. The besiegers brought up reinforcements and the bombardment started again, with the result that the end of the Civil War found only the main gateway and a portion of the castle walls still standing.

Berkeley Castle, where the murder of Edward II took place, was more fortunate, Cromwell returning it to its owners on condition that the battlements were destroyed. In those days entrance to the castle could be gained only by passing through three gates, each protected by a portcullis. Even so it surrendered to the Parliamentarians after a siege of only nine days. In the west door of the church may still be seen bullet-holes made by the firing of the besiegers. This castle was also the subject of a number of unusual sieges by the plaintiffs during a lawsuit starting in the fifteenth century between Lord Berkeley and his cousin and lasting for almost two hundred years.

Sieges, it will be seen from this, were not only caused by war in those times of unrest. Caister Castle was besieged for over a year by Thomas Mowbray, Duke of Norfolk, who, ten years after the death of Sir John Fastolf, claimed that that bluff old knight had given the castle to him. The Pastons, who were occupying the castle at that time, held out for a year before they surrendered "from sore lack of victual and gunpowder." When Mowbray died five years later, however, the castle was eventually restored to the Pastons by the King.

Castle Rising, the finest specimen of a ruined Norman castle in Norfolk, was besieged at one time by the citizens of the near-by port of King's Lynn. The citizens strongly objected to the fact

IN PENDENNIS CASTLE

Pendennis is specially distinguished in that it was one of the last few castles to hold out for the Royalist cause during the Civil War against overwhelming forces of Parliamentary troops. It was defended heroically by one John Arundell, who rallied his garrison for nearly six months through the whole summer of 1646 against the Parliamentarians under the command of John Fairfax. The castle lies at the eastward end of the Falmouth peninsula and was built in the reign of Henry VIII.

that one-third of the customs they paid went to the owners of the castle. They must have had either might or right on their side, for it is on record that the siege brought this state of affairs to a sudden end.

Do not imagine for one moment that a besieged garrison always submitted tamely to the process of being invested by the besieging troops. Far from it. The Royalist garrison of Borstall House indulged in many a daring sally when they were besieged during the Civil War. They forced labourers from all parts of Buckinghamshire to join the garrison. They raided farms to obtain crops and cattle to supplement their dwindling provisions. They even kidnapped several of the principal inhabitants of the district and held them to ransom.

Kenilworth Castle was sustained by a similar intrepid garrison during a siege of six months in 1265. The garrison sallied forth time and time again, and once at night, while away from their

THE CASTLE OF STIRLING

The Scottish lowlands, rather than the border country, were the cockpit of fighting between the English and Scots for hundreds of years. Stirling was one of the castles on the fringe of the lowland belt which witnessed some of the fiercest engagements. To the north the highlands were usually under Scottish control, to the south the lowlands remained disputed territory. Among the many sieges which the garrison of Stirling suffered was one when it was held by the English in 1314 and was besieged and captured by the forces of Robert the Bruce. Its last siege was in 1746, when it was attacked by Prince Charles Edward, who was compelled to raise the siege before overcoming it.

EDINBURGH CASTLE

Strikingly similar in its situation to Stirling, which it faces, as it were, across the fertile lowland belt, Edinburgh Castle has also suffered many sieges, including an unusually prolonged and savage one in 1545, when it was unsuccessfully attacked by the English forces who had, however, captured and burnt most of the surrounding town. The English forces again laid siege to it in 1573 and were this time successful in capturing it. In the Civil War it was held for the King, but surrendered in 1650.

stronghold, they were surprised by Prince Edward, who sent them racing back to the castle minus several of their number and with their leader, Henry de Hastings, forced to swim the moat in order to get back safely.

In the Civil War Kenilworth cast in its lot on the wrong side. And how bitterly it has paid the penalty! Today it is a ghost to which Sir Walter Scott has given immortality. Moss and ivy grow on the crumbling walls. Staircases end in mid-air and grass carpets the great banqueting hall. Ruined though Kenilworth is, it needs but little imagination to picture it as it was just after the battle of Evesham, when de Hastings and his little band withstood that six-months' siege. They were a saucy band, those defenders of 1265.

When the Archbishop of Canterbury arrived to ex-communicate them they arrayed their own chaplain in a borrowed cope and stationed him on the walls to excommunicate the archbishop! For week after week they held out until the whole castle was roofless. Even then it was the enemy within—hunger and disease—rather than the enemy without which brought about the castle's fall.

Arundel Castle, which has been constantly rebuilt so that it is now a palatial residence rather than a stronghold, once withstood a long siege—little short of a year—when it was held by Robert of Bellême during his struggle for the throne occupied by Henry I.

Anyone who has seen Edinburgh Castle, perched high on its great mass of volcanic rock, will understand why even Cromwell, whose troops reduced so many other fortresses, was daunted at the thought of having to besiege it. He persuaded the garrison to surrender

THE CASTLE OF BRAMPTON BRYAN

The little castle of Brampton Bryan in Herefordshire was in the great Civil War most gallantly defended against the Royalists by a woman, Lady Brilliana Harley, while her husband was away fighting for Parliament. Several times she was called upon to surrender, but despite the hardships of the garrison refused. At last the Royalists retired, but, worn out with the strain, Lady Brilliana died shortly afterwards. The following year the siege was reopened and the castle surrendered.

ALNWICK CASTLE, NORTHUMBERLAND

Alnwick Castle is here photographed from the Lion Bridge. There was a Norman castle on the site, one of the many fortresses built for the Norman barons to defend their flanks from insurgent English and Scots. Early in the fourteenth century the Percy family took possession of the castle and rebuilt it. Though there have been many modern additions, parts of the medieval stronghold still survive. The castle suffered several memorable sieges by the Scots during the border wars.

by threatening to undermine the rock itself and blow up both rock and castle.

Women played a prominent and heroic part in many a siege. Brampton Bryan Castle was heroically defended by a woman, Lady Brilliana Harley, against the Royalists at a time when the whole of the surrounding district was predominantly Royalist. When news of the intended siege reached her she strengthened the defences, had the moat refilled and laid in stores of food and ammunition. The garrison was placed under the joint command of the family doctor and a sergeant named Hackluyt. Six hundred Royalists besieged the place for a month, but achieved so little that reinforcements were sent from Gloucester. The besieging troops were then placed under the command of Colonel Lingen, himself a Herefordshire man, who brought personal enmity into the prosecution of the siege. But he achieved no greater success than Sir William Vavasour before him and finally withdrew when news of the Royalist defeat at Gloucester was received. Lady Harley lived to witness

CARRICKFERGUS CASTLE, COUNTY ANTRIM

The picturesque and important castle of Carrickfergus, situated on Belfast Lough in County Antrim, has been the scene of many serious sieges such as those in 1315, 1642 and 1689. The last of these was during the same campaign by the forces of James II that included the siege of Londonderry (see page 305), and the Battle of the Boyne. The castle was built in the late twelfth or early thirteenth century.

her triumph, but worn out with the strain died soon afterwards. The following year the siege was reopened, heavy artillery being used to break down the defensive outworks, and surrender followed.

Another gallant woman defender during the Civil War was the Countess of Derby, who held Lathom House for three months against Parliamentary troops commanded by Sir Thomas Fairfax himself. So successful was her defence that when the siege was raised because of the approach of Prince Rupert the besiegers had lost over six hundred men out of a force of three thousand, while only half a dozen of the three hundred defenders had been killed. Several times the countess was called upon to surrender, but each time she refused. And, although her children were with her, she even refused to take advantage of a free passage from the besieged building which her husband had requested Fairfax to offer her.

The defence of Lathom House was a spirited one. Several times the defenders took on the role of attackers. During one of their sallies they killed thirty of the enemy and took six prisoners. On another occasion they killed fifty of the besiegers and succeeded in spiking several of the guns which were bombarding the mansion.

Corfe Castle, the ruins of which occupy a commanding position overlooking a gap in the Purbeck Hills, was also defended by a woman, Lady Bankes, wife of the Lord Chief Justice, who held it for the King. It was, in fact, one of the last places to hold out for Charles and was finally captured only through treachery.

The castles which sprang up all over Britain in Roman and Norman times were built with only one object in view —to resist attackers, and if necessary to withstand a prolonged siege. Few of the Roman castles are left today. Much more numerous are the massive strongholds which were built between the Norman conquest and the reign of Henry VIII. For the most part these medieval castles are of great size, thick walls linking several defensive towers to enclose the courtyard. From slits in the towers the archers could open fire on the besiegers. Outside the walls is a moat which in those days could be

crossed only by the drawbridge. The massive entrance gate was covered with plates of iron and further protected by a portcullis which could be let down in front of it. Sometimes there were two or even three portcullises to protect the main entrance. From a projecting parapet overhead molten lead and boiling water could be poured down on the attackers. Water could also be poured from this parapet on to any fire which the besiegers might start in an attempt to burn down the castle doors.

With castles so strongly defended it is no wonder that the attackers in the days before artillery came on the scene were often content, once their first attack had been beaten off, to settle down so that supplies could not reach

SIEGE OF LONDONDERRY

James II had already fled from England. His Catholicism and his persecution of the Covenanters had proved too much for the patience of his English subjects and he had taken refuge in France after William of Orange had been invited to assume the throne of England. He spent most of the rest of his life in retirement, but in 1689, the year after his flight, he attempted an invasion of Ireland, lay siege to the ancient walled town of Londonderry and was finally defeated at the battle of the Boyne. He retired once more to France and made no further efforts to regain the throne. Cannon is seen here on the ancient walls. The town was heroically defended during the siege of 1689.

the garrison and wait for time to do the rest.

But when time did not seem to be working in their favour they would bring up battering-rams and primitive tanks in attempts to breach the castle walls. Huge catapults would be used to hurl rocks and boulders among the defenders, while movable towers and scaling ladders were used in attempts to surmount the walls.

When he besieged Bamburgh Castle, where the Earl of Northumberland was holding out, William Rufus had the idea of building a mound from which he and his men could see right into the castle courtyard. From this mound they watched all the preparations made by the defenders, and were able to make the necessary countermoves whenever the besieged garrison looked like preparing to sally forth in search of fresh provisions. Traces of this mound may still be seen.

Bluff and counter-bluff, trickery and betrayal—all played their part in these sieges of old. Edmund, besieged by the Danes for so long in one of his castles that the garrison were on the verge of starvation, bluffed the enemy by causing the only bull left in the castle to be fattened with what little wheat

PEMBROKE CASTLE

Almost all medieval castles utilized as the first line of defence some natural feature of the countryside. So Pembroke is defended on three sides by a natural moat and on the fourth by the steep cliff on which it is built. The first castle on the site was built by the Normans when they were seeking to add Wales to their dominion. A new castle was built in the thirteenth century, from which most of the present ruins date. It played a major part in the conquest of Wales by Edward I. In 1648 it was one of the last Royalist strongholds, but was captured after a short and sharp siege of seven weeks.

FORTRESS OF THE MEN OF HARLECH

Yet another castle in an almost impregnable position, Harlech was one of the line of fortresses built by Edward I to consolidate his victories in Wales. It linked with Caernarvon and Conway in the north and with Aberystwyth in the south. The siege which inspired the song, Men of Harlech, *took place during the reign of Edward IV in 1468, when victory for the Yorkists was complete in many parts of the country and the Wars of the Roses seemed to be drawing near to their close. Harlech was held by the Lancastrians with fearless courage and in the face of great odds. Harlech was one of the last castles in Wales to hold out in the Royalist cause during the Civil War.*

remained. The bull was then allowed out of the castle as if it had wandered away by accident and was caught by the Danes, who, eyeing its splendid condition, concluded that the defenders had provisions enough to withstand the longest siege and accordingly withdrew their forces.

Alnwick Castle, one of the most formidable strongholds in northern England, was saved by a trick when it was held by the Earl of Northumberland against Malcolm III of Scotland.

A member of the garrison rode out as if to surrender, the keys of the castle dangling from his lance. But when Malcolm himself advanced to receive them the lance was immediately lowered and thrust through his heart. In the confusion which followed, the King's eldest son, rushing to avenge his father, was also killed, and the intrepid horseman who had initiated the exploit swam his horse across the Aln at a spot which was afterwards named Hammond's Ford in honour of the remarkable deed.

307

The strength of Harlech Castle, which with Conway ranks as probably the finest castle in the world, may be gauged from the fact that in its early days it was once held—and held successfully—by a garrison of only twenty-five. It was the last fortress in Britain to hold out for the House of Lancaster and the last in Wales to surrender to Parliament during the Civil War. Of its surrender to Henry IV there is an interesting tale. The garrison commander, who boasted that he would hold out so long that the siege would be talked about even across the sea in France, was finally induced to surrender by Sir Richard Herbert on honourable terms, which included the sparing of his life. But the King at first refused to honour the terms. Sir Richard countered that by demanding that either the garrison should be returned to the castle and the siege commenced afresh or that his own life should be taken at the same time as that of the garrison commander. Faced with these alternatives, neither of which suited him, Henry agreed to honour the terms.

THE TOWN WALLS OF TENBY

Many who think of Tenby in Pembrokeshire as a holiday resort are surprised to learn that it also is one of the most historic towns in South Wales, with a history which goes back to before the Norman Conquest. The medieval town walls shown here have been restored, but some at least of the fabric of the towers is original. Tenby also has the ruins of a medieval castle. During the Civil War Tenby, with its castle, was a stronghold of importance, and was taken and retaken by each side several times. When Cromwell laid siege to the place in 1647 it was most heroically defended by Royalists, though like other Royalist castles it fell finally to the Parliamentarians.

CHAPTER 16

WITCHCRAFT

BELIEF in witchcraft was once almost as widespread amongst Christian people as it is today amongst backward and uncivilized races. Three centuries ago many people in Britain believed that witches existed in large numbers and constantly used their sinister powers to harm or help their neighbours. Every unexplained calamity was put down to their work. If a man died suddenly, went mad, or suffered from a wasting disease, he was thought to be bewitched. If murrain broke out amongst the cattle or the crops failed, if ships were wrecked at sea or a barn caught fire in the village, some local sorcerer was blamed, and so it was with minor mishaps like the souring of ale or the refusal of butter to "come." On the other hand, if a young girl wanted a love-potion or her mother needed a remedy for some ache or pain it was to the white witch that they turned in faith that he or she could help.

Stories of once known and dreaded witches are told in every part of Britain. Some are very old, but others date only from a comparatively short time ago. The Image House at Bunbury, in Cheshire, is a visible proof that people still believed in sorcery as late as the mid-nineteenth century, notwithstanding the educational advances that had already been made by then. This cottage stands by itself on the high road outside the village. It is quite an ordinary small dwelling and would scarcely be noticed at all but for the

fact that its walls are covered with curious stone faces and figures. It was once the home of a poacher, who having been caught red-handed was transported for seven years. When he returned to England he settled in the Image House, and there he fashioned images of everyone connected with his trial. Judges, policemen, gamekeepers and witnesses were all included. When they were finished he solemnly cursed them and set them on his house-walls for all to see. He firmly believed that by so doing he was bringing evil on his enemies, and there is little doubt that most of his neighbours believed it also.

Later instances of a belief in sorcery are found. In 1863 an angry crowd in the Swan Inn at Sible Hedingham seized an old French fortune-teller named Dummy and hurled him three times into a near-by brook, because a woman declared he had bewitched her. He never recovered from the effects of this brutal treatment and died soon afterwards; and his persecutors were extremely lucky to escape with only six months' imprisonment.

Again, in 1879, William Butler of Etling Green was charged at East Dereham Petty Sessions with striking a woman because, as he declared, she had enchanted him by burying a "walking-toad" near his house. The magistrate was so astonished at this survival of witch-belief at that late date that he asked if Butler was quite sane. He would probably have been even more surprised had he known that nearly seventy years afterwards another East Dereham justice would be hearing a similar case. In 1947 an Army pensioner assaulted a woman for bewitching him by means of a bunch of flowers.

But if traces of the old faith still linger here and there they are happily now only rare exceptions. In former centuries everyone accepted magic as a fact, and the witches themselves believed as firmly in their supposed powers as did their victims. Almost every parish contained at least one sorcerer, and dabblers in witchcraft were then to be found amongst people of all ages and both sexes, and in every rank.

Even royal blood was no guarantee against the taint of sorcery. In North Berwick Church a witch-coven held midnight meetings under the leadership of Francis, Earl of Bothwell. If James I and VI had died without an heir, Bothwell might well have succeeded to the throne, and there seems little doubt that he and his associates plotted the death of the King by magic, and perhaps by more practical means also. When the plot was discovered Bothwell fled to Naples, leaving his followers to suffer for crimes in which he had shared.

In 1441 Eleanor Cobham, Duchess of Gloucester, and aunt of Henry VI, was charged with attempting the King's death by image-magic. In the rookery of buildings round the Palace of Westminster dwelt a certain Margery Jourdemayne who was known as the

SYMBOLS CONNECTED WITH WITCHCRAFT

Many of the signs and material objects associated with witchcraft had one purpose, to avert the evil eye. Here on the left is a witch cross made of rowan wood and treasured for its magical properties until comparatively recent times at Goathland in Yorkshire. It was credited with absolute power to prevent the evil eye from being directed towards the farm animals. On the right is a mould, typical of those once used for making charms to avert the evil eye. Both exhibits are from the Castle Museum, York.

THE WITCHES' STONE AT FORRES

The north-east coastal districts of Scotland, particularly remote from central govern-
ment until quite recent times, were a lingering stronghold of legends and tales about
witches and of superstitious belief in their powers for evil. Far into the Middle Ages
it was the custom to roll witches downhill from the summit of Cluny Hill in barrels
through which sharp spikes were driven. Where the barrels came to rest they were
burnt, together with the torn remains of the witch, in order to exorcise the spirit of
witchcraft as well as the witch herself. This stone marks the spot of a burning.

Witch of Eye. To this woman the Duchess went to obtain a waxen image. She also persuaded a clerk named Roger Bolingbroke to find out by divination how far she would rise in life. This was a highly suspicious question for one so near the throne, and helped to convince the judges of her guilt.

Her enemies declared that the image represented the King and was to be used for his murder. She swore that this was not so, but that greatly desiring a child she had had it made to use in a fertility rite. This defence may well have been true, for image-magic could be used in many ways.

Innocent or guilty, however, she and her accomplices were convicted and condemned. Margery Jourdemayne was burnt at Smithfield. Bolingbroke was hanged at Tyburn, and his head was set up on London Bridge as a warning to

PEEL, IN THE ISLE OF MAN

The photograph shows Peel Castle, with fishing-boats in the harbour. This peaceful and beautiful scene recalls the case of Eleanor Cobham, Duchess of Gloucester, and aunt of Henry VI. Convicted of attempting the death of the King by image-magic, the Duchess was forced to walk barefoot through the streets of London carrying a lighted candle to exorcise the devil in her. She was imprisoned for the rest of her life, at first in Chester Castle and then in grim ghost-haunted Peel Castle.

all future sorcerers. The Duchess was forced to walk barefoot through London's streets, carrying a lighted candle; and afterwards she was imprisoned for the rest of her life, at first in Chester Castle and then in the grim Peel Castle in the Isle of Man.

UNRELIABLE EVIDENCE

In Tudor and Stuart times the fear and hatred of the witch increased steadily, and for nearly a hundred years hardly anyone was safe from wild accusations inspired by terror, hysteria and sometimes by malice. Any suspected person was liable to be seized by a furious mob, ducked, beaten, searched for "devil-marks," and handed over to the magistrates for examination. The latter were often quite as credulous as the general public, and most unreliable evidence, including that of young children, was freely accepted in the courts. In 1616 nine people were hanged in Leicester on the word of a thirteen-year-old boy, and six more would have perished had it not been for the timely visit of James I. James believed wholeheartedly in witchcraft and wrote a book about it, but he was a stickler for genuine evidence, and was not easily deceived. He insisted on questioning the boy himself with the result that the young wretch broke down and confessed himself a malicious liar. The prisoners were thereupon released and the judges severely reprimanded by the King.

In 1604 the villagers of North Moreton in Berkshire were deeply shocked to hear that young Anne Gunter had begun to foam at the mouth, to suffer from goggling eyes and a variety of other ills, and most significant of all to vomit and sneeze out pins. She declared she was bewitched by three local women, and this was readily believed because the women in question already had bad reputations. Anne was taken to Oxford and lodged in the Rector's quarters at Exeter College. There she was examined by a number of eminent physicians, most of whom diagnosed witchcraft. A few, however, were doubtful, and some even thought her fits were faked. This uncertainty stood the accused women in good stead, for when they were tried at Abingdon the jury refused to convict them. Nevertheless, they were kept in prison at Windsor, and worse things might have befallen them had not King James examined young Anne and formed the impression that she was lying. Eventually she confessed to Dr. Jorden, in whose charge the King had placed her, that her fits were in fact counterfeited and that she had practised the deception to please her father, who was at enmity with the three women.

PRICKING OF WITCHES

One horrible feature of the witch-prosecutions was the existence of prickers, who went about the country "proving" guilt by sticking pins into their victims in the hope of finding some insensitive spot which was at once declared to be the Devil's mark. As these men were paid twenty shillings or more for every "proved" witch, they usually did find it, and hundreds of innocent people were thus placed in deadly peril. Matthew Hopkins and John Stearne spread a positive reign of terror throughout East Anglia and the adjoining counties in 1645 and 1646. According to his own tale Hopkins was first drawn to witch-detection by observing the activities of some witches in Manningtree, where he lived. At the Chelmsford Summer Assizes in 1645 no less than twenty-nine women were condemned to death as a result of his evidence. Flushed with this triumph, he began to style himself "Witch-Finder Generall," and with Stearne travelled through Essex, Suffolk, Norfolk, Cambridgeshire, Huntingdonshire and Bedfordshire. By pricking, bullying, keeping his victims awake, and other cruelties, he induced many confessions. At Framlingham an old man of eighty was "swum" by his orders in the castle moat, and wherever he went he practised numerous brutalities of like nature. He and his accomplice were responsible for at least two hundred executions in the course of two years, and it was the excesses of which they were guilty which finally drove the authorities to forbid pricking altogether. It is often said that Hopkins was himself suspected in the end, and drowned whilst being swum, but this is not true. He died in undeserved peace in 1647 and was buried at Mistley in Essex.

LANCASHIRE WITCHES

Though many innocent people suffered during the persecutions, it would be a mistake to suppose that all witches were falsely accused. The famous Lancashire witches of 1612 had certainly practised black magic in the depths of Pendle Forest for years before they were arrested. Led by two ancient hags known as Old Demdike and Old Chattox they terrorized their neighbours, meeting to lay their plans in a lonely building called Malkin Tower. At their last meeting, when some of their number were already in prison, they plotted to blow up Lancaster Castle and murder the Governor, and helped a visiting witch from Gisborne-in-Craven to plan Thomas Lister's death. But these projects they had no time to complete, for within a few days they were all in prison. The two old women died there; the rest were

brought to trial, and ten were hanged.

The old church at Auldearn in Morayshire is associated with Scotland's most celebrated witch, Isobel Goudie, who was almost certainly guilty o attempted witchcraft and the destruction of men and goods. She was a young and pretty girl, the discontented wife of a farmer near Nairn. In 1662 she made one of the most detailed confessions ever recorded, recounting without shame or repentance how she had been baptized a witch in Auldearn Church by a mysterious Man in Grey, and how thereafter she had committed innumerable crimes by magic and other means, including murder, devil-worship and the blasting of crops. She was hanged at the West Port of Elgin, and her body was afterwards burnt to ashes, according to the belief that only fire can finally destroy a witch's power.

Exeter claims the doubtful distinction of being the scene of England's last execution for witchcraft, as Ipswich probably can that of being the last place where an English witch was burned. In 1645 Mother Lakeland was burnt in the latter place for the crime of bewitching her husband to death.

LAST EXECUTION FOR WITCHCRAFT

Alice Molland, who died at Exeter in 1684, was the last of a long line of men and women to perish on the scaffold for witchcraft. In 1712 Jane Walker of Wenham was condemned to death at the Hertfordshire Assizes, but she was reprieved and lived for twenty years thereafter on a pension paid to her by some charitable (and presumably sceptical) individuals. Some few years later, in 1735, the penal laws against witchcraft were swept away. Henceforward it became illegal to prosecute anyone for sorcery, the only penalties allowed by the Act being for persons who

A WITCH AND HER FAMILIARS

This reproduction from a manuscript in the British Museum brings home the fact that in former times witchcraft represented a very real belief which was not just confined to ignorant or grossly superstitious people. Not a few who were avowed Christians and understood the meaning of Christianity nevertheless had an implicit belief in the satanic power of witches. In those times witches tended to be blamed for anything abnormal in nature, as well as for any misfortunes that fell on the countryside and the calamities that beset individuals and their families. This artist invented monstrous birds and animals as indication of the unnatural nature of a witch's spiritual make-up. There are records of persons, accused of witchcraft, actually confessing to association with these monstrous spirit-animals, often called familiars.

315

"pretended" to possess occult powers.

This Act did not, of course, immediately destroy the popular belief. In 1751 a poor old couple named Osborne were torn from a Hertfordshire workhouse by an angry crowd and hurled into a pond at Long Marston. The woman floated, and the ringleader, Thomas Colley, thrust her down with a pole. When she was taken out she was dead; her husband died later from his injuries. Colley was justly hanged for murder, but there were many who thought he ought to have been acquitted, since in their view he had committed no crime but had merely rid the neighbourhood of Long Marston of two dangerous witches.

With the passing years, however, the ancient faith declined. Only fragmentary remains now linger here and there in Britain, like starfish stranded by the receding tide. White witches are still sometimes consulted for simple cures or love-charms; a few horse-charmers yet exist; and wart-healers are not difficult to find. Now and then a woman may be suspected of black magic as we have seen, but this is very exceptional; and in general we can truthfully say that at least one primitive and long persisting terror has vanished from our lives.

IN THE FLEECE INN, BRETFORTON

Here and there in the countryside today, though belief in witchcraft has probably finally disappeared from the minds of all but the most ignorant and superstitious, the customs of a bygone age arising out of a genuine belief in the power of witches are retained self-consciously as matters of folk interest. This photograph shows witch circles being marked out in the Fleece Inn at Bretforton. Originally in witch mythology there were a number of signs which were regarded as a protection against witches.

INDEX

Numbers in italics indicate illustrations

ACKNOWLEDGEMENTS

The publishers wish to thank the following for permission to reproduce copyright material: Aerofilms, Ltd.; Aero Pictorial, Ltd.; Ashmolean Museum; British Museum; The Controller, H.M. Stationery Office, for Crown copyright photographs; Courtauld Institute of Art; Mrs. T. H. Crozier; *Picture Post* Library; *Sunday Mercury*, Birmingham; Valentine, Dundee.